THE McGILL
REPORT
ON MALE
INTIMACY

Also by Michael E. McGill

The 40 to 60 Year Old Male
Changing Him, Changing Her

THE McGILL REPORT ON MALE INTIMACY

Michael E. McGill, PH.D.

HOLT, RINEHART AND WINSTON ▪ NEW YORK

Copyright © 1985 by Michael E. McGill
All rights reserved, including the right to reproduce this
book or portions thereof in any form.
Published by Holt, Rinehart and Winston,
383 Madison Avenue, New York, New York 10017.
Published simultaneously in Canada by Holt, Rinehart
and Winston of Canada, Limited.

Library of Congress Cataloging in Publication Data
McGill, Michael E.
The McGill Report on Male Intimacy.
Includes index.
1. Men—United States—Psychology.   2. Intimacy
(Psychology)   3. Love.   4. Interpersonal relations.
5. Women—United States—Psychology.   I. Title.
HQ1090.3.M38   1985   155.6'32   84-9053
ISBN 0-03-063297-8

Design by Dalia Bergsagel
Printed in the United States of America
10 9 8 7 6 5 4 3

ISBN 0-03-063297-8

To My Sons, Jim and Adam:

May you know the love of many and show your
love to all. With all my love, Dad.

There are such astonishing things to be told about men and women, and hardly a man or a woman to whom one dares to tell them.

—Logan Pearsall Smith, *Afterthoughts*

Contents

Acknowledgments   xi

Preface   xiii

1   How Do I Love Thee?   1

2   Husbands and Wives: The Man That's Missing
   in Marriage   35

3   Men and the Other Woman   75

4   Family Man or Phantom Man?   117

5   Man to Man   156

6   How Do Men Love?   185

7   Why Aren't Men More Loving?   212

8   Why Should Men Be Loving: What's in It for Men?   235

9   How Men Can Be More Intimate   256

Appendix   283

Index   295

Acknowledgments

I am greatly indebted to the many men and women who have shared with me their thoughts, feelings, and experiences of intimacy. Throughout the book I have drawn upon their stories to illustrate points from the research. In every instance I have altered names, occupations, and locales to protect the privacy of respondents. It is unlikely that those who contributed will recognize themselves in these pages, but I hope they will accept my words of recognition and respect for what they have shared.

Several people have made specific contributions to this book, which I would like to acknowledge. Dominick Abel, my agent, championed and guided the project from the outset. Ann Phillips typed the manuscript with great skill and sensitivity to the subject. Marian Wood, my editor, read the manuscript with uncommon care. Her efforts to sharpen the focus and the form of the book have made it immeasurably better than it could ever have been through my efforts alone.

Throughout this project I have enjoyed the support of intimate, caring friends. Alice Acheson, Kathy and Tom Barry, Sharon and Tom Hofstedt, and John Slocum have all shown an interest in my work that I have drawn upon for motivation on many occasions.

Research and reflection are but two of the many ways we can learn of love and intimacy. I believe that the fundamental lessons of love are learned through living in loving relationships. Those things that I really know of love and intimacy I have learned from my wife, Janet, and the love she has shown me through the many years of our marriage. It is to Janet that I am most indebted for the inspiration for this work. It is because she has loved me that I am able to write of love.

Preface

I set out to do something quite simple in this book. I wanted to explain why men love as they do in their intimate relationships with their wives, lovers, families, and friends. How I came to this purpose, and where the process led me, is not quite so simple a story.

As a man involved in loving relationships, it would be natural for me to have a strong personal interest in the subject of male intimate behaviors. In truth, until I became professionally interested in the subject, I, like a great many other men, had given relatively little thought to how I loved others. I had long taken for granted the loving relationships I enjoyed, and for just as long I had been oblivious to my own behavior in those relationships. It was only as I began to study the loving behavior of men that I became fully aware of my own loving behavior as a man.

As a university professor specializing in organization behavior, and as a consultant to businesses for nearly twenty years, in my training and experience I have been primarily concerned with the behavior of groups and individuals in organizational settings. What is it that people do in organizations? Why? What are the consequences? Over a period of years, my research and writing began to focus more and more on the behavior of specific individuals in specific circumstances.

In 1977 I completed the first of three major studies on

the behavior of men. That initial study was an attempt to discover why and how men dealt with the issues of midlife. My career experiences in teaching and consulting had made it clear to me that a large number of organizational actors were middle-aged men. Their behavior as workers seemed at least in part to be dictated by issues elsewhere in their lives, and I wanted to learn what those issues were and how men dealt with them. It was during this research that I first developed an appreciation of the relational problems of men. One of the contributing factors to male midlife crisis is the absence of intimate others with whom a man might share his midlife concerns. I concluded that research with some prescriptions for how men might change to deal better with the issues of midlife. One recommended change was that men develop close caring relationships with others.

My second major inquiry focused on *how* men could change. It was a broad examination of behavior change in male-female relationships: men changing the behavior of women, and vice versa. Once again I drew on data collected from my many organizational contacts, together with the research population of audiences that my earlier work provided, particularly the many national groups and associations before whom I was invited to appear. As a part of this investigation I attempted to discover the change agendas of men and women. What are those things about men that women would most like to change? What are those things about women that men would most like to change? Again, as in my earlier research, the relational behavior of men emerged as a key issue. I found that with few exceptions women wanted men to be more expressive of their emotions and feelings, their love. Woman after woman said, "I want him to show me that he loves me." By contrast, men asked for more understanding from women: "My wife should know that I love her without my having to show her." There appeared to be a standoff. Five years of research with hundreds of men and women convinced me that I would not truly understand the behavior of men until I had come to an understanding of why men love as they do and what their behavior means for men and those they love. All other questions seemed secondary to this fundamental issue. So it was that three years ago I began research aimed at explaining male intimate behavior.

Early in my research on intimate behavior I discovered that individual experiential data banks are rich with incidents and anecdotes in which the intimate behavior of men and women differs greatly. It has become almost the conventional wisdom that men and women love differently. As pervasive and often profound as conventional wisdom is, it is no substitute for sound empiricism. Assumptions, no matter how widely held, must be tested. Hence, before I could explain *why* differences existed in the intimate behavior of men and women, I had to determine whether or not such differences existed.

I was somewhat surprised to learn that relatively little research had been done on intimate behavior. I had thought, perhaps naïvely, that something so fundamental to male-female interaction would have been thoroughly studied, making my task that much easier. I discovered instead that studies of intimate behavior have been infrequent, fragmentary, and far from the eye of the general public. Indeed, there was evidence of fundamental problems with defining intimacy and measuring intimate behavior. Intimacy has been variously approached by academics in terms of the depth and breadth of social penetration or personal knowledge exchanged; the duration, value, uniqueness, intensity of feeling, or sense of oneness in a relationship. Few researchers have taken a comprehensive view of intimate behavior, integrating these many perspectives, and fewer still have spoken to a general audience. I set out to do both.

Drawing upon existing views and established research methods, I developed the Intimacy Questionnaire (see the Appendix for the questionnaire and a detailed discussion of its design and administration). The Intimacy Questionnaire is designed to measure the loving behavior of an individual in four specific relationships: with the spouse or intimate other, and with parents, children, and friends. Six dimensions of these intimate interactions are measured: breadth of exchange, depth of exchange, significance of exchange, exclusivity of the relationship, duration of the relationship, frequency of interaction, and value attached to the relationship. Results from the questionnaire reveal who it is that men and women love, and how they love them.

Responses to the Intimacy Questionnaire were obtained from 1,383 people: 737 men and 646 women ranging in age from 18 to 73 (see the Appendix for a complete discussion of the sample technique and demographics of the sample). Respondents included a broad range of occupations and incomes—insurance workers, community volunteers, geophysicists, clerks, homemakers—from nearly every state in the country. While not a random sample, it is nonetheless highly representative and allows for generalization from the findings.

In addition to describing the behavior of men in intimate relationships, I wanted to be able to explain the reasons for their behavior. To do this, I chose seventy men, seventy women, and twenty couples from respondents to be interviewed for a more detailed, personal view of those with whom they were intimate, and how and why. Throughout this book, the stories of these individuals are used to illustrate issues in intimacy. In every instance, names, places, and incidentals have been altered so as to thoroughly protect the anonymity of the respondents.

What began as a simple explanatory exercise three years ago emerges now as a well-researched, relevant, and readable study of intimate behavior. The results of this study reveal some fascinating insights into the ways in which men and women relate intimately to others. Some conventional wisdom about male relational patterns is supported, and some is shattered. The data and the personal stories of men and their wives, lovers, families, and friends, show that the problem with men is the problem of men, and that the difference between men and women is that women show their love and men do not. The data and interviews also pinpoint the many reasons why men aren't more loving and why they need to be.

If you are a man, you will find yourself in these pages as husband, lover, father, friend, son. If you have ever loved a man, he is here, as are the ways, whys, and wherefores of his love. Man or woman, if you have ever loved or sought love, there is a message here for you.

Mick McGill
Dallas, Texas

THE McGILL REPORT ON MALE INTIMACY

1 How Do I Love Thee?

They do not love that do not show their love.

—Shakespeare

In 1850, Elizabeth Barrett Browning, in her *Sonnets from the Portuguese*, wrote, "How do I love thee? Let me count the ways." Were the ways of love so easily enumerated, we would know much more of love than we do. But love has always given itself more easily to meter than to measurement. Love is the subject of sentiment, not of statistics. Still, as Shakespeare and Browning noted long ago, we *want* to be able to measure love. We want to know in tangible ways just how and how much we are loved. When a husband says to his wife "I love you," her likely response is "Show me," or "How can I be sure?" Words alone are not an adequate expression; we want and need to see and feel another's love for us in their actions.

   In large part, we have no one to blame but ourselves for bankrupting the language of love. In the 1960s, we made love a collective response to political and social concerns; it was the era of the "love-in" and the "love generation." In the

1970s, love was little more than an amalgam of sophomoric aphorisms: "Love is never having to say you're sorry," and "Love is a warm puppy." Today, declarations of love are ubiquitous, emblazoned on T-shirts and bumper stickers, "I ♥ NY," "I ♥ My Cocker," or "I ♥ Country Music." What does it mean today when we trumpet in traffic in response to the bumper ahead of us, that reads "Honk if you love Jesus"? What does it mean when we close a letter to a casual friend with "Luv ya"? What does it mean when we leave home in the morning with a quick kiss and "I love you" to spouse and children? There is little wonder that we demand a behavioral show of love in a time when declarations of love are so commonplace and inconsequential.

For many, the definitive show of love has become sex. This has only served to confuse the meaning of love. Is making love the ultimate expression of loving? For some, sex clearly is a significant demonstration of love; yet, in an era of casual sex, for many others making love is little more than recreation. Men seem to be particularly confused about sex and love. It is difficult for most men to talk about love without talking about sex, though such an association limits their concept of love and loving behavior. In the interviews we conducted, women were much more likely to view sex as a potential expression of love, one among many such behaviors. These reactions to sex and love underscore the need, in researching this area, to rise above the limitations of language and the varieties and vagaries of current usage and to start with a clear concept, devoid of prejudicial and peculiaristic meanings. That concept is intimacy.

Intimacy is the state of being close. It suggests private and personal interaction, commitment, and caring. The concept of intimacy captures the breadth and depth of the relationships that are important to men and women without being burdened by the contemporary baggage that freights the language of love. We can speak as meaningfully of intimate friends as we can of intimacy in a marriage. There are still those who will confuse intimate behavior with sexual behavior, much as they confuse sex with love, but intimacy embraces a broader, less exclusive range of close, caring relationships than does love. It is an important aspect of intimacy that it opens many more possibilities for measuring behavior in these relationships. By grounding our research in intimacy, we are better able to see the ways in which men and women express themselves in significant relationships, and why they express themelves as they do.

THE ELEMENTS OF INTIMACY: WHAT MAKES US CLOSE

It is possible to identify the elements of a relationship that are associated with intimate interaction. From these elements we can construct measures of intimate behavior and begin to account for differences (if any) in the intimate behavior of men and women. Our conversations with men and women about what makes them feel close to others reveal that in general women are much more aware of, and sensitive to, the many elements of emotional bonding than are men. This difference in perspective accounts in part for the number of intimate relationships men and women have, the kinds of relationships they have, and their behavior in those relationships. The incidents that follow, drawn from interviews, illustrate the elements of intimacy and set the stage for our discussion of the consequent differences in the intimate behavior of men and women.

Time Together

There is a certain intimacy that develops between people in proximity to one another over time, the simple duration of their relationship frequently giving rise to a strong emotional bonding that is felt by both parties, often in the absence of any other real attraction.

"Velma over there is my closest friend here at the bank, maybe my closest friend anywhere. We go back a long way— almost fifteen years now. She came to work three weeks before I did, so she's forever telling everybody how she's the real veteran down here. The truth is, we're the only veterans there are here, or ever have been, or probably ever will be for that matter. Most of these girls just cashier till they get married or, if they are married, till they get pregnant. The managers don't stay around much longer. But seems like no matter how many come and go, me and Velma stay right here.

"We haven't always been so close—in some ways we aren't all that close even now—but it seems like if you're around someone for just a whole lot of the time you can't help but get to know them after a while. That's how it's been with me and Velma. For the longest time I didn't even like her very much; she's always been sort of uppity, if you know what I mean. I'd make friends with the new girls and so would she, but then they'd leave and I'd have to start all over again. I think that after a while we both sort of just decided that since we were the only ones who were here to stay, we might as well get along. Now that we've been here so long, we're kind of the bank's 'old biddies.' We talk a lot about who's come and gone and how it used to be, but we're the only ones who listen to us, 'cause we're the only ones who've known everybody.

"A funny thing about Velma and me is that away from the bank we hardly ever see each other. Oh, we maybe do something together at the holidays, or if some special show comes to town that we both want to see we'll go together, but mostly away from the bank we just don't have that much in common. She has her friends and I have mine. Of course, we talk about them all the time, but we never mix 'em. Isn't that funny, how we are? I think that it's just that we're together so much at the bank—we even take all our breaks together— that we sort of get enough of each other. Then, too, Velma can kinda get on your nerves. Heaven knows, she probably feels the same way about me.

"Still, there's nobody I'm closer to than Velma. It's all those years together behind that counter. We've often said if one of us ever leaves, the other one will have to leave too, 'cause it just wouldn't be the same. We've only lasted this long because we've had each other."

Time often weaves the fabric of the ties that bind us. Jane Battis's description of her friendship with Velma at the bank is a good example of the kind of intimate relationship that comes from time together. If familiarity can be said to breed contempt, we ought to recognize that it can also breed consistency, comfort, and, ultimately, closeness. The intimacy between Jane and Velma is commonly seen in work relationships, in neighborhood or community friendships, and even in some familial relationships. The depth and breadth of exchanges in these relationships, the amount and quality of personal information people have about one another, which is the medium of intimacy, comes as a by-product of simple exposure over time. As Jane noted, "We're the only ones who listen to us, 'cause we're the only ones who've known everybody." Time together sets a framework for friendship that at some point almost compels two people toward closeness.

"When you live next door to someone for seventeen years, you almost have to become close, whether you like each other or not." Patricia Tugger is talking about her relationship with her neighbors of many years, Linda and Marshall Manis. They live side by side in a suburban Northwestern neighborhood. Both the Tuggers and the Manises moved into their homes shortly after the development was completed. They've seen most of the other homes change hands once or twice, families break up, kids grow up and move away. Linda and Marshall separated for a year and a half, but have been together again for the last two years. As Patricia describes it, "We aren't what you'd call close; still, we care a lot about each other. Linda and I more so than the guys.

"We've been through everything that's happened to either one of our families, side by side if not exactly together over seventeen years. That's a long time! You get to know an

5

awful lot about people in that time, and you can't help but grow to care a lot about them, too. We're not the sort of neighbors who are in and out of each other's houses all the time, having coffee or backyard cookouts. We're more the sort of neighbors who are there if you need them, like when you're away on vacation and need someone to watch the house, or if there's an emergency of some kind. In seventeen years there can be a lot of emergencies—accidents, lost kids, births, even death. Linda's dad died while visiting them about three years ago. When someone's been there all the time through all of those things, you get close."

As far as the women are concerned, proximity plus time create a condition in which "you can't help but get close." But men somehow seem to keep from getting close under the same circumstances. Women take shared experiences and use them as a base for further sharing. They use proximity and time to develop broader and deeper relationships. Men tend to take shared experience and treat the resulting relationships as both time and experience-bound. This necessarily renders their relationships somewhat narrow and shallow. Men view time together and shared experiences as if to say, "We shared those experiences at that time, but it doesn't mean any more than that." Women are more likely to use the same sort of shared experience over time as the basis for further intimacy.

Jim and Sue Harrell live in the desert Southwest where Jim is a high-school coach and Sue teaches in the public schools. A young couple in their late twenties without any children, Jim and Sue have lived far from their families since leaving college six years ago. For those six years, the Harrells have spent the summers in the Great Lakes area in the small town where both sets of parents still live. Jim's folks own some lake cottages, which he and Sue manage for them during the summer season. Most of their friends from college come up for at least a week, and many of their childhood friends still live in the area.

The first few years, both Jim and Sue eagerly awaited their summer homecoming, but lately they've argued about just how much fun it is. This year Jim doesn't want to go at all. He explains why:

"We've gone for six years straight, and I just don't see the sense in going again. It's always the same thing year after year, with the same people. Not that there's anything wrong with them. They're a great bunch, always have been, but after we've relived old times, I'm ready to go, because there's nothing else to talk about. It's all so predictable. We'll talk about the team we had in high school, then the team we had in college, and tell the same lies about the parties in the old days. We don't talk much about girls, because everybody ended up marrying somebody that someone else had dated, so that might get kinda sticky. We'll wonder about why so-and-so moved away and are they ever coming back. It's like every reunion you ever went to, only it lasts all summer long. It's not worth it anymore, and I don't see any sense in going back again."

Sue has a different view of the summers at home. To her they still have value, more so each year. The value is in the relationships she has at the lake, relationships that are not frozen in time because she hasn't allowed them to freeze. "If all I did when I went home was to talk about the good old days, the way Jim does with his buddies, I'd be just as bored with it as he is. But I've kept up with my friends. When I'm home we spend all of our time talking about who we are now and what's going on with us, instead of rehashing who we were and what happened way back when. These old friendships are all the more important to me because all the time we've spent together gives us a sense of perspective on what's happening now. It's like people I meet now know me for who I am, but they don't know who I've been, what-all has happened to me, and why I am the way I am now. But my old friends that I've stayed close to over the years know who I am now and why I am that way because they've

7

known me all along. I say you can have old friends who are good friends and new friends who are good friends, but the best friends are the good old friends that you keep renewing.

"The trouble with Jim and his friends is that they never take the trouble to find out who they are now. They keep relating to each other the way they were in college or even high school. I know at the time they were really close, but it's not that time anymore. If they're going to be close now, I think they have to find out who they are now. I don't know why they don't. I've told Jim what I think he ought to do, but he just sloughs it off. Maybe the guys are afraid they'd find out that all they have in common is the past. It's probably true, but they've let it happen to themselves. No wonder Jim is bored with them. I'm sure that they're bored with him, too. Maybe this summer I'll go home alone. It might be easier on everybody that way."

Is intimacy "time-bound" for men? Do women work harder at keeping old relationships renewed? Sue thinks so, and so, too, do many women as they reflect upon the differences in those of their relationships that have persisted as compared with the relationships of their husbands, brothers, and lovers over the same time:

- "Mike (husband) doesn't have any old friends. Outside of his family, he has absolutely no contact with anybody he knew before we moved here three years ago."
- "Thank God he's not around his old friends much. Jerry (husband) was a real hell-raiser in college, and when he's with his old buddies he thinks he has to be like that all over again. When he's like that, I really don't like him all that much. If his friends saw him the way he really is now, so conservative and staid, they wouldn't even recognize him. So when he's with them he's the old, obnoxious Jerry."
- "If it weren't for my sister-in-law, I wouldn't have the slightest idea of what's going on with Dan (brother) these days. He treats me just the same as when he last lived at home, and that was fourteen years ago! I know from Gail that he's changed a lot, but he's never told me anything. As far as

he's concerned, I'll forever be the spoiled girl who took too much time in the bathroom. I'd really like to bring our relationship up to date, but I don't think he wants to."

▪ "The way I see it, men (lovers) sort all of their relationships into pigeonholes with time and topic labels. Once they've slotted you, they never take the trouble to see what else there might be there. All their relationships are one-dimensional, and that's the way they want to keep them. It's easier on them that way, 'cause they don't have to keep the relationship current. They just relate to you like you were frozen in time or something."

The intimacy that comes from time together and shared experience really emanates from the way in which time and experience are used. Men tend to view time together and shared experiences as defining the limits of a relationship: at this time, for this experience, here are the rules for relating. Male relationships are time-bound. Time and experience form a barrier to any real intimacy that might transcend that time and experience. Women view their time and experience together as a bridge, as a means to broader and deeper exchanges, and hence to greater intimacy. The man who boasts that he's known "old so-and-so" for twenty years is more than likely saying he met so-and-so twenty years ago, and the way he knows him now is the way he knew him then. The woman who has known a friend for twenty years has known who her friend was in each of those twenty years. Time freezes what men know of one another; it expands what women know of one another. For that reason, women see the closeness that comes from breadth of knowledge of the other, from the variety of exchanges. Men are much more limited in their perspective.

Intimacy and Variety: The Breadth of Interpersonal Exchange

"I think that men have just as many friends as women. There's no difference at all. I know that I have more friends than my wife has—quite a few more, actually. She spends all of her time with the same three or four gals. Hell, I must have five or six times that many guys I would call my friends. There are the guys at work, of course, then my lodge buddies, and George and Ray from here in the neighborhood, and then my hunting buddies that get together two or three times a year. That must be about twenty right there, and there are probably another half-dozen or so I can't think of right off the bat. No sir, I can't say that men and women are all that much different where friends are concerned, except that probably men have more friends."

Don Palmer is an engaging, gregarious insurance salesman from the Southeast. His easy, outgoing manner with everyone he meets is inviting and attractive, and leads to a great many friendships that he works at keeping through his involvement in a wide range of activities. Harriet, Don's wife of twenty-four years, is quiet and demure by comparison. She is slower to form friendships and more thoughtful about what her friendships mean.

"It's certainly true that Don has a lot more friends than I do. Being the way he is, Don has a lot more friends than anyone I know. But all of Don's friends have a purpose, like a label. He has his work friends and his lodge friends and his neighborhood friends and his hunting friends. Do you see what I mean? He only talks to his hunting friends about hunting, his work friends about work, and so on. I don't think that he has any one friend that he can talk to about everything; each of his friendships has its own very special purpose. I may not have many friends, but the ones I do have are all-purpose friends. I can talk to any one of them about anything that I want. I don't have one friend for this thing and another friend for that thing; every one of my friends is for everything. I think that's a big difference between men and women. Men seem to have certain friends for certain things, where women have just friends, period, friends for all things.

"It's the same way in our marriage. Don only talks to me

about certain things—the kids, the house, what's going on around town. Just like his friends, I have my purpose too. I wish he would feel free to talk to me about everything, but he doesn't. He says he just doesn't need to talk to me about 'everything under the sun,' the way I do with my friends. Sometimes I feel a little used. Thank God I have friends I can talk to when I get to feeling that way."

As one measure of the closeness of a given relationship, women use the variety of things they can disclose and discuss in it. For women, the closest of their relationships, romantic, familial, or based on friendship, are those in which the greatest variety of things are exchanged. Men typically view relationships in a more unidimensional fashion. There are certain things men talk about in some relationships and certain other things they talk about in others. Rarely, for men, are there relationships in which all things are open to discussion. These limits on disclosure necessarily limit the relationships men develop, and lead to the sentiment commonly expressed by wives, that "sometimes I feel as though I hardly know him at all."

Two stories are illustrative of the frustration that women feel over their fractional relations with men. The first is that of Judy Beccar, a young wife who is repeatedly embarrassed when she hears about her husband from others:

"What makes me the very maddest about Jerry is that I'm always hearing things from other people that I think I ought to hear from him. I'm not one of those Pollyanna-type young wives who think a husband and wife ought to share everything. Jerry and I have been married almost nine years, and I long ago lost any illusions about how much real communication goes on in a marriage. Still, I don't think it's too much to ask him to share the things that are mutually important to us. He has his life so compartmentalized, with his friends for this and his friends for that, that no one knows all of Jerry, including me. What happens is that someone will talk to me about something Jerry's told them, thinking of

11

course that he would have told me too, but he hasn't. I'm hearing important things about my husband from a stranger, pretending I've known it all along, and feeling really foolish. A good example is when his secretary asked me over the phone what I thought about Jerry's promotion. I had to pretend I knew all about it, when really I didn't have the slightest idea what was going on. Another time I heard from his mother that his brother had been in town to see him, three weeks after it happened!

"When I get on Jerry about these things, he shrugs it off and says, 'Don't make such a big deal out of nothing,' To him it isn't a big deal. He really doesn't think it's necessary to tell me everything that goes on with him. I think that if we're going to be close at all, I need to know more about more of him."

To Shirley Cassion it's not just that men don't need to share all of themselves in a relationship. She's convinced that they don't care to know more than one dimension of her: "I've been divorced for six years plus, and I've dated a lot of men of all kinds—older, younger, professional, blue-collar, widowers, divorced, and even a couple of married men. When it comes to communicating, as far as I'm concerned they're all alike. They find one thing to talk about with you, and that's it. They never care enough to find out anything else about who you are. Some want to talk about work or hobbies or movies or sports—all things I'm interested in, but I never met one yet who took the trouble to find out that I was interested in *all* of those things. They just latch on to the first one we have in common, and that's going to be it for as long as you see them. What's more, they don't seem to mind. A one-topic relationship is just fine with them. As far as I'm concerned, a one-topic relationship is no relationship at all!"

Coming to the defense of men is Robert Spann. Robert is recently divorced and, by his own admission, is "struggling with dating" after thirteen years of married social life. At thirty-seven, Robert has the lean good looks of someone who is used to physical labor. At the same time, he has the social polish that comes from the white-collar business world. He attributes this combination to his job as owner-operator of a large wholesale nursery in one of the Gulf States. His looks and demeanor, as well as the number of unattached women of all ages in his town, make it easy for Robert to get dates. But enjoying himself on those dates is another matter. "Maybe it's just me. After all, it has been some time since I dated, but it seems like women today want to know everything there is to know about you on the first date. I don't mind talking some about my work or my interests away from the job, but some of the stuff I'm asked I never even told my wife, and we were married for thirteen years! I don't believe that any one person can be everything for any other person. A little mystery in a relationship is natural and even desirable. My male friends at work don't demand to know all about my personal life, and my friends away from work don't care about my job. Why shouldn't it be the same with the women I date? But it's not. The women today aren't satisfied until they've wrung every last detail of personal information out of you. That's just not something I've ever looked for in a relationship with a woman. I don't want my life to be an open book to anybody."

A great many men agree with Robert Spann:

- "So we (men friends) don't talk to each other about everything—is that bad? Maybe we wouldn't like what we found out; then the whole thing would be shot. A little bit of a good thing is better than a lot of nothing at all."

- "First, she (wife) doesn't need to know everything about me. Second, she wouldn't understand all of it. And third, I don't want to tell her."

- "I think it's better to have a lot of friends, even if you only know a little bit about them, than it is to have only a few friends. It's not good to be too dependent on people, because they're not always going to be there."

The intimacy that comes from knowing a great deal about another person, from sharing all aspects of each other in the relationship, is an important source of closeness for women. Women frequently judge the intensity of their relationships by the variety and breadth of knowledge of the other, by how much is exchanged. Women use shared interests as a springboard from which they can dive into the breadth of possibilities a relationship might present. It is not uncommon for a woman to say of a woman friend, "She knows everything there is to know about me," or "She knows me better than I know myself." Men rarely speak of one another in such terms. For most men, breadth of knowledge of another is not a measure of intimacy. Male relationships are based not on variety, but rather on specific shared interests. These interests circumscribe the emotional and behavioral interaction that can take place in the relationship; they limit intimacy.

Intimacy and Value: The Depth of Interpersonal Exchange

The time we spend with others, and the variety of things we know about them, bond us together, creating the interpersonal exchanges that lead to intimacy. A third important source of this emotional bonding comes not from time spent together or from the breadth of the relationship, but rather from the value of what is exchanged, the depth of disclosure. The revelation to another person of something that is very important to us, central to who we are, constitutes an intimate exchange, regardless of the history of the relationship or what else the other may know about us.

A common example of intimacy that comes from the disclosure of personally valued information is what I call "in-flight intimacy." Perhaps you have experienced something like it. You've just found your seat on a crowded plane and are curiously scanning the remaining boarding passengers as they move along the aisle. You've brought along a

14

book or a magazine for the flight, both to pass the time and to buffer you from unwanted conversation with fellow travelers. But before you can get into your reading, your attention is caught by your seat mate, who is visibly upset. Initially you politely ignore her, assuming she would prefer some privacy and a chance to regain her composure. She remains distraught, and so you ask, "Is there anything I can do to help?" In response she tells you why she is upset. It's rarely anything casual, and soon this total stranger is revealing to you the most intimate details of her life. You are witness to her confession of divorce, abandonment, betrayal or deceit for the remainder of the flight.

The remarkable thing about these in-flight intimacies is that your first inclination is to feel put upon, even trapped, but out of politeness you listen, and as you listen you come to care. The flight ends and you part. There is no exchange of names—no effort made to continue the relationship in any fashion. Yet, strangely, you leave feeling closer for the moment to that stranger than to many of the people you see every day, because for that brief, anonymous time you shared in her intimacy.

In-flight intimacies and their variants—waiting-line intimacy, hospital intimacy—testify to the bonding strength of deeply personal revelations. Of course, we are far more interested in relationships of greater duration, scope, and significance than that offered by the chance encounters spawned by air travel or waiting rooms. The incidents reported by men and women in established relationships suggest that men seldom reveal deeply valued personal information, even to long-term partners. As a result, men seldom know the kind of intimacy that comes from such valued exchanges.

Barbara Reed has been in the company of men all her life. She is the only daughter in a family where there are three sons. She's married, with two teenaged sons of her own, and she has worked for ten years as the only woman in an office of oil company landmen in West Texas. Barbara has some strong feeling about just what one can and cannot expect to hear from a man:

"I don't care how close you think you are to a man, you will never know all there is to know about him, because he won't let you. I saw it between my mother and father, I saw it with my brothers, I see it with my own husband and with my boys. They may tell you a lot about what's going on with them, but there will always be that important something they don't tell, something hidden that really makes the difference. You can push and pry all you want, but you are never going to find out all there is to know about a man, because they are never going to tell. That's just the way they are."

Barbara Reed's sentiments are echoed by many women who express the feeling about a husband, father, lover, brother, or friend that there will forever be something about him, some part of him, that is inaccessible. Some women are still societally conditioned to expect a man to be reserved; such women do not desire this kind of intimacy, and may convey that through their actions. Other women do not expect full disclosure from men, because they don't think men are capable of it.

A mother of six—three boys and three girls, all grown and on their own now—had an interesting perspective on this issue. "I never expected that my boys would confide in me like the girls would, not because I'm their mother, but because I just don't think boys—or men, for that matter—think very much about real personal sorts of things, not anywhere near as much as girls or women do, anyway. It's unfair to expect them to tell you things about themselves that they don't even *know* about themselves, don't you think?"

A much younger woman, whose experience of men is largely confined to those she has dated over the last five years, has come to share much the same view. "Men will tell you a lot about what they are, their job, their hobbies, what they like to do, but damn few will say much about who they are as a person. I've pretty much decided that most men don't know *who* they are, they only think of themselves in terms of '*what.*' Maybe it's expecting too much to want to know more about a man than he knows about himself."

Whatever the motives behind male reticence, the lack of personal depth in men's relationships creates barriers to intimacy, particularly with women. Rightly or wrongly, women expect a depth, a value of exchange, commensurate with their own personal investment in the relationship.

"It really is unfair. A woman lays herself open to a man, she's willing to tell him anything and everything about herself, and what does she get in return? She gets screwed, that's what. Literally and figuratively screwed!"

Jan Wanick is, by her own description, "twice-burned" in her relationships with men. She has once been divorced, and once rejected on the eve of marriage. Beneath the bitterness of her remarks runs a concern for equity that is at the core of many women's complaints about the lack of depth and intimacy in male-female relationships. "We women think that because we're in love and he's in love, he's going to match us stride for stride in the relationship. I tell him my favorite movies and he tells me his. I introduce him to my friends and he introduces me to his. It all works great until you get to the stuff that really counts. Then I tell him what I'm most afraid of or what I really want out of life, and he tells me, 'That's interesting.' There you are, completely exposed, completely vulnerable. You've given him everything he needs to hurt you, and you've got nothing in return. It's like you've got your whole existence invested in the relationship, and he's into it for pocket change! It's just not fair, but it's men!"

For real intimacy, there must be an equitable exchange. Both parties must bring comparable value to the relationship. In-flight intimacies are equitable because, for the limited time of their duration, listening is valued as much as revelation. If these relationships were to persist, the roles would have to be reversed and the listener would have to become a confessor of comparable value. Anything less would be a departure from intimacy. In their relationships with women, men seldom bring comparable value to the exchange. This limits intimacy and limits the loving that women experience.

Men have several explanations for their failure to engage in valued disclosures. There are those who assert that men are raised to be self-protective. Some argue that they simply don't need the same depth in a relationship that women do. Others say that women set the ante too high, requiring a level of disclosure that men, for whatever reason, can't attain. The following incidents speak to these male perspectives on intimacy and value.

Bob Pecher works as a buyer for a Chicago-area department store chain. Most of the other buyers are young women who, like Bob, are recently married and struggling with the complexities of a two-career relationship. At their bull sessions, talk often turns to some very personal topics in a way that makes Bob uncomfortable. "I don't know exactly how to handle it. We're all pretty close and I want to stay friends, but it seems like the more we talk, the more personal things get. I tell you, nothing embarrasses those girls! The problem is, I feel like if I don't volunteer something equally personal, I'll be left out. They don't understand that guys don't talk about those things the same way that girls do. I think about a lot of those same things, but I'm not going to talk about them. The cost is just too high—there's no telling what somebody might do with that information. Maybe I'm not as trusting as I should be, or not as honest, but if the cost of being 'in' is describing how my wife and I most like to have sex, I think I'll just choose to be out."

One husband, who admitted that he and his wife frequently fought over the issue of the extent of his involvement in their marriage, wrote, "Why should the woman always be the one who sets the rules for what's a *real* feeling and what's not? Who made her judge of my feelings? Where does she get off saying these are good feelings and these are bad, and these you need to work on. I'll decide what my feelings are, thank you, and what ones I want to talk about when. That's the way it ought to be, for any man."

One dimension of the issue of the depth of personal exchange that men bring to relationships is the relative definition of depth, the "ante," as we've seen it described above. Who determines what is a valued disclosure and what is not? Who will say what is "personal" enough? Men and women clearly disagree as to what kind of personal information a relationship requires. This observation suggests a larger issue, which has to do with the relative needs of men and women to reveal issues of depth in their relationships.

The nine-year-old son of Dave and Carol Brandt was killed in a boating accident eleven years ago. Waterskiing on a lake near their summer place in the Catskills, the boy failed to drop the tow rope as the boat turned dangerously close to the dock. He was slammed against the pilings and killed. In the ensuing year, the Brandts sold their lake house, Dave changed jobs, and the couple moved to the Midwest. It is Carol's claim that Dave has never talked to her about the death of their son.

"To this day, eleven years later, I don't know if Dave ever thinks about Bobby or what he thinks about Bobby. I just don't understand how he could not think about it. But then, if he thought about it, how could he keep it bottled up inside for all of these years? Why won't he talk about it? I think I've finally pretty much worked through it after a lot of soul-searching, hours and hours of tears with good friends, and a small fortune on therapy, but as far as I know, Dave's never mentioned it to a single soul. It has really driven a wedge between us, because I won't be able to really resolve the whole thing until Dave and I can talk about it."

Dave's response is that he has dealt with his son's death in his own private way, and he doesn't need to "bring it up all over again."

"I understand Carol's need to talk about our son's death, because her way of dealing with things is to talk them out. I have my own way of dealing with things—within myself—and just because I don't talk about them doesn't mean I feel things any less than she does. Frankly, I resent her implication that it does. I have resolved my son's death my way for me. It is only an issue between Carol and me to the extent that she makes it one. As far as I'm concerned, it need never be mentioned again."

In less dramatic fashion, men and women in pairings of every form—husband/wife, father/daughter, mother/son—struggle with their differing needs for personal disclosure in a relationship and the different disclosures they are prepared to make. The Brandts' trauma is the sort of event that can be an anchor point in intimate relationships. Such events provide an opportunity for yet another kind of bonding, the exclusivity of exchange, the sense that whatever is received from the other can only be received from *that* other. Here again, men and women differ in their views and their behavior, with predictable consequences for their loving relationships with each other.

Intimacy and Exclusivity

We have a special attachment to those people we feel offer us something special, something that no one else can or will bring to a relationship. This exclusivity is another source of the positive emotional bonding we associate with intimacy. Exclusivity describes one of the bonds we feel with family members: "When all is said and done, you've got only one mother and father." Exclusivity describes a source of intimacy in long-standing relationships: "After all these years, who else would have me?" Exclusivity is also at the root of the kind of emotional attachment we feel for someone when we share an intense experience with them: "If you weren't there, you couldn't understand." In each of these circumstances, the relational exchange is character-ized by a feeling of uniqueness; there is a perception that we have something special in the relationship that cannot be replicated by others.

Women seem to strive for exclusivity in their relation-ships; they value it, protect it, and build other dimensions of intimacy upon it. In contrast, men neither seek nor savor exclusivity. When it occurs in their relationships, they rarely use it as a bridge to other forms of intimacy. Rather than valuing exclusivity, men are made to feel vulnerable by it.

"Sometimes I get the feeling that we're just not that spe-cial to Harry, none of us, me or the kids. It's like if we weren't here his life would go on pretty much uninter-rupted. If there were some certain something he missed about us, he would just go out and get some replacements." Fran Depple is a thirty-four-year-old homemaker and mother of three. She and her husband, Harry, a furniture salesman in New England, have been married for fourteen years. Harry has done some job-hopping, and Burlington is their fourth home since they were married. Fran thinks it is Harry's fear of dependency that prevents him from making real commitments to anything, including his job and his family. "I'd like to think that there is something special about every relationship I have— with Harry, with the kids, with my friends. For example, each one of the children is different from the others, and I have a special relationship with each one of them. Tommy, the oldest, is so serious he needs me to loosen him up. Lisa, the youngest, is too loose and needs a little discipline. Then Jessica, she's real emo-tional, I try to help her calm down and be more rational. Their father treats them all alike, as though they weren't in-dividuals with their own special gifts and needs. I don't think any one of them would say they have a really 'special relationship' with their father. He's no different with me. Outside of the fact that we have been married for fourteen years, there's nothing special about our relationship. I cook for him, clean for him, raise his kids, and have sex with him every couple of weeks, but if I dropped dead tomorrow, he'd just go out and hire somebody to do all of that and not think anything of it.

"Maybe it's not really that bad, but that's the way I feel, and that's what counts, isn't it? I just don't feel special, because he never does anything to make me feel special. What would be so wrong if he just admitted how important I was to him? If he just said once, 'I don't know what I'd do without you?' Is that too much to ask, to be needed? To be special? The way I see it, if you're not special, you're not loved."

Harry sees the issue in purely pragmatic terms. "Fran's overdramatizing the whole thing. Of course I love her and I think she's special. Just because I don't say so every day doesn't mean anything. Look, the fact of the matter is, if something were to happen and she weren't around, the kids and I could manage. She may not like to hear that, but it's true. Life would go on. She'd do the same if I weren't around. I don't think any of us should get too dependent on anyone else, because when it really comes down to it you can't depend on anybody but yourself. It's like every time we move, Fran goes into this big thing about how she doesn't know how she's going to get along without so-and-so. 'There'll never be another friend like so-and-so,' she says. The simple answer to that is you don't *make* a friend like so-and-so! See what I mean? You don't put all your eggs in one basket, no matter whether it's money or friends or family or anything else."

The difference between Harry and Fran's views of marriage may be the clash between romance and reality. A number of men commented that they feel women carry a lot of illusions about romance, looking for the "knight on a white charger" who will meet their every need. Men report themselves to be much more realistic about relationships, recognizing that no one person can be everything to any other person, and that to expect that kind of "specialness" or seek it is unrealistic and dangerous: unrealistic because you're unlikely to find it; dangerous because if you do find it, you're likely to lose it just when you come to depend on it. One man said, "If my wife was my lover, my best friend, my companion and partner in everything, the way she'd like to be, and she left me, then where would I be? This way, if she leaves me, all I've lost is a wife. I'll be hurt but I'll still be whole!"

Men frequently confuse "exclusive" with "all-inclusive." Actually, very few women today expect or desire to be all things to their spouses or vice versa. Most women however, would like to feel that there is something about their relationship with a man that cannot be replicated elsewhere, by either one of them. This exclusivity is a yardstick by which women measure intimacy and loving. It may be romantic, but for women it is also very real.

There are men like Harry Depple who avoid exclusivity in their relationships as though it were dangerous, but most men do not *avoid* exclusivity so much as they simply do not *seek* it. They are ever wary of becoming too dependent. Shared experiences, particularly those that carry a degree of emotional intensity with them, create exclusive exchanges and, hence, intimacy. In such instances men are quick to treat the experience as time-bound and unidimensional, minimizing its potential for the development of intimacy.

Mike Lockner is a Vietnam vet. Mike is now active in Vietnam veterans' affairs. His comments on relationships among Vietnam vets are illustrative of male responses to the kind of "event exclusivity" described here:

"The thing about Vietnam is, if you weren't there you can't talk about it, and if you were there you can't talk about anything else. I guess for just about anybody who went over, it was the most emotionally intense time of their life. I know

23

it was for me. I thought the friends I made there were the only true friends I had ever known or would ever know. When your life is on the line you get real close real fast and you just hope and pray that it will last. Over there, friendships didn't break up, they got shot up. I thought, like everybody else, that when I got back and we saw each other I would be just as tight with those guys as ever. It isn't like that, though. We get together now, at meetings or something, and as we talk about over there, there is that same close feeling. You remember how much you loved those guys, but you realize that you can't bring that closeness back except as a memory. I remember being close to those guys then, but I don't feel that way now. I figure it can't be that way now or ever again, no matter how close we were. It's a different time, different place. The old closeness is old and you have to let it go. Christmas cards and a phone call from the airport, 'just passin' through,' is about as close as any of us get now."

Of course, there are many wartime friendships that endure, college comrades who become friends for life, and boyhood relationships that withstand the test of time, but the extension of an incidental intimacy beyond the incident requires an effort to explore other bases of intimacy. It is an effort that most men simply don't make. Women are much more opportunistic in their relationships in this way; they tend to use incidental intimacies to build other bonds. Many an enduring relationship has been born between women who share a maternity room in a hospital, or who confront a common family crisis. Marilyn Farmer describes how one such relationship came about:

"A few years ago our oldest boy, John junior, got into a lot of trouble with drugs. It was destroying him and our whole family along with him. We spent more time with the schools, the police, the probation people, and the counselors than I care to remember. Mostly out of desperation we joined a parents' support group. It proved to be a godsend. It helped to straighten John junior out, it helped our marriage, and I found one of my best friends ever. Ginny and I first started talking because it turned out our kids were at the same school so of course we had something in common right off the bat, plus we were both about to go out of our minds. The more we talked, the more we found we liked each other. Soon we were sharing things that didn't have anything to do with the kids or drugs but were just about us. Luckily the kids got that all behind them and we've had five or six relatively normal years now. I never would have thought that anything good could come out of such a terrible time in our lives, but in a lot of ways my friendship with Ginny is one of the best things that ever happened to me.

"The odd thing is that my husband and Max, Ginny's husband, never developed much of a relationship. It's strange, because with their jobs and all they really have more in common than Ginny and I do. It's not that they dislike each other or anything. It's more that they just never took the time to see if they might like each other. But I guess women are more likely to take that kind of time, especially when you think you might have found a 'soul sister' who knows firsthand the hell you've been going through."

John's response to Marilyn's observation is that he and Max simply never sought a relationship outside of the support group. "I'm not sure who it was who said 'misery loves company,' but if it wasn't a woman, they were talking about women. A man in misery wants to be alone. I wasn't wild about the support group. I just went along with it because Marilyn wanted to, she didn't want to deal with John junior's problem 'all alone.' I'm sure Max felt the same way I did. Just because we shared the same problem was no reason for us to become super-close friends."

If men do not value exclusivity in relationships in the same ways that women do, it is not because they lack exposure. Rather it is because, like John and Max, they do not use their experiences to create that exclusive "we" feeling. This

collective concern, expressed in thinking and talking about a relationship in we/our/us terms, is the final form of intimacy, and in many ways the most telling.

Intimacy and "We"

To an outsider looking in on a relationship, it is very difficult to judge the degree of intimacy the people in the relationship enjoy. The observer may see what are assumed to be signs of loving—a golden-anniversary couple walking hand in hand; a mother and daughter, heads bent together, sharing a private laugh; a father with his arm about a son— but these physical signs may belie the nature of their bonds. Perhaps what is seen is only a moment of comfort or closeness amid years of conflict, or perhaps it is merely habitual behavior that has long since lost any real meaning for either party. We see behavior we associate with intimacy, but we can only guess at the duration, breadth, depth, and exclusivity of others' relationships. Important relational dimensions that actually define intimacy are known only to those who share in a relationship and who experience one another's loving. There is one meaning of intimacy that frequently gives a public face to the personal, private feelings two people share for one another: it is their use of "we," the evidence of collective concern.

If we were to develop a relationship, you and I, there would be in our coming together I, you, and we. Each of us would have an identity separate unto ourselves, and as a relational pair we would have an identity: we. In the initial stages of our relationship, our conversation would be peppered with "I" statements, each of us revealing ourselves in declaratory disclosures: I do this, I like that. As our relationship developed through these revelations and as we shared experiences, more of our expressions would be in "we" terms, with relatively less "you" or "me" language. The use of "we" would signal a collective concern, a message that the identity of the relationship is valued as much as we value our individual identities. The emergence and expres-

26

sion of this collective concern represents yet another meaning of intimacy and yet another difference in the ways men and women view love.

"I remember a movie called *Yours, Mine and Ours* or something like that. In it, a man and woman each had a lot of kids by other marriages. Then they got married to each other and had even more kids. Jeff and I don't have any kids yet, but we still have plenty of 'yours, mine, and ours' kinds of problems."

Jeff is Jeff Campbell, a twenty-nine-year-old architect with a large Eastern seaboard firm. Talking about Jeff is Kim, his wife of less than a year. Jeff and Kim lived together for more than two years before they decided to get married. Kim thinks that a lot of their current problems stem from patterns they established during their live-in years.

"Both Jeff and I value our independence. That's part of why it took us so long to make up our minds about marriage. While we were living together we made it real clear that we weren't going to be one of those couples that do everything together. You know the types I'm talking about—you never see one of them without the other. They finish each other's sentences and pretty soon they start looking alike. That wasn't for us. Jeff had his things—his work, his money, his friends—and I had mine, and that was just fine. We both figured there would be plenty of time to have 'our' things later. Well, now it is later and we're married, but it's still 'his things' and 'my things.' I thought getting married would create something special for us, make us a real couple, but Jeff goes on like we're just two people who live together. Just once I'd like to hear him talk about *we* or *us*, but it's all still my things and his things as far as he's concerned. It's gotten to the point now where I'm afraid to start a family for fear that they'll be 'my' kids, not 'our' kids. He says I'm being foolish and putting too much stock in words. If it were just words he might be right, but he acts just like he talks—he acts like he doesn't think about 'us' at all."

Collective concern as a dimension of intimacy does not

mean that the individuals in the relationship must subordinate their own identities to that of the relationship, but rather that the three identities in the relationship receive equal emphasis, that "we" is fully as important as "you" or "me." In truly intimate relationships, there is an evident collective concern in word and deed. Language is not the only measure of a sense of union in a relationship, and in fact can be a false measure: Many men speak of "our decision," "our time," "our hope" when it is clear that they've not consulted their spouses on any of these matters. Still, it seems reasonable to suggest, as Kim Campbell does, that if there isn't at least some talk of "us" or "we," there's probably not much collective concern in thought or action. Where words, thoughts, and actions come together, collective concern is greatest. That usually is the case for women, not so for men.

Cynthia Nover is a manager with a large national accounting firm. Married, with a three-year-old girl at home, Cynthia has had a very successful career and hopes to become a partner in her firm within the next couple of years. She speaks candidly about the struggle of being a wife, a mother, and a professional. "Because of my work, most of the women I know are career women. Probably two-thirds are married or have been, although I would guess that less than one-quarter of them have children. What makes it tough on a career woman is that we have to consider everything in terms of what it means not just for ourselves but for our marriages and children, too. I don't think most men do that, they just think about themselves. For example, if I'm faced with the choice of working late or coming in on the weekend, I always stop and think what would be easiest on Jennifer and Tom, and most of the time I call Tom and ask. The men around here don't even consider calling home to ask, and my husband wouldn't, either. I would never make a social obligation without checking it out with Tom first, but he makes plans constantly without consulting me. He just assumes I'll make whatever arrangements need to be made

—shopping or getting a sitter or whatever—without a thought for what I might want to do. He would never think that *together* we might decide what to do. I'm really not asking him to think of me first. I wish just once he'd think of us, the whole family—him, me, and Jennifer—first, before he thinks of himself."

Working women like Cynthia are particularly attuned to the kind of intimacy that is reflected in expressions of collective concern. Their experience is that few men know or express a sense of "we."

■ A professor wrote: "My work suffers from the sacrifices I make for my marriage. His work never suffers because he never thinks about how what he does might affect our marriage."

■ From a secretary: "To hear him talk, he's the moneymaker and the money manager, and I'm the spender. *We* make the money and *we* spend it. He just won't admit it."

■ A legal aide said, "There's his work and there's my work and there's not much energy left at the end of work for *our* marriage. That's why we don't have much of a marriage."

■ A housewife said, "To hear him talk, you'd think everything in our household was the result of a joint discussion and conversation. He's forever announcing, 'We think this,' or 'We've decided that.' But all of these 'we thinks' are his decision alone; none of the rest of us are ever involved in any way. I used to challenge him on it, but he always would say that he knew what was best for us, so after a while I just gave up. He never will accept that he doesn't make any room in our marriage for 'us.'"

Even many younger men who have been exposed to a broader set of role models and who may be more intellectually sensitive to a sense of shared obligation in a relationship behave in self-absorbed ways.

■ A high-school English teacher writes of her husband, "He believes the best thing for our relationship is for him to get into his thing as much as possible and for me to get into my thing as much as possible. Somehow by going our separate ways he thinks we'll be stronger as a couple. It doesn't make any sense to me."

■ The wife of a postal worker says, "He talks a good game of sharing—there's a lot of 'we' this and 'we' that—but I don't see much sharing. As near as I can tell, he still thinks of himself first and us second, if he thinks of us at all."

In defense of their alleged self-absorption, men are apt to cite traditional male roles or the pressures of work, time, or money. Men give the impression that they would show more collective concern if only circumstances permitted. These protestations of intent and innocence aside, the evidence suggests that men simply don't think of the relationship. And where men do have the time and circumstances to demonstrate their collective concern, they rarely do.

Margaret Barran's doctor-inventor husband is retired and they are able to live handsomely on royalties from his many patents. They have ample money and time, but Margaret complains that little of either is spent on "them."

"I guess I should consider myself lucky. I don't want for anything, except time with my husband. He encourages me in anything I want to do, travel, hobbies, whatever, so long as it doesn't require 'us' to do anything because 'we' simply don't do anything together. You should read our Christmas letter. Brian writes it every year, and every year he lists what he did and what I did and there's not one word of what we did together, because we didn't do anything together. It's embarrassing. I'm sure some people must wonder if we're still together at all. Well, we are and we're not, not in any way that really counts. He just doesn't think that a sense of being together is all that important, I guess."

If Margaret Barran's experience is an indicator of a common pattern, it is more than mere convenience that keeps men from displaying their collective concern. It is a matter of consciousness. Men simply do not think of relationships in the same ways that women do. Collective concern may be communicated by time together, by talk of we/us/our, or by acting in any way that shows that the relationship itself is valued as much as either party in it, perhaps even more so. Unlike many of the other meanings of intimacy introduced here, collective concern can be readily measured. We can literally see and hear this kind of loving. But is that proof of love? With the many meanings of love and ways of loving that there are, how can we know when we are loved? With so many meanings of love and ways of loving unknown to men, how can we know when men love?

HOW DOES HE LOVE? YOU CAN COUNT THE WAYS

We know that love, intimacy, and being close mean very different things to men and women. For men, sex seems to be the supreme intimacy, the context in which all issues of relational closeness are considered. Other dimensions of emotional bonding—time together, variety of exchanges, value of exchanges, exclusivity, and collective concern—are unknown to most men; their loving is limited to their narrow knowledge of what love is. By contrast, women are aware of the richness of loving relationships in all their dimensions. For women, sex is but one aspect of intimacy alongside shared experience, depth and breadth of personal knowledge, exclusivity of exchanges, and a common concern for the relationship. Women both exhibit and expect a full range of loving behavior. Little wonder, therefore, that when faced with men's limited loving, women—certain that they love men more than they are loved in return—have reason to wonder if they are loved at all. Men claim that they love as much as women, but in different ways. How can we know if we are loved or how we should love?

The language of intimacy is a start. When we learn that love stems from the duration of a relationship, the variety and value of relational exchanges, the exclusivity of the relationship, and the extent of collective concern, we can look for evidence of these dimensions in our relationships and the relationships of others. Of course, it will not always be the case that where conditions of intimacy exist, there are feelings of intimacy. We all, men and women alike, have known relationships that persisted for some time without any real caring developing. It is possible to engage in varied and valued exchanges with another without love. We even come to depend upon others for exclusive exchanges without feeling affection, or use the collective where there is little sharing. What is missing in these relationships which have the circumstances but not the caring of loving relationships, is the disclosure required by intimacy and love, the voluntary revealing of oneself to another that is the real basis for closeness. This voluntary disclosure is the "giving of oneself" that we associate with loving relationships.

Considerable work has been done in psychology and social psychology with "social penetration theory" or, as it is popularly known, the "onion skin theory" of personality. The central theme of this work is that an individual's personality is structured in a layered fashion, much like an onion: as one layer is peeled off a new layer, deeper, closer to the core, is revealed. Getting close to a person means moving toward the core, uncovering more and deeper layers of a personality. Using this approach, it is possible to measure intimate behavior by measuring how many layers have been revealed in a relationship.

We actually can measure the loving behavior of others by noting how much they give of themselves in their relationships with us. What do they reveal to us? How much have they told us about themselves? As important as *what* is revealed in a relationship is *how* it is revealed. Real intimacy and love rely on voluntary disclosure, not only because that is the only hope of accuracy, but because it is literally the giving of oneself to another. Much of what we know about others is drawn from inference and implication. We think that a spouse is having trouble at work because of his or her behavior at home. We sense that a child feels left out and alone at school because he or she seems withdrawn. These are important sources of information in a relationship, and we rely upon them so that we may act effectively. But as important and accurate as these secondary sources of information are, they tell us little about how we are loved or how our relationship is valued. They are not voluntary disclosures. They represent no "giving of oneself" on the part of the other.

If you truly want to know how you are loved by another, how intimate you are with a spouse, family member, or friend, you must ask yourself, "What has he told me about himself?"

■ Do you know his tastes and interests? His hobbies? His favorite music, films, foods?

■ Has he told you his attitudes and opinions? His political and religious views? His ideas on marriage and the family?

■ What has he revealed to you about how he feels about work and money? What about his job does he really like? What does he dislike?

■ Has he made you aware of his thoughts about himself? His own personality? His sense of self-esteem?

■ Has he confided in you about his sexual fantasies and fears?

These categories of personal information are not arbitrary; they have emerged from more than twenty-five years of social psychological research. Despite the use of different labels, there is general agreement as to the order of these informational layers. The outer circle constitutes the "public arena," that information about ourselves which we make readily available to others. This arena consists largely of tastes and interests, attitudes and opinions. These points of personal information are often made available to even the most casual of our acquaintances. Inside the public arena is the "private arena," that information about ourselves which is closer to what we most value, and therefore is more guarded. Here are feelings about work, money, relationships with others. At the core is the "personal arena," the repository of our thoughts and feelings about ourselves. For men, sexual fantasies and fears are deeply personal information. Women are more likely to treat this aspect of self as existing somewhere between private information and personal information. Everyone has at his core his sense of self-esteem, his feelings about who he is as a person.

For some individuals in certain circumstances, the order of information may be altered to account for individual taboos. These exceptions notwithstanding, in general we can say that the more exchanges in a relationship occur in the personal arena, the more intimate the relationship. Using disclosure patterns as the primary measuring device, it is possible to determine both who it is that men love and *how* men love. When combined with information about the duration of relationships, the significance of exchanges, the frequency of interaction, and the value attached to relationships, these patterns give us the most comprehensive picture to date of the loving behavior of men.

2 Husbands and Wives: The Man That's Missing in Marriage

Every man can have a woman—many women can have a woman—but to have had a man! That no woman has ever had.

—Dalton Trumbo, *Night of the Aurochs* (1979)

"Is that you?"

"Yes. I'm home."

"You're home so early. Is there anything wrong?"

"No."

"You feeling okay?"

"Sure."

"Things go all right at work today?"

"Yes."

"Well, it's nice that you could get home a little early for a change. Actually, I tried to call you about an hour or so ago, but they said that you had already left."

"Oh?"

"Yes. I was really upset this afternoon. I ran into Marjorie at the store and she looked like she'd been crying for days, so I offered to buy her a cup of coffee and she really let go. She told Bill to move out and she's decided to get a divorce, can you imagine that? Did Bill say anything to you about it at work?"

"No. He didn't mention anything."

"That's strange. Of course, I knew they were having problems but I didn't think it was anything all that serious. I just never thought that they would actually split up. Did you know that they've been married almost as long as we have, fourteen years?"

"Uh-huh."

"Do you know what Marjorie said when I asked her why it happened?"

"What?"

"She said that she and Bill hadn't talked to each other for ten years. According to her, they never had a real conversation. They just got by with whatever was necessary to live in the same house and no more than that. She said if it wasn't for her friends she would have no one to talk to at all. Can you imagine that? They always seemed to be as close as anyone else, but Marjorie says they hardly know each other at all. Apparently he never has talked to her and she just finally got tired of living with a stranger. So they're getting a divorce. I just can't believe she actually threw him out. I've been on the phone all afternoon and everybody else is as surprised as I am. Doesn't it surprise you?"

"Huh?"

"Doesn't it surprise you that Marjorie told Bill to leave? Did you expect her to do anything like that?"

"No."

"No what?"

"No. I didn't know about it."

"You don't sound very surprised."

"I just haven't thought about it much, I guess."

"Well, what do you think about it now?"

"I don't know."

"How can you not know? Bill and Marjorie are two of our closest friends. You yourself have said how much we have in common with them. Now I tell you that they're getting a divorce and you don't know how you feel about it? I just don't understand that at all."

"There's nothing to understand."

"What do you mean by that?"

"I don't mean anything by that. It's just that I don't spend a lot of my time thinking about other people's marriages."

"Do you spend much time thinking about our marriage?"

"I don't need to spend time thinking about our marriage."

"You don't, huh? Why not?"

"Because our marriage is fine. Don't you think so?"

"Yes, I do, but I like to hear it from you. Sometimes I'm not so sure that we aren't just like Marjorie and Bill. We never talk anymore. I need to know how you feel about us, about me."

"Here's how I feel about you."

"Come on, don't do that now. I'm not talking about sex. Don't you ever want us to have a real conversation?"

"What do you call what we're doing right now?"

"This isn't talking. This is interrogation. If I didn't ask you questions, you wouldn't say anything at all. I have to drag every word out of you."

"That's not true."

"Yes, it is. You never share anything with me. I never really know what you're thinking or feeling. I can never be sure that things are okay between us."

"Look, honey, don't make this into a bigger deal than it is. Bill and Marjorie have their problems, but that's got nothing to do with us. So enough of this talk. I'm going to get cleaned up. What's for dinner?"

No single dialogue can capture the infinite variety of ways in which men and women relate together as husbands and wives, but the above exchange, though fictional, is illustrative of a pattern of interaction that is recognizable to anyone who is married. It is a pattern rich in data about intimacy between husbands and their wives. Initially, the husband is a Reluctant Revealer, not readily volunteering to

37

his wife his feelings or thoughts. He must be drawn into disclosure by her questioning. Eager to know him, the wife watches his reactions, looking for clues to the mystery he presents. She draws inferences from the slightest information and presses him for affirmation of her conclusions, but he is a Cautious Confirmer, always in control of her knowledge of him. The closer she comes to the emotional, feeling dimensions of their relationship, the nearer to his "personal self," the more he attempts to escape: he is an Emotional Evader.

In their relationships with their wives, men are Reluctant Revealers, Cautious Confirmers, and Emotional Evaders. These patterns are practiced with varying intensity, depending on the issues involved: the deeper the wife probes beyond his public self to find out who a man is, how he views himself, and the way he views himself in the relationship, the less disclosing he is likely to be. These disclosure behaviors have significant implications as to how husbands love and how wives in turn feel loved by their husbands. They lie at the root of what is reported to be missing from so many marriages.

A HUSBAND'S PUBLIC SELF

On a recent weekend morning, as I was reading the sports page, I was surprised to learn that my office neighbor at work had won first place in his age group in our local marathon. I have worked next door to Martin for more than eight years and knew him to be a jogger, but I never imagined that he was a serious runner. Later that week at a dinner party with Martin and his wife, Carol, I expressed my surprise at learning that Martin had won a marathon. Carol replied, "You're surprised? I didn't even known he had entered!" When I said that she surely must have known he was in training, with long, time-consuming runs every day, she answered, "He never said anything to me about a race or a marathon. Running does take a lot of his time, but to tell you the truth, I've always thought that was just because he was such a slow runner!"

A husband's public self, his tastes and interests, attitudes and opinions, are usually well known to his wife. Rare is the instance in which a wife cannot name her husband's favorite foods or movies, list the ways he would prefer to spend his leisure time, or know where he stands on social issues, politics, or religion. Even allowing for those consciousness-raising (and often embarrassing) moments that occur in all marriages—"you mean I've been serving this dish for seven years and you never have liked it?" or "And all this time I went along because I thought you liked Westerns!"—we expect a wife to know what her husband likes and dislikes, and most often she does. In many instances this knowledge is the result of declarations on the part of the husband—blunt assertions, often dogmatic and opinionated, of what his preferences and views are. But the same man who, for instance, speaks his mind on political issues may be tight-lipped about his religious views.

The intimacy survey revealed that less than one-fifth of the husbands responding had fully disclosed all items in the public arena to their wives; three-fifths reported disclosing some in most details, but a remaining fifth disclosed almost nothing. In interviews we learned that even in the absence of voluntary disclosure, wives come to know the likes and dislikes, attitudes and opinions of their husbands. What a wife knows of her husband's likes, dislikes, opinions, and attitudes comes from her observation as well as from his revelation. If nothing else, the time she spends with a man gives a wife an opportunity to learn these public parts of him. Wives who would know their husbands' public selves must be opportunistic, attentive to the nuances of his behavior, because many husbands do not voluntarily tell their wives even the most obvious information about themselves.

Emily Markton, a wife of fifty-two years, mother of three

girls, and grandmother to another five, writes of the advice she has given each of her daughters and granddaughters on the occasion of their marriages: "Keep him well fed, but don't expect him to tell you what he likes to eat, because he won't know. If you make only what he tells you he likes, you'll end up cooking the same three or four things his mother made over and over again. You just fix lots of different things at the beginning and watch what he eats all of and what he leaves on the plate. After a while you'll know just what to cook. To this day your father couldn't tell you what foods he likes and doesn't like, but I could. You have to give your man what he likes to keep him happy, and you have to learn what your man likes, because he won't tell you."

Emily captures the experience of many women who commented that in the absence of a man's volunteering information about his preferences, the only way to really know his likes and dislikes in food, clothes (his or hers), books, movies, or even his taste in friends is to offer lots and pay close attention to what he rejects.

- "He never tells me what he likes but he never fails to tell me what he doesn't like!"

- "If I waited for him to line up things that he likes to do, we'd never do anything. I'm much more interested in finding out what he's interested in than he is."

- "I don't think he's hiding anything from me, I just honestly think that he doesn't give much thought to whether or not he likes certain things. At restaurants he has me order for him, because I know his tastes better than he does. I can understand that; after all, he's got a lot on his mind."

- "It's sort of like a game for men. All their lives some woman, first their mother, then their wife, has been trying to please them without their telling her what will please them. Men say, 'See if you can guess what will make me happy.' And we women fall all over ourselves trying to guess. If we guess wrong they give us hell, and if we guess right they say, 'Now see if you can do it again.'"

In the area of a man's public self—tastes and interests,

attitudes and opinions—the challenge facing a wife is to get her husband to overcome his reluctance to reveal his preferences. Many men implicitly or explicitly play the "see if you can guess what will please me" game. In order to know her husband at even the most superficial level, a wife must continually offer things—meals, entertainments, friends, her own appearance, herself—for acceptance or rejection. It is a game most women find easy to win, for the likes and dislikes of men are not hard to divine. But the price of winning is very high. As one woman noted, "It is hard to feel loved when you're always being judged."

Roberta Rouark has run out of patience with her husband's reluctance to reveal his preferences. After only two years of marriage, she's stated her intent to begin acting on her own interests rather than try to cater to her husband's unspoken desires. "Our relationship has been through a complete cycle in the space of about three years. When we were first dating, Jake would plan an evening or a day together and ask me if I was interested. Then, as we got more serious, it was more of a mutual thing, we'd talk together about what we wanted to do. Ever since we've been married, though, it's been clear that I'm the one who is supposed to think of the things that he would like to do, the places he'd like to go. It's my job to figure out what will please him. At first I stuck with the kinds of things we did while we were dating. Then he told me we weren't dating anymore and didn't need to do dating kinds of things. Everything new I've tried, he's rejected. It's gotten to be a serious problem with us. I don't feel like I can be me if I'm always trying to please him. If I can't be me, then I wonder how much Jake really loves me. I guess I'll find out because I've decided that I'm going to do the things that I like and the hell with trying to figure out what he likes!"

Roberta has described the major consequence of a relationship where one partner is placed in the position of always trying to please the other: "I don't feel like I can be me if I'm always trying to please him. If I can't be me, then I wonder how much Jake really loves me." When the reluctance of husbands to reveal their likes and dislikes to their wives leads those wives, wittingly or unwittingly, to offer alternatives in their search for acceptance or rejection, there is a sense that love is conditional:

- "He loves me as long as I please him, but he never tells me ahead of time what will please him. I'm always afraid I'll lose his love by doing the wrong thing."

- "I never feel loved just for me, for who I am, because I'm always trying to be something for him. If I stop trying, he'll stop loving."

- "The constant effort to figure out what he wants to eat, where he wants to go, who he wants to be with, wears you down. The only way you know you've done right is when he doesn't tell you you've done wrong. Is that love? I don't feel loved."

In every marriage, however intimate the partners, there can be areas of undisclosed likes and dislikes, attitudes and opinions. Where these exist, one partner often takes the initiative, offering up alternatives in the hope of discovering the preferences of the mate. In most marriages, pursuing this public information, on either a small or a large scale, is done by the wife. Over time, the one who continually initiates exchange begins to feel put upon by the other's selfishness, to feel taken for granted. The statements above speak to the feeling of conditional love that comes with always trying to please someone who won't reveal what pleases him. In some cases, this sense that love is conditional pervades the relationship; for most of us, however, it is a circumstantial feeling associated with that part of the other we would like to know but cannot—his true interests, opinions, likes, dislikes. When a man makes these small public disclosures, it is an expression of intimacy. When a woman is kept guessing, challenged to "see if you can please me," she may know that she is loved, but in that one arena of their relationship she will say, "I don't *feel* loved."

A HUSBAND'S PRIVATE SELF

The disclosure pattern of reluctant revelation, cautious confirmation, and emotional evasion that is used by husbands is intensified when the disclosure issues move from the relatively public arena of tastes and interests, attitudes and opinions, to the more private arena of work and money. Reluctant as men are to volunteer their likes and dislikes, their behavior provides ample clues to their inclinations. Such is not always the case with work and money, where a man's thoughts and feelings may not be telegraphed by his actions. Here what stands in the way of intimacy between husband and wife is not only his reluctance to reveal but also his reluctance to confirm conclusions she draws from the subtle clues available to her.

Women talk about work and money. Much more freely than do men, women exchange information about their work, their thoughts about money. Men view these issues as far more personal, more revealing of self than do women, and as a consequence give little data to others, even their wives. Because women receive so little real, firsthand information about their husbands' work and money concerns, they are forced to make a great many presumptions from secondary and even tertiary sources. Does he seem to look forward to going to work in the morning? Is he down at the end of the day? Does he get irritable when he has to pay the bills? Knowing that these presumptions at best only approximate the truth, wives constantly seek confirming evidence. They talk to other wives, they listen to their husbands' conversations at parties, and they confront their husbands with their conclusions. But confirmation is seldom forthcoming.

"Here's what I don't understand. How can somebody do something all day, five, sometimes six days a week, then come home and never want to talk about it? I mean never!" Ginger Crites describes herself as a "working homemaker." She is thirty-six, the mother of two boys, and works full time as secretary in a construction firm. Ginger's husband, Norm, is manager of a clothing store. In almost sixteen years of marriage, to Ginger's recollection they have never had a conversation about Norm's work. "I'm almost embarrassed to say it, but do you know that I don't even know how much money Norm makes? I have a general idea, of course, but I don't know for sure, because he deposits his paycheck directly and he keeps the checkbook. Whenever I ask he just says, 'It's enough.' That's just part of what I don't know about his work. I don't know whether his career is going up or down, if business is good or bad, I don't know any of the people he works with. Once, years ago, I went to the shop, but he made it very clear that I wasn't welcome there, so I never went again. For all I know about his work, he could be some sort of underworld character or something. That whole side of his life is a mystery to me.

"With me it's different. I tell him everything that's going on at work, who's doing well, who's not, who's sleeping with whom, who gets on my nerves and why. He gets a blow-by-blow report of every working day over the dinner table at night. I need to talk about it, to unload. I guess he doesn't have the same need, or maybe it's just that he doesn't need me that way. It doesn't seem natural to me that he wouldn't need to talk about his work to someone, but he says he doesn't and that's about all he says about work, no matter how many questions I ask."

Norm Crites may be the extreme, a man who tells his wife *nothing* about his work. But if that is extreme, the mean falls very close to it. Most men reveal very little about their work to their wives, and once again wives must become detectives, drawing on a variety of clues to track down their husbands' private identities. Cindy Kendrick, another working homemaker, has a husband who is only slightly more communicative about his work than Norm Crites. But Cindy thinks she's figured out a way to know when his job is getting to him, even though he won't tell her:

"Because we both work, we have a deal that we'll divide up the chores around the apartment. Usually I have to nag Greg to get him to do his share, but I've noticed that when he gets super-depressed about his sales, he throws himself into all the stuff around here, he dusts and vacuums like crazy, cleaning everything two or three times. If I ask him if things are going okay at work, he'll always say yes, but his cleaning is a dead giveaway that something's wrong, and the more he cleans, the worse it is at work. I still wish that he would talk about it with me, but at least I can tell when it's getting to him."

Many wives report the giveaways that signal what's going on at work in lieu of an admission from their husbands:

■ The wife of a professional athlete in the South writes, "Over the years I've learned that if it's a game that he's particularly up tight about, he'll wash the car. It's a simple thing, but it tells me that he's feeling the pressure and of course he'd never come right out and tell me that. It's a much more accurate predictor than whatever he says. Why, once when our car was in the shop and he had a big game, he washed the neighbor's car!"

■ From the Midwest, the wife of a plant foreman says, "If he's not eating, I know it's something at work. He won't talk about it, but he won't eat and that tells me as much as he ever could."

■ For a Rockies attorney who is married to another attorney, work is discussed as long as it's good: "If things are going well with his work, he'll ask about mine knowing that I'll ask in return and he can tell me how great things are going. But I know that if things aren't going well for him, he won't ask about my work. So the way it works out, we only talk about work when there are good things for him to say about his work. That, of course, is the easiest time to talk about something. I need to be able to talk about the not-so-good times as well, but he won't hear of it. And when it's clear to me that his work is not going so well, because he won't talk about it, there's nothing I can say that will get him to admit it."

These are only some of the behavioral clues that wives use to read their husbands. Others cover the full range from subtle to substantial—from the man who has two drinks before dinner instead of his customary one, to the man who kicks the dog he has named after his boss! Men may not talk about work and money, but they communicate volumes through their behavior. Wives, sincerely interested in sharing both the good and the bad with their husbands, are sensitive to these clues. They use them to form conclusions about how things are going in these mysterious parts of their husbands' lives, conclusions that require confirmation. These conclusions are typically presented by wives as observations of behavior and invitations to disclosure:

- "You're pretty grumpy tonight. A bad day at work?"
- "That's your third drink tonight. Is there something wrong at work?"
- "You got up in the middle of the night again and didn't come back to bed. Is something bothering you?"

The husband's response to these observations and invitations is, predictably, a curt, conversation-closing "No." Because confirmation would constitute disclosure of these personal concerns, the male response is defensive: he disclaims and denies even in the face of his own behavioral evidence to the contrary.

The persistent spouse who doesn't give up at her husband's initial defensive reaction, but piles behavior on behavior until the case is overwhelming, may be rewarded with a grudging acknowledgment that she has hit the mark. However, lest she think that she has discovered some basic truth about how her husband deals with work and money and has therefore moved closer to knowing him, the man will typically vow that the condition is inconsequential, circumstantial, temporary, entirely within his control (or at least entirely outside of her control), and therefore not the subject of further discussion or disclosure:

- "It's not worth talking about."
- "I guess you're right, work hasn't been so great lately, but it's nothing I can't handle."
- "I am a little worried about money, but once I get us over this hump, I think I'll have us in pretty good shape. It's nothing for you to worry about."
- "Things are terrible at the office, but I don't see what you can do about it."
- "I'll work it out."
- "It'll pass."

The effect of these cautious confirmations is that a man's work and money concerns remain shrouded in mystery. What his wife knows of these things is only what she can deduce from subtle and secondary sources. When her deductions do mount to a conclusion that might bring her closer to her husband, he's quick to remind her that what she thinks she knows about him is only true at that one time, in that one instance. Her conclusion, then, and the "closeness" she derives from it, is only circumstantial. For some women, the conclusions about their husbands' work and money selves are less than circumstantial; they are illusionary. Their husbands have misrepresented themselves to their wives; they have lied. Men are more likely to misrepresent themselves in the arena of the private self than in any other arena:

"My husband never told me anything about our money situation. I gave him my paycheck every two weeks and he handled everything, all the deposits, all the bills, everything. We weren't well off or anything, but we always seemed to have enough to pay for the things we really needed. It wasn't until after he died that I realized how much financial trouble he had gotten us into." Gina Griff has been widowed for two years. Her husband was killed when the car he was driving the wrong way on a four-lane highway was struck by an oncoming truck. It was late at night, but the highway was well lit and police hypothesized that Carl Griff must have been drunk or suicidal. Gina is only now beginning to work back toward some degree of financial security in the wake of the situation Carl left.

"Soon after Carl's death I found out that we had no money at all, and what's more, we owed—or I owed—everybody for everything. There was no money to bury him because he had borrowed to the limit on his life-insurance policy. He had taken out a second mortgage on the house, hadn't made a car payment in over three months, was delinquent on our taxes, and had even pawned some of my jewelry—heirlooms from my mother. It seems Carl was a big gambler and a big loser. He gambled away everything we had, and I didn't even know it. Looking back, I really blame myself for being so trusting, so naïve. I see now that I made it so easy for him because I believed whatever he told me about our money, I never doubted, never questioned, because it never entered my mind that he would lie about it. I've made arrangements with all the legal creditors, the bank, the mortgage company, Carl's employer—he had borrowed against his salary—but there are lots of others. Before I moved and went back to using my maiden name, strangers would call, saying, 'Your husband owed me and I expect you to pay.' It got pretty scary at times.

"It's odd to think that you can live with someone for so many years [six], loving them and believing that they love you; then, just when you're missing them the most, you find out that you really didn't know them at all. The Carl I grieved for simply never existed, it was all a lie."

Miles away from Gina Griff's Midwestern home, Katherine Burnette, from the West Coast, tells of her husband's misrepresentations: "Hugh and I never were the sort of people who got together a lot with friends from work. With both of us working, we always had little enough time for each other, let alone for other people. Then, too, our schedules usually meant that the time we had available, other people didn't. I was working nights at the hospital and he was on the day shift at the refinery. We kept saying to each other that the sacrifice was worth it because every spare penny went into savings so we could buy a house. So he had his work and I had mine and we had the odd day or two together, that's the way it was for almost four years. Not ideal maybe, but not so bad either, if you've got a goal in mind.

"I guess I tell you all this so you'll understand how it is that Hugh could have been out of work for almost six months before I discovered it! It's true. Hugh got fired and he didn't tell me for nearly half a year. Actually, he didn't tell me at all. I found out and confronted him with it and he finally had to admit to what he had been doing. There was a patient who had been admitted to the hospital, and looking over his forms I noticed that he worked at the refinery where Hugh did. I casually asked him if he knew my husband, and he said, "Yes, I know Hugh. I was real sorry they let him go. We had some good times together at work. What's he been doing?" Well, of course I thought he was mistaken, so I asked some more questions and it came out that some six months ago Hugh had been put on probation and then fired for something or other. The next morning, after Hugh supposedly went to work, I called the refinery, pretending to be an employer checking up on Hugh's references, and they told me they couldn't give him a good recommendation because he had been fired.

"That night I stayed home from work and confronted Hugh. He didn't even try to deny it—he couldn't. He had been pretending to go to work for all that time, not even trying to get a job—just spending his days going to the movies, the library, bars, anything to pass the time until it was time to come home. He had been drawing money out of our savings and then banking it like it was his paycheck. I never noticed because he always handled the bank accounts. When I asked him why he never told me, he said he just couldn't bring himself to admit to me that he had lost his job. He was just going to pretend that he hadn't until he found something else.

"Maybe we should have talked more about work all along, but when you're both working so hard every day, it's nice to come home and leave all of that behind you. I always thought it was kind of nice that we didn't talk about work, but I guess if you don't talk about something that's as much a part of someone as work is, you don't really know that someone. I sure didn't know Hugh, and now that I do know him, I'm trying to figure out if I can still love him."

The stories of Gina and Katherine are uncommon, to be sure, but the elements are not that rare where husbands' work and money selves are concerned:

- "I remember the first year I actually read the income tax forms before I signed them. I was shocked to learn that we were rich! He had me pinching pennies for years, never going out, never buying new clothes, and all the time he was making money hand over fist. When I figured out what was really going on, I got mine. Then I got out."

- "He always made out like he was in a very important position. From everything he said, I thought he ran the office. I guess I was shocked and a little hurt when I found out he wasn't much more than a clerk. I was hurt for him more than for myself. Why did he think he had to lie to me about his work?"

- "You get to a point, after you catch them in a little lie here and a little lie there, that you don't believe anything they say, especially about things like work and money. Where I am with him now is, if I don't see it for myself, I don't believe it, no matter what he says."

The nature of the public self is such that even without voluntary disclosure the dimensions can be accurately ascertained. A man's behavior is evidence of his likes and dislikes; further confirmation is not necessary. This is not the case with the private self. A man's behavior may give clues to his feelings and thoughts about such things as work and money, but inasmuch as these arenas of activity may be removed from the view of his spouse, she needs direct confirmation of her conclusions, confirmation that in the main can come only from her husband. Since confirmation would be tantamount to disclosure, it is seldom forthcoming; when present, it is likely to be circumstantial or even misrepresented. At times the misrepresentation is willful and purposeful, a lie. At other times it is the withholding of information, such as how much money he makes or how well he's doing on the job. Some husbands allow their wives to form a conclusion about their work or money selves without either confirming or denying, letting her think what she will. The effect of these forms of behavior is to undermine the trust that intimacy requires. The wife feels that her husband does not trust her enough to reveal important aspects of himself, and in the absence of confirmation she begins to mistrust her own judgment and knowledge of him. Lacking trust, it is difficult for her to feel loved.

When a man makes a mystery of his work and money self, he makes a maze of getting close, being intimate. Traversing this maze is made more difficult by the fact that the closer one gets to the center, the more elusive the target becomes.

As mysterious as a man may be about his work and money self, it does not approach the evasive behavior he engages in when the topics of disclosure are his personal self—his self-esteem, his own personality, and his sexual thoughts and desires. Here, in the areas that lie closest to his core sense of self, nearest to who he is, getting close to a man can be an elusive goal.

A HUSBAND'S PERSONAL SELF

Beneath a man's public self, his tastes and interests, attitudes and opinions, beneath his private self, his orientation

51

toward and experience with work and money, lies his personal self—the way he thinks and feels about himself. A wife may learn of her husband's public self, reluctant as he may be to reveal it, through the preferences he makes apparent in his public behavior, the choices he makes that communicate his likes and dislikes, the opinions he expresses (usually in reaction to others). A wife may learn of her husband's private self by deducing how he feels about his work and about their money situation from the subtle clues he gives her. A wife can learn about a husband's personal self only insofar as he allows her to know how he feels about himself and how he deals with his feelings about himself. Disclosure of one's personal self to another is, for any man or woman, the most intimate, most loving behavior he or she can express.

We know that men are reluctant revealers of even the most public of information about themselves. We have seen that men confirm others' conclusions about their private selves only with the utmost caution. From this prior knowledge, one might anticipate that men would be even more reluctant and cautious where dimensions of their most personal selves are concerned. This prior knowledge and experience notwithstanding, nothing can quite prepare one for just how evasive men can be where their feelings and thoughts about themselves are concerned:

"Arnold has always been a very private person. Even when we were first dating, he was quiet and reserved. I think that's part of why I was so attracted to him; he seemed so much more mature than all of the other boys I knew, more stable, more secure. And Arnold has provided me and the children with a very stable, secure life. I have no complaints about that whatsoever. If he hasn't always been the most exciting person to be married to, or the most demonstrative father and husband, I have pretty much accepted that that is just the way he is, and I remind myself that that's why I married him to begin with. But ever since he retired, I've become less accepting and I find myself asking more and more often just why I did marry him."

Claudia Finnick has been married to Arnold for forty-two years. They have two children and three grandchildren. Within the last year, Arnold has retired from his job with the local school district and Claudia has cut back on the hours she spends selling real estate, in part because of the state of the economy and in part to spend more time with Arnold. For Claudia, their new time together has served only to underscore what strangers they have become.

"All during our marriage, each of us has had something else. For Arnold, there has always been his work—forty years with the schools, starting at the very bottom and ending up at the top. For me, there were the children, and when they were gone, I went to work. With Arnold being such a private person and both of us being so busy with our own things—not that he wasn't involved with the kids, but they were mainly my responsibility—I guess we sort of lost touch with each other over the years. When he retired and started spending time at home, I realized that in so many ways we were really strangers.

"At first I just put it down to his retirement. I had read how difficult it can be for a man to go from work to retirement, so I was anticipating some problems. What I didn't anticipate was that I would know so little about the man I had lived with for more than forty years! As an example, Arnold and I had never had a discussion of what he wanted to do when he retired, he just always refused to talk about it. To this day I don't know how he feels about himself these days, whether he thinks retirement is a reward or a punishment, if he has any goals or ambitions now that he's not working. I push and I probe, but he either avoids me or gets defensive or downright petty. One of our biggest fights was over why I had so many loaves of bread in the freezer! Can you imagine? Here I am, all of a sudden living with someone I feel like I don't even know anymore, begging for some communication from him about who he is now, how he feels about himself, how he feels about me, and he wants to argue about what I've got in the freezer.

"It's just so frustrating. We've invested too much to give up. I don't want a divorce at my age, but I don't want to live with a stranger, either. I can't just avoid the whole thing like Arnold does. I want to know who he is after all these years, but he won't let me know him."

Claudia's discovery of the distance that has developed between her husband and herself is not an uncommon occurrence among couples who have been married for some time but who have not really communicated. When external events—the children leaving home, retirement, major illness—force husband and wife together, it becomes clear that the years of declining communication have left them virtual strangers. They have changed since they last really knew each other (if indeed they ever did), and they must either become reacquainted or resign themselves to being together without being close. The problem is exacerbated by the fact that it is rarely viewed as a problem by the man involved; he feels he neither needs nor desires the kind of closeness that comes from the disclosure of one's personal self. The result is that the woman feels unloved and she experiences no appreciation or action from her husband to assuage her feelings. Rather, he is defensive and evasive in response to her attempts to learn who he is after all these years.

The cumulative effect of years of withholding oneself from another can be devastating for a relationship. But the same feelings of emotional estrangment and abandonment at the hands of a man are evident in isolated events. Deborah Lasser describes her situation:

"Before we were married, I got pregnant. I knew Don wasn't ready to get married and have a family and neither was I, so I got an abortion. We never really talked about it before or after. I just did it. About two years after that, Don and I got married. Within months I was pregnant again, but I miscarried. The doctor told Don and me that something was wrong inside of me (probably from the abortion) and I would never be able to have children. When he heard that, Don got up and walked right out of the doctor's office without saying a word to me. He never has in three years.

"I went through a year of pure hell, blaming myself for what had happened. I became a recluse. I didn't go anywhere or talk to anyone. I cried constantly. After two years of therapy, life is getting back to normal for me, or as close to normal as it ever will be; at least I can talk about it. Don still can't, not even to me.

"In all these years the only thing Don has ever said about not having children is 'It's not your fault.' There was a time when that was enough; I was so guilt-ridden that I needed every reassurance from him that he didn't hold me responsible. As I got more in control of my own reaction, though, I began to wonder how he was dealing with his reaction, but he refused to talk about it. Whenever I would bring it up, he would simply say, 'I don't want to talk about it right now.' As though it were just the time I had picked that kept him from talking about it. But in three years there never has been a 'right time' for Don to talk about it. Gradually my wonder over how he was dealing with it turned to concern. It was such a big part of me that I couldn't help but think it was eating away at Don. I urged him to go see a counselor and talk about it there, but he just got defensive. 'I'm dealing with it fine by myself,'" is what he said. Lately, in the last year or so, my concern has given way to anger. I am mad as hell that he won't discuss what happened to us. The abortion completely changed my life; I am a different person because of it. It had to have some effect on Don. If he loves me, he should share that. If he can't or won't talk to me about it, either because it didn't faze him—which I just can't believe—or because he doesn't want to tell me, then we don't have much of a marriage.

"You always hear about how tragedy brings people closer together. I think that is true only if both people will share how the tragedy touched them, otherwise tragedy drives people apart. At least that's what I see happening to Don and me."

Traumatic events such as the death of a child, the death of a spouse, the loss of a home, and the like frequently highlight the differing emotional responses of men and women. The ability or inclination to show emotion in the moment is not the measure of love here; rather, it is the ability or inclination to share one's personal response, to discuss the why and how of one's personal emotional reaction, with a loved one. Men characteristically avoid such disclosures and discussions, leading women to believe that men have no emotional responses to events or that men are dealing with their responses on their own. In either case, a wife is likely to feel shut out and hence, less loved. This pattern of evading emotional disclosures may be most evident in times of crises, but it can be seen in the day-to-day, commonplace interactions of husbands and wives as well:

"Stephen says I get too emotional, that I take everything too personally. That may be, but he takes nothing personally at all, at least not so you'd know it, and it drives me crazy." Lucy Crolind has hit on what she thinks is the basic difference between herself and her husband, perhaps the basic difference between men and women, and she's not at all happy with what she has discovered. "I just happen to think everything that happens to Stephen or me is important to both of us, whether it's at home or at work or wherever. I'm forever telling Stephen how different things that happen affect me, what I think about them and how they make me feel. Most of the time I might as well be talking to myself. For one thing, he never responds to what I tell him about me, and of course he never tells me anything about him. It's like he goes through life and nothing ever touches him. If it does, he never tells me about it. I used to worry about it a lot, I thought there was something wrong with our marriage, but my friends all say the same thing about their husbands. I've decided it's just another one of those ways that men are different from women. I don't like not knowing how Stephen thinks about things, especially how he thinks about himself, but I guess that's just the way men are. I'm not going to be able to change that. Really, I've got it better than a lot of my friends, because nothing really bad has ever happened to either Stephen or me—nothing that I know of, I should say. If it did, I don't know how we would deal with it, because I wouldn't be satisfied until I knew for sure what it meant to him, and I know for sure that he wouldn't tell me."

Women typically do relate even the most commonplace events and experiences in a way that reveals something about themselves, how they were affected, what those events meant to them personally. By contrast, men, if they relate events and experiences at all, are likely to do so in an impersonal, "just the facts ma'am" manner, with no hint that they were affected, or in what way. Many women commented on their husbands' impassiveness and the implications:

- "If I wanted to be kind, I would say that he's stoic. It gripes the hell out of me, though, because his stoicism comes off as indifference as far as I'm concerned, indifference to me and our marriage, and I just can't accept that."

- "Because I care about things and show it, he says that I overreact. He never shows what he cares about, so I've come to the conclusion that he doesn't care very much about anything, including me."

- "I don't know what it would take to move him emotionally, because I've never seen any emotion from him, unless you can call swearing at football teams emotion."

- "He has a way of belittling the things that really mean something to me by never talking about what the same things mean to him, as though they weren't worth the effort. It makes me feel foolish."

- "I feel sorry for him. I don't think he knows himself well enough to know what is important to him and what's not—let alone to tell me."

Underlying these comments and countless others in the same vein is the sentiment shared by women that the personal self is an emotional self, and the most important "self" in a relationship. In the behavior of men, women miss both an acknowledgment of the personal/emotional self, in the form of some response to their own revelations, and a concomitant disclosure. When a man ignores (or worse, ridicules) the personal emotional disclosures of others and/or evades disclosures of his own, he is withholding himself from the relationship. He is not loving.

For men, the personal self is also a sexual self. They are as evasive in sexual disclosures as they are in emotional issues. This is not the case with women, who are more likely to view sexual disclosures as a dimension of the private self. This important difference in the way men and women deal with their sexual selves is a source of many problems in loving between husbands and wives.

Few issues are as volatile in marital relationships as the issue of sex—sexual identity, sexual satisfaction, sexual relationships. This volatility is largely latent, below the surface, often acted on and experienced by each partner, but rarely talked about. There are many reasons why the sexual concerns of couples are so seldom discussed, but as influential as any other is the male's evasiveness regarding his sexual self. Research data illustrate that fewer than two out of every ten men have disclosed their favorite forms of sex play, their former sex partners, or their sexual fantasies, even to their wives. It would seem that at the very core of a man's personal self is his sexual self.

Here, three women describe the difficulties they experience in getting close to their men, in loving, because of the inability or unwillingness of their husbands to bring their sexual selves into the relationship. The women represent three different generations, as do their marriages, but the problems they discuss apply across age groups, to marriages of all lengths.

58

Rebecca Pulber is fifty-seven; she has been married for thirty-six years to Leonard. Neither of them had ever dated anyone else before their marriage, nor have they had relations with anyone else since their marriage. Their entire sexual experience has been gained with each other. Rebecca talks about their past and present sexual relations. "In the last three or four years there's been a real change in our sex life. For some years now there has been a gradual decline in how often we had sexual relations. I know that this is normal for people our age. I don't have any idea of what the average would be, but I'm sure that Leonard and I had relations far less often than most. Still, it wasn't an issue until almost four years ago. That was when we stopped having any sex at all. I think in the last four years we have been sexually close no more than eight or nine times, few enough that I can remember each occasion. This has caused me a great deal of worry and tears, but Leonard won't talk about it.

"I should tell you that in all our years of dating and marriage, Leonard and I never have talked about sex. Never. I guess we're both sort of old-fashioned that way, but I, for one, never felt sexual relations were something that needed to be talked about, even between a husband and wife. I've always felt that sexual intimacy ought to come naturally in a loving relationship. If you talked about it, it made it dirty somehow. Leonard has felt the same, or at least I have always taken his silence on the subject to mean that he has felt the same. That attitude may seem strange to a lot of younger wives today, but most women my age were brought up the same way and they have treated sex the same way in their marriage. Now that sexual relations are not occurring naturally for Leonard and me, I have to believe that something has gone wrong with our loving. I thought that he loved me less now, and that was why he stopped having relations with me.

"I have been so upset over this whole thing that I finally

broke down and told my daughter. It was very difficult to do, because I had never talked with her about sexual relations between her father and me. But I needed to talk to someone, and one day when she was over I just found myself pouring out my heart to her. I cried and cried. She said that the whole thing was probably caused by changes Leonard was going through, sort of like a menopause. She was sure he didn't love me any less; he was just feeling different about sex. She was the one who said that I should talk to him about it. I still wasn't sure, but I read some articles and I decided that she was probably right, at Leonard's age he might be experiencing some signs of impotency. I've learned that many men do, and I think that might make him shy away from sexual relations. That helped me feel better about myself, and I tried to get Leonard to talk about it, thinking it would help him too, but he refused. He simply will not talk about sex at all. He actually gets up and leaves the room if I even so much as bring the subject up. At other times he accuses me of being 'obsessed' or 'sex-crazed.' Imagine, sex-crazed at my age. I've finally become convinced that it's his attitude toward sex that is the problem, not mine, but I can't get him to talk about it. Maybe that alone says something about how much he loves me or doesn't love me anymore. When I start thinking like that, I'm right back where I started. I just wish that all those years when we were doing it but not talking about it, we would have been talking about it too, because now we're not doing it and he can't talk about it. It's driving me half out of my head with worry. I just don't know how it can possibly get better if we can't even talk about it."

Jane and Craig Holt have been married for only one-fourth of the Pulbers' thirty-six years. Like Rebecca Pulber, Jane is uncertain of her husband's sexual self, but the source of her uncertainty is quite different, as is the language she uses to describe the problem:

"To watch Craig with other women, you would think

that he is the world's greatest cocksman. He's constantly flirting. His conversations are filled with sexual innuendos. He's always touching, patting, turning women on. The thing is, it's all just a front. At home in bed with me he has nothing at all; half the time he can't get it up, and I have to take care of myself. After we were first married, I thought it was all me, that other women were exciting to him but I wasn't. I would get so jealous and we would fight like crazy. Then we'd try to make up in bed, but that only led to sexual frustration for both of us and reinforced the feelings I had in the first place.

"Craig wasn't much help. He denied that his way with other women was anything more than innocent flirting, but he would never deal with his inability to do anything with me in bed. It got so bad that I threatened divorce more than once if he didn't either stop flirting or start fucking—preferably both!

"There was no one big thing that made me realize what was really going on with Craig. It was just that I began to see that nothing ever did come from all his flirting. It was just his way of relating to women. At the same time, I had a couple of experiences with men that assured me there wasn't anything wrong with me as a woman, in or out of bed, so whatever problem there was, I decided it definitely was on Craig's side of the bed, so to speak. The way I have figured it is that Craig compensates for his sexual problems by putting up this cocksman front. It works, too, because no one who knows him would ever doubt that he's great in bed. The two friends I have told the truth to were astonished, they couldn't believe it. But it is so obvious to me now that that is his way of dealing with the problem, which of course is not dealing with it at all.

"There's a world of difference between my knowing what Craig's problem is and his knowing what it is. He still won't even admit that he has a problem. He puts up this sexy front with me just like he does with every woman, but when

I get him into bed he's got nothing to put up at all, if you know what I mean. Where we are now is that I've told him if he won't talk to me about it, he has to get some professional help—and if he won't do that, I will divorce him. I simply will not live with someone who treats sex like some kind of secret. It's no secret to me that he's got a problem. I don't know who he thinks he's fooling besides himself."

As a newlywed, Amanda Kerlow has a lot of ideas about how she is going to keep her marriage to Bill alive and vibrant into their twilight years. At twenty, it is her first marriage. Her husband, Bill, who is twenty-three, was married once before, for less than two years. Knowing that Bill has already had one marriage that didn't work, Amanda is determined to be the kind of wife that Bill wants, in every way:

"I think the most important thing in a marriage is for each person to try to please the other. It's so obvious that the reason people get divorced is because they stop trying to make each other happy. That's not going to happen to Bill and me. I know we've only been married a short time—almost ten months—but I think we're already doing things that will ensure a long, happy life together. The only place where we're having any problems at all is around sex. The reason we're having some problems is because I get such mixed messages from Bill about what he really likes.

"When we're having sex, Bill really talks a lot, dirty-like, you know? And he likes for me to talk the same way. It's a real turn-on for him. He'll tell me about things he wants me to do or say, and I'll do it and he really gets excited—we have great sex. The problem is, outside of bed he never wants to talk about it, he even gets mad if I do or say the things that turn him on so much in bed. Do you understand? I don't want to go into all of it, but I'll give you an example that's not too embarrassing. The other night in bed he was playing with my breasts, telling me how pretty they were and how I ought to go braless all the time because then he could see them and all. Well, the next night we were going out to a party and I dressed in this low-cut blouse without a bra, just like he said he liked the night before in bed. I thought he'd really be happy. Instead he got mad. He said some really shitty things to me, like 'What are you advertising?' and 'You look like some hooker!' I changed, and we went on to the party. Then, later that night in bed, he told me how good I looked before, without a bra, and how much it turned him on when I dressed like that. What am I supposed to think? I'm damned if I do and damned if I don't!

"The thing of it is, I really do want to please Bill and I'll do whatever it takes to make him happy, but the only time I can get him to talk about sex is while we're doing it. I've learned that I can't trust that what he tells me he wants when we're in bed is what he really wants. Outside of bed he just won't discuss it at all. The subject never comes up except when I do something I think he'll like, only to find out it makes him mad. If we could just one time talk rationally about how each of us felt about sex, when we weren't all wrapped up in it, we wouldn't have such a problem. The way it is now, I'm getting more and more inhibited in bed, and he's getting more and more demanding. Lately he's been talking about some really kinky kinds of things. I don't know whether he's serious about them or not—I'm afraid to try them and I'm afraid not to. How can I know how to make him happy? That's really all I want."

Certainly there are wives who are as inhibited and guarded about their sexual selves as are the men described here—women who, like these men, have a difficult time disclosing their own feelings about sex, sexual identities and sexual fantasies to others, even to their spouses. As a rule, however, women are much freer in this regard than are men. Research shows, for example, that women view sex, in concert with work and money, as a dimension of the private self. Men treat sexual issues as the most personal of personal information, the last data to be disclosed to another—if, indeed, it is disclosed at all. A contributing factor here is the male tendency to associate intimacy with sex. It was noted earlier that there is a feeling among men that the sex act is evidence of intimacy, and further sexual expression is not necessary. More than one man expressed the sentiment that intercourse was the only interaction necessary to deal with sexual issues in a relationship:

- "All she needs to know about my 'sexual identity' is that I'm one horny son of a bitch, and if she can't keep me happy I'll get somebody who can."

- "It is just this sort of question that is the real problem with sex in relationships today—all this analyzing and theorizing is just inviting trouble. Time was, the act alone was proof enough of love; in my house it still is."

- "You can't screw 'em if you don't first convince 'em you really love 'em—then they want more of you than just screwin'. The so-called liberated woman wants more than any man can give. Why can't they be satisfied with just sex, like men are?"

- "Desire is enough proof for me. It ought to be for her, too."

- "There's more to love than sex? What?"

Just as intimacy is not solely expressed sexually, so sexual expression is not limited to the sex act. Women are much more conscious of this than men are. Husbands who do not express their sexual selves other than through intercourse (and husbands engage in remarkably few non-intercourse-oriented physical sexual expressions) are experienced by their wives as limited lovers withholding yet another part of their sexual selves:

- "Sometimes a woman feels sexy but she doesn't want sex. She wants some loving attention and affection. With men there's no such difference; when they feel sexy, they want sex."

- "He never just pets me, it's all or nothing at all; lots of times I'd rather have nothing at all."

- "Sex gets in the way of love, at least having sex gets in

the way. Sometimes I think if we touched more and made love less, we'd really be closer. My husband says that's crazy."

- "Men only know one way to be sexy—screw. They can't understand that a woman wants some physical attention that doesn't always end up in the missionary position."

The notion of a sexual self is not limited to physical sex, but can also include one's sense of sex identity—what it is to be a man or a woman. Women today are much more expressive of their sex-identity concerns than are men. Countless wives are struggling with what it is to be simultaneously spouse, mother, homemaker, and careerist. Women involve their husbands in their struggle, airing issues before them, testing alternatives. It seems logical that men might be dealing with similar questions regarding their own sex identity, if for no other reason than to relate to the "new woman." A few men are struggling with questions of sex identity (though far fewer than movies and television situation comedies would have us believe). Their struggles may be manifest in the behavior of men toward their spouses, but they are rarely a topic of discussion between spouses. In other words, a wife will share her sex-identity struggle with her husband, while a husband, if he's struggling with sex identity at all, is more likely to subject his wife to it than share it with her:

One woman said, "I keep thinking we ought to work out the roles for our relationship *together*. We at least ought to get our priorities straight. But I'm conducting a monologue. I talk about what I'm trying to be, but I get zero response from him. I wonder—can you be a 'new woman' if your husband's not a 'new man'?"

The reluctance of men to bring important aspects of themselves into their marriages has some predictable consequences for husbands and wives. The mystery of a man leads many a woman to comment, "I don't really know the man I'm married to," or, "After all these years I still never know quite what to expect from him." Or, more dramatically, "I'm married to a complete stranger."

The cautious commitment that is so characteristic of male disclosure patterns, with their grudging acknowledgment of their own private and personal selves, results in many women feeling that their husbands' love for them is at best circumstantial and at worst conditional:

- "I feel like the minute I stop pleasing him he'll leave me."

- "I don't know from one minute to the next what it is that does please him; I'm always being tested."

- "Just when I think that I've got him all figured out, he changes on me."

Finally, the emotional evasiveness of men, particularly as regards their personal selves, leaves many wives with the feeling that they give much more to their relationships than they receive. Ultimately, this perceived inequity in what is presumed to be a partnership leaves wives wondering just how much they are loved. Some wonder if they are loved at all:

As this woman commented, "I feel like I've met him more than halfway. I give and give and give and get nothing in return, nothing of him. The way I see it, I give much more of myself—like *all*—to the relationship than he does. I love him more than he loves me. Sometimes I wonder if he loves me at all. Why does he do this to me?"

There is little behavior from their husbands to which women can look to know their love. Reluctant Revealers, Cautious Confirmers, and Emotional Evaders, men withhold their public, private, and personal selves and in so doing withhold their love. One cannot help but ask why.

WHY DO HUSBANDS WITHHOLD THEMSELVES FROM THEIR WIVES?

In attempting to discover why husbands are not more intimate with their wives we must look first to husbands themselves. We find that the reasons they give are as varied as the kinds of behavior they defend. When confronted with their wives' feeling unloved, the first response of most husbands is defensive. "She knows how I feel, I don't need to tell her or show her." This defense is really twofold. On the one hand, it implies that the man does engage in loving behavior already and that this is adequate (and ought to be acknowledged), so that further expressions of loving are not necessary. Such a defense also implies that there is something slightly unreasonable about women's demands for more intimacy. The proof of the unreasonableness is that the husband doesn't experience the need for further intimacy. In other words, he's satisfied with the way things are and the fact that she is not puts her in the wrong—it's her problem, not his. This attitude that "I don't need it, and if she were being reasonable she wouldn't, either" is seen not only in the general issue of the amount of loving in a relationship, but also in the more specific disclosures that make up loving behavior, especially in those critical personal self-disclosure areas.

Deborah Lasser has been distraught for some years over her abortion and subsequent inability to have children. But what bothers her more is the fact that her husband, Don, has never discussed their problem with her. She argues, "How close can we be, if we can't talk about something as important as this?" Don Lasser acknowledges that he has never talked about the issue with his wife, but it is his claim that he has never needed to. "Of course it was a tremendous loss and of course I have been affected by it, but I have dealt with all of that in my own way, as Deborah has in hers. I don't need to keep rehashing it over and over again, and I don't see why she would want to. We're both better off just letting it go and getting on with our lives. At the time, she needed to talk with someone about her own feelings and I listened and helped her deal with what she was going through. I didn't need to talk to anyone about my feelings, and I still don't. That doesn't mean that I don't love Deborah, it just means that I have different needs. She shouldn't judge my feelings by her needs."

In thirty-six years of marriage, Leonard Pulber has never discussed sex with his wife, Rebecca, and is now, by her account, experiencing some sexual problems. He, too, imposes his own needs as the parameters of intimate disclosure between himself and his wife. "I have never had the need to talk about sex, in or out of my marriage. I don't have that need now, and if I don't need to talk about it, I don't know why she would." Throughout male reports that further intimacy is not necessary, there is an undercurrent of a basic difference in the needs of men and women. A great number of men, when asked why they are not more intimate, point to this difference and say, "That's just the way I am." Leonard Pulber amplifies the difference in this way: "Men and women are different. It's as simple as that. Women want to analyze everything; they can't take things just as they come, but always need to look for some hidden meaning. So I don't reveal a lot to my wife, so what? It doesn't mean anything. It's just the way I am, and I don't think that I'm any different from most other men. We're just more private than women are. Maybe we don't show a lot of love, but that doesn't mean that we don't love. It also doesn't mean that we are going to change. Our privacy is just one of those things that women are going to have to accept. Hell, we accept a lot of stuff about women that we don't especially like, at least I do about Rebecca. So if she thinks I'm not loving enough, I'm sorry, but that's just the way I am, and she's going to have to live with it."

Is it the natural order of things that men are not as loving as their wives would like them to be? Most men seem to think so. Jim Rouark, the young husband whose reticent behavior forces his wife to divine his unspoken interests and desires, defends his behavior with some conventional male thinking:

"First of all, I'm not a very talkative, outgoing sort of

person. That may be wrong, but that is the way I am and I don't think that's going to change. Roberta knew that when she married me, so it's not like it's any big surprise to her or anything. Of course, there are certain things that I like and certain things that I don't like, but I'm not the sort of person to go advertising them around any more than I want other people to advertise what they like and don't like. I can't stand all those T-shirts and bumper stickers with 'I like this' or 'I like that'—I mean, who gives a shit, really? The point is, maybe I don't make it too easy for Roberta to figure out what I really like or what I really want to do, but that's who I am and that's who she married. I see it as sort of her duty, just like it's my duty as her husband to try and please her. But I can't be somebody I'm not and I'm just not a very public person."

In many ways, to accept a certain degree of reticence as regards the revelation of a man's public self may be relatively easy for women to do, because there are many other ways in which the public self is disclosed. Where the issues are much more private, however, a wife is often asked to accept an absence of intimacy and disclosure, which has the effect of closing her off from an important dimension of her husband because there is simply no other way to get the information that intimacy requires. Such is the case where personal issues of sexual identity are concerned, as with Jane and Craig Holt. Craig who has problems of impotency with his wife, refuses to discuss it. He speaks here without knowledge of what Jane has revealed:

"I don't know exactly what Jane has told you about our relationship, but I can guess that if she talked about problems at all, she complained about my flirting. I'll tell you exactly what I tell Jane. I do flirt, I don't know why, but I do. It doesn't mean anything at all; I never would get involved with another woman. It doesn't mean I love Jane any less. It's just one of those things that I do. It's a part of me that I've accepted, and I think Jane is just going to have to accept it too. I was the same way with my first wife, but that's not why we got divorced. There were other things involved. If Jane asked me to stop, I'm not sure that I could. It's just the way I relate to women. I think she can accept that as long as it doesn't lead to anything else. I think she has accepted it, 'cause we don't even talk about it that much anymore."

Craig Holt's ostensible ignorance of his own behavior should be familiar to many women. Once challenged, it forms the basis of a commonly heard excuse from husbands: "I didn't realize I hadn't told you." "I didn't know you wanted to know." "I don't know why I did that, I didn't mean anything by it."

As with the other reasons men give for not being more intimate with their wives, men use ignorance (and their presumption that it is evidence of innocence) to defend withholding every dimension of themselves from others— public, private, and personal:

"I guess I thought that she knew I was getting ready for a marathon, so I didn't bother to tell her. It isn't as though I was trying to hide anything from her, I just didn't think to tell her. I really don't know why. In retrospect, she made it into a much bigger deal than it was. She acted as though I was trying to shut her out of some important part of my life or something. As I said, I really didn't give it much thought and I certainly didn't mean anything by it one way or the other."

Martin's simple neglect or oversight was, by his account, innocent. He claims he was ignorant of what he was doing even as he was doing it. In the sphere of the public self, such behavior is perhaps benign if not acceptable to wives. When the sphere of self moves from the public to the private, a husband's ignorance/innocence is a bit more difficult to take at face value. Consider Hugh Burnette's comments about why he hid his unemployment from his wife, Katherine, for six months before she found him out:

"This is probably hard for someone else to believe, but

all the time I really wasn't trying to hide anything from Kathy. It was more like I just couldn't find the right way or the right time to tell her what had happened to me. Many times during that six months I would say to myself, 'Okay this is it, tonight I'm going to tell her that I lost my job.' Then the night would come and she'd be tired after work and somehow it just wasn't the right time to tell her, so I wouldn't. I was able to carry if off because I was using the savings like income, but the whole time I was doing that I thought it would just be another day or two until I got a job, then I could put the money back and Kathy would never know the difference. After a while I kept it up without even knowing why I was doing it. I mean, it was pretty clear that I wasn't going to get another job anytime soon, but I just kept on pretending I was still working, and all the time I was using up our savings for a house. Still, I wasn't really trying to lie to Kathy, at least not in my mind. I can see how she would see it differently, but like I said at the time, I was sort of crazy, I didn't really know what I was doing, so how can she blame me for trying to do something to her?"

In the personal arena also, male protestations of innocent withholdings are somewhat suspect. Bill Kerlow, for example, claims to be unaware that he presents his sexual attitudes and inclinations any differently to his wife in bed or out: "On this point she's way off base. I don't want to go into the details, but I can tell you that I've never given Amanda any reason to doubt exactly what I wanted from her sexually at any time. I just can't imagine what she's talking about or where she gets the idea that I might say one thing at one time and something else some other time. There may be a lot of things in our relationship she can nail me on but this is not one of them. I'm absolutely innocent."

In effect, what these men who claim ignorance/innocence are saying is that they are being unjustly accused of not being loving, because it was never their intent not to be loving; they simply didn't know any better.

Yet another excuse heard from husbands for the absence of intimacy is that the effort is not worth the reward. There are men who admit that they may be less than completely disclosing and even less than completely loving, but who argue that to be otherwise is, in their words, not worth the trouble. Of the men introduced in incidents in this chapter, both Norm Crites and Arnold Finnick cite this as the reason they have not confided more of their work selves to their wives.

Ginger Crites complains that her husband never talks about his work. Norm's explanation is deceptively simple: "She wouldn't understand. First, I'm working all day at a job that is not exactly a bed of roses. When quitting time comes, I quit thinking about what a lousy job it is. If I have to come home and rehash it all with her, it's just like being there again. Even if I did tell her, there's no way she could understand all of the shit that goes on down there, so why should I bother? So that she'll know that side of me? That's what she says, but, hey, I don't even like that side of me, so why should I want her to know it, huh? No, there's nothing she can do, and telling her just makes it worse for me, so I'll keep it just like it is. I am not going to bring my work home. There's just no percentage in it."

For many of the same reasons, though perhaps with less vehemence, Arnold Finnick has not discussed his retirement with his wife of many years: "I am having some trouble adjusting to retirement, but nothing traumatic. I think any man who has worked all his life does. I don't see any need to burden Claudia with all of that. It would only depress her and she has enough to deal with already. What's more, there is nothing she or anybody else can do about it. Talking about it cannot possibly make things better, and it could make things a great deal worse. It seems easier just to leave things as they are. It may be difficult on her in the short run. I know she feels like I should reach out to her in my time of need, and wonders why I don't. However, I think it is really best even if it is a little awkward now; believe me, it would be so much worse if I tried to go through with her everything that I'm going through, and I would be no better off for it. Not because she wouldn't try to help, but because she *couldn't* help. So I'll take the easy way out and handle this myself. She may be hurt for a while, but she'll get over it—she always has."

In some instances the absence of intimate disclosure on the part of men may be warranted. There may be times, as Crites and Finnick note, when withholding of themselves is both prudent and protective, the best thing to do for the relationship. At other times women may not be truly desirous of disclosure or able to handle what would be disclosed. We must be open to the possibility that withholding of himself may seem to a man to be an honest expression of love.

An alternative interpretation sees the many rationales for the absence of intimacy as self-centered and self-serving. Because he thinks that he does enough or that disclosure would not help him or be worth his effort, he chooses not to do it. Little thought is given to how the relationship, the marriage, might be helped, or how his wife might be helped by his disclosures, how she might be made to feel more loved.

Whatever the reasons may be, we know that most men withhold something of themselves from their wives, and many withhold a great deal. Among the respondents to our survey, less than 10 percent reported that they had been fully disclosing with their wives in every arena—public, private, and personal. The majority, over 65 percent, were partially disclosing, while nearly 25 percent disclosed very little.

There are men who share openly of themselves with the women they love and behave in self-disclosing ways that make those women *feel* loved. There are other men who may not now be disclosing and intimate but who are responsive to the needs of their wives and who are making every effort to bring more of themselves and their wives and who are making every effort to bring more of themselves and their love to their marriages. But most wives live with and love men who are in some very fundamental ways strangers to them—men who withhold themselves and, in doing so, withhold their loving. These wives may be loved, but they do not feel loved because they do not know their husbands. They do not know love.

Is this the natural order, the way men are? To take men at their word, yes. But how then do they explain the many self-disclosures and invitations to intimacy they make to other women, women who are not their wives? The wife who wonders if she is loved by her husband may have reason to fear that he loves someone else more—the other woman.

3 Men and the Other Woman

The reason why lovers and their mistresses never tire of being together is that they are always talking of themselves.

—La Rochefoucauld, *Maxims*

"The only problem with our relationship is that Gary tells me everything and he only tells his wife some things. I always know more about Gary and what's going on with him than his wife does. For her and for Gary, that's a problem."

It is often thought that any relationship a man has with a woman other than his wife has but one purpose—sex. Certainly, extramarital sexual liaisons are a problem for any couple, but a more common problem may be a man's *friendships* with other women. Often in these relationships a man discloses the very intimacies that he withholds from his wife. Knowing that her husband is intimate with another woman, even though the relationship is sexually innocent, is likely to be a problem for any wife. It is this sort of threatening "other woman" relationship that Sally Thelbert describes here.

"Gary was my husband Bill's friend at first. They were good friends when Bill and I first started dating. We used to

75

go out together a lot, Bill and I and Gary and his date. Gary never did go out with any one special girl all that much, and it was sometimes awkward for a strange girl to fit in with the three of us, with all of our in-jokes that were funny only to us, or all of our stories about things we had done together. Most of the time Gary's dates felt pretty left out. After a while he stopped asking girls along, and just the three of us would go out. Gary and I talked a lot about who he might date and I set him up with a lot of dates. He and I started to get really close then, because he would tell me about his experiences with girls and all. I guess I was kind of like a big sister for him. When Bill and I got married, things didn't change at all except that Gary was around even more. When Bill was out of town on business, Gary was real company for me. Bill always said that with Gary around, he didn't have to worry about me and other guys, and of course there was nothing between me and Gary.

"One summer, Bill had a four-month job in another city and I went with him. While we were away, Gary got married, just like that! He met this girl one night at a party, and two months later they got married. At first Bill and I were a little hurt that Gary hadn't let us know what was going on, but we promised ourselves that we would make every effort to get to know his wife, Lucy, and make her feel as welcome in our home as Gary was.

"I guess I was a little shocked when I first met Lucy. She wasn't anything like what I expected. From a distance she was very pretty—almost too pretty, if you know what I mean, because up close you could see that it was all manufactured, lacquered hair, false eyelashes, a pound and a half of makeup, you know the type. What surprised me so was that Gary had always said he liked natural girls, like me. I guess my surprise showed because I'm afraid I wasn't very gracious to Lucy and she didn't exactly warm up to me, either. It didn't help that Gary kept describing me as the only woman who knew everything there was to know about him.

"Things didn't get any better as time went on. The four of us would try to do things together, but with Lucy there it never felt like old times. She didn't even like to do the same things that the rest of us did. The one thing that didn't change was that Gary kept talking to me, except that he talked mostly about himself and Lucy and how things were going between them. Gradually, Lucy began to find reasons for not going along with the three of us, so it got to be pretty much like it was before. Whenever Lucy is around, things go sour. It seems like we're always right on the edge of fighting but we never let it out.

"I know what the problem is, of course. Lucy is jealous of how close I am to her husband. She'd like to know as much about him as I do, and she wishes he'd talk to her the way he talks to me. I've tried to make it clear that there is nothing between Gary and me except a lot of caring and a really close friendship, but the fact of the matter is that I am closer to him as a friend than she is as a wife. I know him better than she does, and she doesn't like it. I can understand just how she feels. I wouldn't like it either, if Bill were as close to her as Gary is to me. No wife ever likes the 'other woman,' no matter how innocent it may be. I guess maybe where our husbands are concerned it is hard for us to believe that any intimate relationship with another woman is innocent."

Sally Thelbert is an "other woman"—perhaps not in the classic sense that we think of the "other woman," as lover, mistress, or paramour. But she is an other woman in the real sense, in the sense that most men know other women—as a close friend, a confidante. The real "other woman" is perhaps a more serious rival to his wife than is the woman with whom he has a sexual relationship, because he shares with her those dimensions of himself that he withholds from his wife.

The very idea of the "other woman" conjures visions of intrigue and illicit sex. This chapter will examine relationships men have with women outside marriage. It will show how commonplace such relationships are, who the other woman is, what these relationships are like—including the sexual dimension—and what these relationships mean.

HOW MANY MEN KNOW AN "OTHER WOMAN"?

It is broadly estimated that 50 to 75 percent of married men have had sexual relations outside their marriages. This covers everything from a brief business trip encounter, a one-night stand, to an actual affair, a sexual relationship that persists for some time, which usually has a degree of emotional involvement in it as well. Even allowing for the breadth of definition of sexual relations, and the statistical vagaries of sex researches, one cannot help but conclude that a significant number of married men have had sexual relations with women outside their marriages. This is not to say, however, that the same number of men have been intimate with another woman. The number of men who share something of themselves with another woman is very likely considerably lower than the number of men who have sex with another woman.

Our own research into the intimacy patterns of men reveals that nearly two-thirds of all men report having disclosed some dimension of themselves—public, private, and/or personal—to at least one woman other than their spouses. This says merely that most men have revealed to women besides their wives information that can be the basis for an intimate relationship. Of greater interest is the finding that approximately one-third of the men in the research reported that they have revealed things about themselves to another woman that they have not revealed to their wives. This suggests that for roughly one out of every three men, there is an "other woman" who knows more and different things about him than does his wife. If the substance of these revelations is significant to the men's sense of self, it would suggest that these men may be more intimate with other women than they are with their spouses. This also suggest that the common male defense of ignorance or inability to be intimate is groundless. Further indications of the degree of closeness that exists in these relationships are to be found in what men have to say about who these other women are, and how their relationships with them evolved.

WHO IS THE "OTHER WOMAN"?

"The 'other woman' in my life is my sister. I don't know how anyone could make anything sordid out of that, although in this day and age I suppose there are those who would try. Anyone in your family is going to know a lot about you that your wife doesn't know, if for no other reason than that they've known you longer, but there's a lot more than just time between Sis and me. She really is my best friend, and she has been for as long as I can remember. Both Mom and Dad worked, so a lot of the time there were just the two of us while we were growing up. It was the kind of situation where you were either going to hate each other or love each other, and we came out of it loving each other.

"Neither one of us ever saw any reason why marriage or our own families should change or get in the way of what we had with each other, and we haven't let it. There isn't anything that I wouldn't tell Sis or haven't told her. And I mean *anything*. I know that whatever is going on with me, however bad it might get, Sis will listen and go on loving me. It's not that way with Valerie, my wife. I don't think it can be. You can only get complete acceptance from your family. That's just the way it is. Valerie may be a little jealous of the closeness between me and Sis, but I don't think so. Anyway, everybody needs somebody to talk to, and like I tell Val, it's better that it's my sister than some other woman."

For a great number of men, the "other woman" is a relative, usually an older sister. Neil Sooner (the respondent above) makes an important point when he says that it is not

79

simply time together that creates the closeness he feels with his sister, but rather the freedom he feels to unburden himself to her without fear of being judged or losing her love. Most of the men who acknowledged that they were intimate with a female relative mentioned this trust factor as the distinctive characteristic about the relationship, which made it possible for them to be disclosing in ways that they could not be with their wives.

- "With someone in your family, you've got to figure that they know everything bad there is to know about you and they still love you, right? So that makes it easier to be honest with them than with somebody like your wife, who may know only the best side of you."

- "People may think it's funny or odd, but my best friend, the person I'm closest to in all the world, is still my mother. At forty-four I don't think you could call me a 'mama's boy.' My wife does when she gets really upset about how close Mom and I are—or really, when she gets upset that Mom and I are closer than she and I are. But I don't mind. I'm actually proud to say that my mom is still my best friend. I wouldn't have it any other way."

- "My sister practically raised me. She was mother, sister, friend all rolled into one. No one will ever be closer to me than she is, they couldn't be."

- "I'm still close to my two girl cousins, even though we're all grown now. It used to bother me when I was younger that I couldn't marry one of them, 'cause I couldn't imagine loving anybody as much as I loved them. I'm still not so sure that it wouldn't have worked out. Lord knows, the two wives I've had didn't work out, but then, neither of them could hold a candle to my cousins."

- "I used to hate it that my sister knew me so well. When we were young she was always using something I told her in confidence against me. But now that we are grown I love it that I can talk to her about anything. We still have 'our secrets'; she's the only woman I can say that about."

Family circumstances create a natural opportunity for the development of intimacy between a man and his female siblings or relatives. If anything, it is somewhat surprising that relatively few of these become intimate, and that fewer still remain intimate into adulthood. For every man who shares a close, caring relationship with a sister or a cousin, there are countless others who are no more intimate with these family members than they are with the most casual of friends. Siblings leave home to start families of their own, and once removed from an environment that provides the opportunity for intimacy, men make few efforts to sustain a relationship. It appears that the situation has a lot to do with where and how men find relationships with other women. Proximity facilitates association with an "other woman," and if the circumstances are right, the association can become intimate.

"I first met Glenda through my car pool. Here in the Houston area, if you aren't in a car pool you simply don't drive to work. What with the distances and traffic and the parking problem, when you finally do get where you're going, car pools make a lot of sense. When we came from the East, where there's plenty of public transportation, it was all pretty new to Ann and me, but a service connected me with three other people in my area, two other guys and Glenda.

"At first for me it was just another ride to work. Most of the time nobody talked much, we read the paper, got a head start on work, or slept. After you ride to work every day with the same people, you can't help but get to know them a little. Still, we weren't anything more than casual friends. What changed all that was that within the space of about six weeks, one of the other guys was fired and the other one transferred, and just like that our car pool was down to just Glenda and me. We advertised for other riders but couldn't find anyone, so we decided we would just ride together, the two of us.

"Glenda is now my closest friend. I don't know how to

explain how it happened. Right from the start, with just the two of us in the car it was different. We actually talked. I remember one of the first things we talked about was whether Ann would mind me riding alone with Glenda. Glenda asked me and I found myself telling her about Ann's and my relationship, things I hadn't even told Ann! That really broke the ice, and from that time on I've been able to talk to Glenda about anything I want—my wife, work, you name it. There's nothing she and I haven't talked about. We're so close now that neither one of us would want another rider, so we stopped looking for one.

"Why can I talk to Glenda and not my wife? I guess I really don't know why. It's not like I'm physically attracted to Glenda or anything like that. Maybe a lot of it is just circumstance, I mean, two hours in the car every day, uninterrupted by anybody or anything, gives Glenda and me a chance to talk that Ann and I rarely have, what with the house and the kids and all. Maybe it's because Glenda is a really good listener. Who knows? I don't spend a whole lot of time analyzing it. I just take it for the really good friendship that it is."

As an increasing number of women work side by side with men, the opportunities increase for a man to associate with women who share common interests with him outside his marriage. More and more men know women not as neighbors or friends of their wives or the wives of friends but as work associates, fellow professionals, peers. Some of these associations become really good friendships, even intimate relationships, as a man discloses to his woman friend information about his private and even personal self, perhaps information he has not disclosed to his wife:

- "The members of any accounting audit team get pretty close because they have to work closely together for long hours, usually under some pressure and often out of town. You have to know the people you work with pretty well, just to get the job done. I suppose that I am closer to

Penny than I am to the other men on the team, but for whatever reason I find it easier to talk to her about the things that
are really important to me than to talk to the guys. She
knows a lot more about my work and how I feel about it than
my wife does, but I think that's just because she works with
me."

■ "My secretary is my closest friend. Before you get the
wrong idea, let me say that my secretary is sixty years old
and I would as soon think of having an affair with her as I
would with my mother. At the same time, I trust her like I
trust my mother. She knows absolutely everything there is to
know about me, because I tell her everything and she is completely trustworthy. In a lot of ways I am closer to her than I
am to my wife, but then in some ways I'm not, too."

■ "My boss is a woman. In a lot of fields that is not all
that common these days, but in retailing there have been
women bosses for a long time, especially on the buying side.
At first I wasn't too keen on the idea myself, but now Betty is
more than a boss to me, she is a mentor, an adviser, a best
buddy. I go to her for help with everything from business to
personal stuff, including how to handle my wife. She listens
and asks questions that help me to see things I'd never look
at as important, and she gives me advice. I wouldn't tell anybody but her just how important she is to me—especially
not my wife—but the truth is, I've become so dependent on
her that I'm a little afraid of being promoted because it
would mean I would have to work for someone else."

"Other woman" relationships that men have at work or
in the neighborhood typically begin with some shared interest, frequently one that is not shared by the wife. It is easy to
see how this might come about at work, but men also reported the genesis of these intimacies in hobbies, sports, or
even in their children's activities. The "other woman" may
be met playing tennis, at a computer hobbyists' meeting,
organizing for the school carnival, in the church choir, or in
countless other places where men and women are brought

together by their common interests. Proximity alone is not the basis for intimacy outside marriage, but proximity and common interest, be it work or play, form a convenient catalyst for communication. Initially this communication is about their shared interest. Many of these relationships seldom delve deeper than the private arena, and much of what is exchanged may be of little interest to the man's wife. Despite her lack of interest and despite the obvious innocence of many of these friendships, wives typically view these relationships with suspicion and jealousy.

One type of "other woman" relationship that is particularly problematical for wives is that which exists between the spouse and the spouse's ex-wife. In this era of no-fault divorce, joint custody, and children's rights, there are an increasing number of men and women who maintain relationships with each other after divorce. Such a relationship is sometimes warranted by their shared interest in the children, their preexisting and continuing involvement in some joint economic endeavor, or, despite the failure of the marriage, the fact they genuinely like each other. This means that some men (perhaps more than are willing to admit it) count their ex-wives as their best friends.

One such man is Joe Coleman. Joe is a thirty-six-year-old sales representative for a line of athletic shoes. He and his first wife, Alice, were divorced two years ago. He has since married Sherry, whom he met while he and Alice were in a trial separation. Joe and Sherry live in Sherry's home from her first marriage. The house is conveniently only a half-mile from where Alice lives with her two daughters from her marriage to Joe, aged fifteen and ten. Joe says this about his relationship with his present and past wives:

"Alice and I split as friendly as any two people who get a divorce can. We had both pretty much come to the point where we felt like we weren't in love anymore, and neither of us saw the possibility of things improving, so we cashed it in. I think I got to that point first and Alice took the position that she wasn't going to love anyone who didn't love her, and that was that. Both of us were determined that no matter what had happened between us, we weren't going to let it hurt the kids, so we opted for joint custody. Living close like we do, it seemed the easiest thing.

"Because of the arrangement for the girls, Alice and I spend a lot more time talking to each other and even being with each other than most people who get divorced do. Sherry has chosen not to get involved in things where the girls are concerned, and I think that's for the best. It's less confusing for the girls, but it does mean that Sherry is left out of a lot of things between Alice and me. We have to talk about the kids, but of course in the process we talk about a lot of other things as well. After all, we did have a lot of years together. We've sort of discovered that it's a whole lot easier to talk when we aren't married than it was when we were married. I don't know why that should be, but it's worked out that way for us. In some ways we're much closer now than we were when we were married. The way it's worked out, my ex-wife has become my best friend. Anybody with any sense can imagine that that creates a few problems in my marriage."

Joe Coleman may be underestimating the problems his friendship with his ex-wife is creating. Sherry Coleman feels that Joe and Alice have put her in a real bind:

"If I complain about Joe's talking to her, he claims I'm trying to get between him and his kids. If I try to get involved and be a part of what's going on, he and Alice remind me that the girls are theirs, not mine. I know he talks to her about everything that goes on between us, probably even our sex life. They may still have sex together, for all I know. It makes me really uncomfortable. I feel like I'm competing with his girls and his ex-wife for his love. They know everything about him, so I'm at a real disadvantage. I can't tell him not to talk to her and I can't control what they talk about and I certainly can't erase what they have had together, so I either have to withdraw from the whole thing and pretend I don't care—which I just can't do—or bitch constantly.

I can't see myself demanding to know what they talk about or demanding to be there every time they are together. Even I see that that's unreasonable. Can a wife tell her husband who he should have for a best friend? Wouldn't any wife feel threatened by knowing that her husband is close to some other woman, especially his ex-wife? That he talks to her about things that he doesn't share at home? I don't think I'm being all that unreasonable in all of this, am I?"

The suspicions Sherry Coleman has about just how close her husband is to his ex-wife are echoed by every wife who has reason to believe that her husband has a relationship with another woman. Wives want to know why their husbands have these relationships. What goes on? Where it is headed? These concerns are expressed in a way that presumes guilt; what the wife really wants to know is just how guilty her husband is:

- "He says all they ever talk about is work. Well, in the first place, I would give my eyeteeth to have him talk about his work to me, but he never does. In the second place, I don't believe that all they ever talk about is work, because they spend too much time together away from work. And why, after fifteen years of working, does he need to talk to her?"

- "I just don't like the idea of him having a close female friend, even if it is all open and aboveboard. It seems to me that if he really wanted to, he could find some male friends who are as interested in his hobby as she is. The fact that he doesn't have any male friends tells me that he's got a lot more going with her than a common interest in gardening."

- "It bothers me that his secretary seems to know more about his life than I do, I don't suspect anything sexual there. Maybe I don't like it that she always seems to know what's going on between us, or with him and the kids. Obviously he has told her these things, and I don't like that because sometimes he hasn't told me."

- "He says they have to talk every now and then because of the property they still own jointly—some rental houses that for some reason they didn't divide up in the divorce. I think they talk together entirely too much, and I think they've even been sleeping together."

- "As far as I'm concerned, there is no such thing as an innocent relationship between a man and a woman. If their is any relationship at all, sooner or later it's going to lead to bed."

- "Of course I have some male friends and we are pretty close. I know that they have told me some things that they have not told their own wives. That doesn't make it any easier for me to accept the fact that he has a close female friend. If anything, I have a clearer picture of what their relationship is probably like, and I get angry thinking that there are things he's told her that he hasn't told me."

Whether the other woman is a family member, a work associate, or a neighborhood friend, there is a great deal of supposition and suspicion about what transpires between men and other women. Wives imagine the worst. Husbands protest innocence: "We're just friends. There's nothing going on." The other women, who might verify or deny just what does or does not go on in these relationships, are rarely heard from except in popular magazine confessions, which serve only to heighten suspicions while adding nothing of substance to the real issue.

HOW INTIMATE ARE MEN WITH "OTHER WOMEN"? HOW ARE MEN INTIMATE WITH "OTHER WOMEN"?

"One of the reasons I hate visiting John's family is that I always get into this competition with his mother and sister over who knows John best. It seems like such a silly thing when I am removed from it and can step back and think about what goes on, but I can tell you, when I'm in the thick of it there's nothing silly about it. It's serious stuff and I'm determined to win."

Becky Patrill is describing how she reacts to what goes

on between her husband, John, and the other women in his life—his mother and sister. John and Becky have been married for six years; their home is only thirty-five miles from the little town where John's family still resides. Despite their proximity, visits to John's parents are few and punctuated by bitter battles between the women in John's life over who knows John best:

"To an outsider it might look like little things, but I know what they're up to. They're trying to show me that even though I may be married to John, they still know him best and they always will. They do things like fix foods for him that he used to like, 'home-style' meat and potatoes, cooking that they know I don't do because I've taught John to like more continental cooking. They are always talking about things he used to do as a boy or people he used to know, anything they can think of that excludes me from the conversation. The worst is when they talk about John's old girlfriends.

"It's a crazy situation. I'm jealous of them for being so close to John and I get upset with John for letting them be so close. I'm suspicious of all that goes on between them that I don't even know about. To top it all off, I get angry with myself for making such a big deal out of it. It's like my friend tells me, I ought to be thankful that the other women he's close to are his mother and sister; at least I can be sure he's not sleeping with them—though in my really crazy moments I have wondered about John and his sister."

The feelings Becky Petrill has about competing with her husband's family for his intimacy are not at all unusual. Most new brides experience acutely the same sense of competition, only to find that the feeling dissipates as they and their husbands build up mutual experience of their own to rival that which exists in the family. In most marriages this cycle plays out rather quickly and becomes an issue only infrequently. It can often be seen at holiday-occasioned family gatherings, where competition to establish who cares the most is at the root of much of the tension that characterizes such events (and, at times, accounts for most of the food on the table). For Becky and John, the issue remains a live one, perhaps because of the emotional closeness between John and his family, combined with their physical proximity, perhaps due to Becky's insecurity about the level of intimacy between herself and John. There is little solace in the observation that she need not worry about John's having sex with another woman when what concerns her most is the fact that John may care for someone else more than he cares for her. The evidence of her exclusion adds some conviction to her concern. This feeling of being excluded is central to wives' experience of their men and other women. Nadine Higgins describes what it is like for her at the many business parties she attends with her husband, Roger:

"They are always together at the parties, Roger and that young assistant of his. I see them with their heads bent close together, laughing, enjoying some private joke. If I go over to join in, they jump back from each other and begin talking business. I'm made to feel like some sort of intruder, invading on their privacy. If I don't go over, I feel like they're watching me, talking about me. Roger says I'm paranoid, but damn it, he is my husband and I shouldn't be the one excluded!"

This feeling of exclusion and the resultant competition and suspicion lie at the core of a woman's concern about her man and the other woman. Information is the medium of inclusion or exclusion. As a man reveals himself to a woman he invites her into a relationship with him, he includes her. When a man withholds information about himself from a woman, he is in fact excluding her. What a wife and an other woman know about a man, what he has disclosed of himself to each, is used by them as a measure of his love. This is why wives want most to know, "What did you talk about? What have you told her?"

In the area of the public self, other women, apart from

family members, know relatively little about the men with whom they are involved. What they do know of a man's public self is often limited to a certain time and/or topic. The reports of other women who acknowledge being close to and intimate with men who are not their husbands indicate that the intimacy they share is not the product of knowing a lot about a man (his public self), but rather of knowing a lot about the things that are most central to a man's identity—his private and personal self:

• "I've been really close to Tom for more than five years, but to this day I couldn't tell you what his hobbies are, or what he thinks about politics or the economy or any of those things. We don't spend any time on the superficial things, but we talk a lot about the special things. We talk about his work and mine, his family and mine, even about us. Those other things just never come up. They're not important."

• "Even though I feel comfortable in saying that there is nothing about Ray and his work that I don't know—from exactly what he does to how he feels about it and what he dreams of doing—in most other ways I don't know him at all. As an example, I drew his name in the Christmas party gift raffle. Now you would think, as close as we are, that I would know exactly what to get him. The truth is, I couldn't think of a damn thing because apart from work I don't know him at all."

• "When you have someone as a doubles partner for a whole season, you get to know him pretty well—you almost have to get to know him. Martin and I are more than just partners, we're really best friends. Some people, Martin's wife for one, probably think we are more than friends, if you know what I mean. But I don't feel any need to apologize for things that haven't happened, not that I haven't thought about it. Anyway, what I want to say is that while I think we can talk about anything, most things we don't talk about at all. I know who Martin works for, but I have no idea of what he does—things like work and religion, even what kinds of food he likes, I know almost nothing about. Now sex, well, that's a different subject, and I think it's better if I don't say anything about that."

■ "The great thing about having a married man for a friend and lover is that there is nothing trivial about the relationship. You don't have to spend time talking about the house, the neighbors, the kids. You can focus on the things that are really important to you. I don't have to be interested in everything that he's interested in, and vice versa. The things I don't care about I don't ask about, he doesn't tell me, and I don't know. She (his wife) may know more about him, but I know him best."

His wife may know more about him, but the other woman knows him best. The evidence from men, from their wives, and from other women suggests that in the area of the public self, wives know more about their husbands than almost anyone else (the exception here may be female members of the man's family). Probably very little of this knowledge is the result of voluntary revelation by the man; much of it is certainly deduced from careful observation over time and by process of elimination. The context of a man's relationship with another woman is a significant constraint on disclosure, by whatever process, of information about many dimensions of his public self. The other woman rarely sees the man in as many settings or over as much time as does his wife. Therefore, her knowledge of him is largely restricted to what he tells her of himself. Since men will reveal little of their public selves of their own volition, other women typically have only limited knowledge of the public self of a man.

There may be some comfort for wives in the realization that in an absolute sense they know more about their husbands than any other woman does. Such momentary security as this may bring is, however, undermined by the awareness that knowing his shirt size or favorite foods may signal familiarity, but knowing how he feels about himself and his identity is a sign of real intimacy. In the important areas of the private and the personal selves, men disclose a great deal to other women, in many instances as much as, and more than, they reveal to their own spouses.

It is probably true that no man is completely open and honest with his wife. Every man has some secrets from his wife—things he has done, thought, or felt, things he knows about himself that he has not revealed. But these things are usually known to someone, in one way or another. They have been revealed by the man, often to the other woman. His secretary has heard the reason why he can't stand so-and-so at work. His sister was there to witness the real reason why he's avoided swimming since he was a child. His doubles partner has seen the sadistic bent that lies just below his "competitive edge" on the tennis court. These little bits and pieces of self, which men withhold from their wives, or misrepresent, or quite innocently overlook, can be a source of embarrassment when they come to light, but they are rarely the stuff of intimate relationships. These secrets are the kind of incidental information that is revealed at a particular time and in a specific situation, but they rarely signal anything significant about the man's self, anything that would bring one closer to him.

A man's secrets are an invitation to intimacy when they disclose something about his private and personal self, something that reveals the way he sees himself. When you know a man as he knows himself, whatever the source of your knowledge, you become intimate with him. There are a great many men who allow women other than their wives to know them as they know themselves.

There seems to be nothing of a private or personal nature that men do not reveal to other women. Reports of confessional conversations between men and women about work, money, sex, their wives, their children, their hopes and dreams, their emotions, their own sense of self, are commonplace. Of course, not all men tell all things about themselves to other women, but it seems as though a man who chooses to reveal to an other woman some dimension of himself that he has not revealed to his wife usually goes on to reveal many such dimensions. One secret leads to another and another and another.

The typical pattern is for these revelations to begin in the private arena—for example, with disclosures about work—and move toward increasingly personal disclosures.

Nearly all men who might be identified as being truly intimate with women other than their wives reported that they had disclosed their satisfaction with their jobs or their career concerns, their money worries, even their household budgeting problems. A Midwestern dentist had this to say about his close relationship with his office manager:

"Since Amy is at the office with me all day, she is obviously going to know more about my work than my wife does, and of course that makes it easier for me to talk to her about work. As office manager, Amy is responsible for the books. She does all the billing and writes all the checks. She knows more about my money situation than even I do. My wife would probably raise hell if she knew just how much I do talk to Amy about our personal finances—she even advises me on how much household money I should let my wife have. I need someone to talk to about work and money and the office. Amy understands the whole picture without really having a stake in it, if you know what I mean. I can be completely open with her, and she can be objective. I'm sure that it has made us closer than we might otherwise be, but I don't see anything wrong with that, either."

From the Great Plains, a mechanic wrote of his relationship with an other woman and their joint planning of his career: "Until Jenny came along I never allowed myself to think a whole lot about another career, and I certainly never talked to Margie about it. I got married right out of high school and jumped at the first steady job that came along. Whenever I did think of getting into something better, it seemed like Margie would get pregnant again and we needed the money too much for me to play around at learning a new job. I met Jenny in night school. She was the tutor for an accounting class I took through Adult Education at the junior college. I had a lot of trouble with the class, and signed up for some extra help. Right from the start, she and I really hit it off, and before I knew it, I was telling her about things I had never had the guts to talk to anybody about. How I wanted to get out from under cars and get into some professional kind of work. How I wished Margie was more encouraging of me doing something besides greasing. What I hoped for my kids, stuff like that.

"I could never talk about those things with Margie. She'd think I was blaming her or sorry we got married so young, or sorry for all the kids. Jenny listens to me dreaming about getting out of the garage and into something really good, and she encourages me to try. She doesn't lay a lot of guilt on me or say, 'Who are you kidding?' or 'Aren't you happy with me?' Talking to Jenny helps me think that maybe I can be what I want to be. She helps me plan instead of telling me to put it off. When I get my plan togther, then I'm going to spring it on Margie."

The inclination men feel to confide in women other than their wives is not related to income or age. From a retirement village in the South came the comments of a sixty-eight-year-old former postal worker:

"Sometimes you don't know how you feel about something until you talk to somebody else about it. You can think about things in your head, but to really test them out you need to say them out loud and hear somebody tell you how it sounds. The somebody shouldn't be too close to you because then you'd be testing it on the same person you were going to use it on, see? Me, I talk to Vera about money. She's the lady two trailers down. On a fixed income, Ruby and I have a hard time just making it one month to the next, but I don't want to worry Ruby with all of that. I've always handled the money for us, and just because there's less of it now is no reason to bother her. Vera's a widow and has managed on her own for a long time. I help her and she helps me without worrying me about it. She thinks I should get a part-time job, so she's going to help me look into that before I say anything to Ruby about it. Like I said, sometimes you need to test things out on someone to see how you really think, and Vera is a real good tester."

As men and women work together as peers, it is only natural that they have occasion to talk about their jobs and their careers. These discussions often lead to the subject of money: how much is earned, how it is spent, how one feels about it. When challenged about their relationships with other women, men frequently point to how "natural" their disclosures are, given the situation. This, of course, does not explain why they do not avail themselves of the situation presented by their marriage, in which discussions of work, career, and money would seem to be every bit as "natural" as those situations outside of marriage. Nor does situational favorableness account for disclosures of a much more personal nature that we know occur between men and other women—disclosures of the man's emotions, his sense of self, his feelings about sex and his own sexual identity. Why do men withhold these significant areas of self from their wives, yet voluntarily disclose them to other women? The question becomes all the more important when we see the kinds of intimate disclosures men make.

Marriage is one of the most common topics of intimate exchange between men and their other women:

- "I've been married for less than a year, and frankly it's nothing like I expected. I don't know whether it's me or my wife, or our marriage. I don't feel like I can really talk to my wife about it because it would be too scary, I might really screw things up. So I talk to Marilyn. She knows me from before, plus she's been married a couple of times, so she knows what it should be like."

- "I don't understand what my wife really wants from me. I hear the words when she asks for something and I try to do what she wants, but somehow it's never quite right. I've been using her best friend as a kind of counselor for a couple of years now, just to try to figure out how to make my wife happy."

- "We disagree on so many things, my wife and I, and it's hard for me to believe that I could be wrong about all of them. Every now and then I run things by my friend just to see if I really am off base."

- "When you've been married for so long to the same person, and maybe, like us, you never even dated anybody else, all of your ideas about the opposite sex come from one person. After a while you wonder if maybe there aren't some things about women that are different from the way your wife is. The only way to find out is with some other woman."

As can be seen in the comments above, men use the other women in their lives as confessor, alter ego, sounding board, verifier, and means of comparison. How much like other women is my wife? How much like other men am I? Each of these interactions requires that the man disclose something of himself, and each disclosure further develops his intimacy with the other woman. The most personal of all disclosures for men, namely sex, is frequently the topic of discussion with the other woman:

- "If your wife has never made love to another man, or you to another woman, how can you know if it is any different for anyone else unless you talk about it? I admit to being just plain curious about what's normal. The best discussions about sex I've ever had have been with Mary Ellen's best friend. She's the one who convinced me that wanting to try something beside the missionary position wasn't perverted!"

- "For some reason I can't really explain, it's easier for me to talk about my impotence with Betsy than it is to talk about it with my wife. At home it's always a big emotional scene; we can't discuss it rationally because she feels rejected and I feel humiliated. Betsy tries to understand and doesn't put me down."

- "I want to know if I'm as good in bed as other guys, but I don't want to ruin my marriage by going to bed with lots of women to find out, nor do I want my wife to sleep around. I have this young friend who dates a lot and, frankly, sleeps around a lot. I talk to her about the different guys she's been with and what they are like. I can ask her anything and it's made me a better lover, I think."

- "Lately my wife has been suggesting some pretty strange things in bed. At least they're strange to me. I don't want to ask other guys if their wives want the same things, because they might get the wrong idea about me or her. I can ask my sister. We've always talked about everything, including sex."

Using the measures available, it must be concluded that many men have intimate relationships with women other than their wives and, further, that some number (perhaps as many as one-third) of these relationships are more intimate than is the man's marriage. The evidence can be seen in the relative amounts of information about self that men disclose, and the kinds of information they reveal. Certainly, when a man admits to revealing his most personal self—his feelings about sex and his own sexual identity—he is acknowledging the intimacy that exists between himself and the other woman. Perhaps because of this, men hide these relationships from their wives. Very few wives are aware of the existence of their husband's friendships with other women. Even fewer are aware of just how friendly these friendships are.

WHAT DO WIVES KNOW? WHAT DO WIVES SUSPECT?

Many men are quite open about the number and nature of their friendships with women. The wives of these men have an accurate understanding of just what the relationship means to their husbands. The Midwestern dentist's wife said of her husband's office friendship, "Of course he talks to Amy about all sorts of things; after all, she is the office manager, she has to know what is going on. I myself often talk to Amy about his schedule when I can't reach him. The work demands that they spend a great deal of time together, but I'm sure that it is all completely aboveboard and very businesslike. I can't imagine that either he or Amy would let it become anything else. When you come right down to it, I'm really glad that he has her to talk to about his work. Teeth are really pretty boring, if you ask me."

Not all husbands are so honest with their wives; some go to great lengths to disguise the nature of their relationships with other women. Judging by the comments from wives about their husbands' friendships, these deceptions are often successful. Margie, who is married to the young mechanic with the night-school friend, is aware of the threat of outside friendships, but doesn't see that her husband has the time to get involved or that she has the time to worry about him:

"I guess I should worry—he spends so much time up at that school, and there are a lot of young girls around there— but with all that I have to do around here, I just plain don't have a lot of time left over to worry about much of anything except money. I worry plenty about money. What bothers me most about his school is that he could be spending some of that time bringing in some extra money instead of studying. I don't know where he thinks all that studying is going to get him, anyway."

The retired postal worker's wife has a different perspective on her husband's friendship with the widow two trailers down: "He and Vera get together and yak for hours, and I say thank God! If he didn't have her to talk to, he'd be around here all day, underfoot and driving me crazy. The worst thing about retirement is that he's home all the time and in my hair. I swear, it's like having kids again. This trailer is only big enough for two if they're both sound asleep. I have to chase him out of here just so I can clean up. At least when he's off with Vera, I've got room to breathe. My friends all think I'm crazy to let him spend so much time with her; they think she'll snatch him away from me. Well, if she does she does, and if he goes with her he wasn't worth keepin', was he? After fifty-three years, I don't think he's going to run off on me. She can talk to him all she wants about whatever she wants, for all I care. At least when he's with her I've got some peace and quiet."

Ruby's friends aren't the only ones who might think that her cavalier attitude toward her husband and his widow friend is foolish. While most women know few of the specific details of their husbands' relationships with other women, they are universally suspicious of extramarital friendships on principle. The commonly expressed belief is that men have only one reason for a relationship with a woman who is not his wife, and that reason is sex:

- "You tell me what there could possibly be that a man could talk to some other woman about that he couldn't talk to his wife about. The only thing is sex with that other woman, that's what! A man shouldn't need to talk to any woman but his wife, and if he does it's because he's looking for something besides a good listener, if you ask me."

- "Look, it's this simple—if he lies to his wife about her (the other woman), you can bet it's because he's layin' her."

- "A man and a woman can only get so close, and then they're going to get into trouble. I don't care who they are or how happily married they are or anything else, it doesn't make any difference. As soon as they start having secrets, it won't be long before they're having sex."

- "I know that if I learned that my husband was close friends with another woman, I would certainly suspect them of being more than just friends. Why? I don't know, I guess because I think that's just the way men are."

There are two interesting points in these and many similar statements of suspicion from women about their husbands and other women. First, many of the same women who reported their suspicions about their husbands' extramarital relationships simultaneously admitted that they were intimate with another woman's husband, and most vehemently denied that there was anything sexual about these relationships, but still felt that their husbands, and, indeed most men, could not be trusted. Apparently wives feel that they can control the sexual temptations of these relationships better than their husband can. Also, women see themselves as more respectful of others' marriages than other women are of theirs. In any event, wives seem to feel that what is good for the goose is not good for the gander!

A second point of interest is that as vehement as these wives were about sex and extramarital friendships, a surprising number of women commented that what was most threatening to them about their husbands' friendships with other women was the idea that they might be more intimate with the other women than they were with their wives. Sex is a concern, but the real worry is that the husband might disclose to another woman things he had not revealed to his wife, and might in fact reveal to the other woman his feelings about his wife:

- "I can't say that it wouldn't bother me if I learned that he was sleeping with another woman. Of course it would. But somehow I think that if it was just a sexual thing, we could work it through. I think that I would have a much harder time if I thought that he was really close to another woman, told her things that he hadn't told me. That seems to me like more of a violation of our marriage. Then again, I haven't actually had to deal with either one, so I suppose I really can't say how I would react if it happened. But to me, sex just isn't as serious as sharing."

- "My first husband did sleep around on me—twice that I know of. I don't think 'accept' is the right word, because it's not the sort of thing you can ever accept, but I did come to understand it. It's only natural to wonder what sex would be like with someone else. He just couldn't wonder without wandering, so to speak. What split us up, though, was when I learned that he had confided some things to a woman friend of his, things that had long been an issue with us but that I couldn't get him to talk about. I don't know whether he was sleeping with this one or not, but I couldn't for the life of me understand why he would need to talk to another woman. Why couldn't he talk to me? I deserved at least that much from him. When I didn't get it, I decided enough was enough."

- "Sex is just something physical, it doesn't mean you're really involved with someone. If he were really involved with someone, I don't think that I could take that."

- "To be crude about it, I don't really care who he fucks as long as he doesn't talk to them about how he feels about it. I don't want any other woman to have something from him that I don't."

WHAT *REALLY* GOES ON?

It is impossible to ignore the subject of sex in extramarital friendships, nor should its role in these relationships be minimized. Sex is certainly on the minds of wives as they think about their husbands' involvements, and there is every reason to believe that it is on the minds of the men and their friends as well. The presence or presumption of a sexual relationship where there is a male-female friendship affects the behavior of everyone involved, the man, his wife, and the other woman. Determining the sexual content of these relationships is a difficult proposition at best. Sex surveys have become something of a journalistic fashion in recent years, as popular magazines have found that they are a sure boost to sales. Estimates are that anywhere from 60 to 80 percent of married men have had sex outside marriage;

for married women the figure ranges from 40 to 60 percent. In this study, an attempt was made to discover the extent to which men and women who were intimate with one another were also sexual partners. The assumption here is that many people may have sex without being intimate, and that others may be intimate without having sex.

Of the men who have had intimate relationships outside their marriages, three in ten reported that they had had sex at least once with the other woman. Of this group, half reported that they frequently had sex with their intimate friend. (It was not possible to verify this with the women involved. But of the women in our survey, only one of every ten who reported an intimate relationship with a man reported that they frequently had sex together as well.) The comments of the men and women who acknowledge being both friends and lovers reveal more about how and why sex and intimacy become linked in their relationships.

■ From a forty-two-year-old man who is currently involved in his second such relationship: "For us it was just a natural extension of a relationship that became closer and closer over time. Going to bed was the logical next step. I think you get to a point in any close relationship between a man and a woman where you can't help but wonder what it would be like to make love to this person you have come to love. Maybe it's not inevitable—I'm sure that there are people who get really close and don't end up going to bed, but I really don't see how. When you've shared so much it seems natural to share sex, too. Now we're friends and lovers, what could be better?"

■ From a young stewardess: "I was the one who kept saying no. It was really nice to have a friend instead of another guy trying to hit on me all of the time. Plus I always thought that once you went to bed with someone, sex took over all of the talking time, and I for one need a friend a lot more than I need another fuck. So he would ask and I would say no. All the time we got closer and closer till finally I figured that we were close enough that screwing wouldn't change anything. For the very first time, I was right! We haven't stopped talking. In some ways it's even better. The sex is not great, but it's good enough for friends. I guess I have to change my thinking. Sex hasn't come between us. If anything, we're closer."

■ A woman who admits to being a veteran of many intimate friendships with married men wrote: "Sleeping together doesn't change a thing. I know, I've been there. If the relationship is good, it gets better. If it wasn't that good, it can still get better—sex sure isn't going to make it any worse."

■ A man who is "really in love for the first time" with his wife's best friend: "Sex does change everything because it brings you that much closer."

■ One woman has given up on friendships with men because of sex: "Sex changes everything. Once you start sleeping together you can't be as close, you just can't. Good friends, men or women, talk about sex. They ask questions, share their feelings, try to figure out what it's all about. People who have sex together never talk about it. They get into performing and proving, none of which was there when they were just friends talking about sex. Every close friendship I've ever had with a man sooner or later became an affair, and the friendship ended when the affair started. Once you've been to bed with a man, he won't let you into his head and when he stops sharing, he stops being a friend and starts being a lover."

Some men have defended their extramarital sexual activity by arguing that it improves their marriages. One line of defense is that it has made these men more experienced, more inventive sex partners. The more common rationale is that a sexual affair alleviates sexual tension in the marriage. Sexual tension is ofter produced by boredom; therefore, changing sex partners is perceived as an effective resolution.

As one man described his feelings, "I have always felt

that my friendship with Charlotte was really good for my marriage, and now that it is a love affair too, in some ways it's even better for my marriage. Charlotte has always been someone I could talk to about things that I couldn't talk to my wife about in that way. She is a great emotional release for me, an outlet that takes a lot of emotional pressure off my marriage. It is the same way with sex. It never was that good with my wife, so it was always a problem, I was constantly demanding something from her and she was always rejecting me. Charlotte satisfies me in every way, so I demand much less at home and things go a lot easier."

Most men stopped short of saying that extramarital sex helped their marriages, asserting only that "it hasn't hurt my marriage."

Sex gets mixed reviews from those who admit to being both friends and lovers. In general, men seem to think that sex is an important and positive dimension of their relationships with other women. The other women are much more critical of the role of sex in these friendships. Most of them argue that sex is a distancing factor; once it enters the relationship, it drives out some (if not all) of the intimacy. It may be that these mixed feelings about sex account for the 60 percent of men who report that sex was an issue in their friendships with other women, but that they had not had sex with their friends. In these relationships, sex is thought about, talked about, often even pursued, but there is no sex between the partners. Here, accounts indicate that the reason sex is an issue is usually that the man wants it and the woman does not. Tom Scully and his friend Susan exemplify what transpires in many extramarital friendships:

Tom says, "Of course sex has been an issue in our relationship. How could it not be? I've told her how I feel about sex, and she's shared with me what goes through the minds of women about sex. We've done all there is to do with sex but have it! I want it but she doesn't. She says it wouldn't be right, it wouldn't be fair, it would change everything. I never knew there were so many reasons for not having sex until I started asking her why she wouldn't go to bed with me. The funny thing is, any other woman—I mean any woman I was after just for sex—if she said no, that would be the end of the relationship. With Susan, it's different. Sure, I want it and I'm disappointed—and plenty frustrated too—but the relationship, the friendship, is important enough to me to hang in there whether I get her body in the deal or not."

As for Susan: "It's not that I wouldn't like to, I think Tom realizes that, it's just that I couldn't. I'm sure it would change everything. If it were great, we'd want more and that would really threaten our marriages more than they already are. If it was terrible, how could I tell him? We've been so honest about everything else. I think it's probably been a mistake that we've even talked about sex as much as we have. We've probably made it into more of an issue than it has to be. But at least we can stop it here. I've told Tom that I can't be his friend if it means giving him my body, and for now he seems to have decided in favor of friendship."

The honesty and openness that they experience in their discussions of sex with other women act as an aphrodisiac for men. Personal disclosures concerning sex are viewed as an invitation to at least raise the issue of sex together. Like Susan, most other women are of the belief that good friends do not make good lovers. Such rebukes leave many men frustrated.

- "You can just talk about sex for only so long, then the talking itself is a turn-on. Twice my close friendships with women have ended because I thought we were at the point where we ought to go to bed and they didn't. I felt cheated; I'd given a lot of myself to the relationships and when push came to shove, they weren't willing to give in return."

- "How can you not want to go to bed with someone you love? If it were up to me, I'd jump her every time we got together. But, thank God, she's in charge and it's hands off. I don't like it, but I know that's the way it has to be to work."

105

- "I guess I may be the oddball 'cause I really don't want to go to bed with her. Most of my experiences with sex have been pretty bad. I make a few passes 'cause I think that's expected. Lucky for me, she's pretty firm about us not sleeping together. If she ever took me up on one of my passes, I don't know what I'd do. I'm sure that we'd both be plenty disappointed."

- "She keeps saying no, but she's weakening. The way I see it now, it's only a matter of time. Pretty soon she'll be the one who brings it up. Then we'll get this relationship to where it really ought to be."

Nearly every woman who befriends a man and becomes intimate with him must sooner or later deal with his sexual desires. When the time comes, the woman holds the fate of the relationship in her hands. She can choose to be friend, lover, or friend *and* lover. If she genuinely cares for the man and for the intimacy they have developed, the matter of sex must be handled with delicacy and sensitivity:

- "The thing of it is, for the average guy, the only women who have ever really cared for him have either gone to bed with him or had some damn good reason not to—like they were his mother or his sister or something. Now along comes me, who really cares for him but won't screw him and doesn't have a really good reason except that I value his friendship. Any way you say it, he's going to feel put down. So the real thing is, how can you stay friends after you tell him you won't screw? Maybe when I learn that, I'll get back some of the good friends I've lost."

- "Sex is always there between a man and a woman, right from the start. The longer you put off dealing with it, the bigger the problem when you finally do. I tell men right up front that that's not what I'm in the relationship for, and if that's what they expect, then I don't want them for a friend. After that it's almost never a problem."

- "The very best way to deal with it is to laugh about it. Every time he makes a pass you pretend it's a joke. They soon get the idea that you are not interested, and it stops being an issue."

- "You have to be honest with yourself first. You have to know what you really want, then if it's no, tell him no, but try to do it in a way that you're not rejecting him so much as rejecting the idea of sex with a friend. It's tricky, sure, but it can be done and it's so much better than going to bed with him just to avoid hurting his feelings. Believe me, I've tried it both ways, and not hurting him always ends up hurting you."

The decision to have sex or not to have it in extramarital friendships is not as one-sided as these statements might imply (he always wants to and she never does). There are relationships in which the woman is the sexual aggressor and the man demurs. There are also relationships in which the issue of sex is subject to a rational, mutual decision process. In fact, many who said that sex was not an issue in their friendships commented that this was so because they had "decided that it would not be an issue":

- "Early on, we decided that we would be like sister and brother. Once we agreed on that kind of a model for our relationship, a lot of things that might otherwise have gotten between us, things like sex, just never were important."

- "Perhaps if we weren't happily married, sex would be a problem, but we have both always agreed that we would never do anything that might jeopardize our marriages, so naturally anything to do with sex was out from the start."

- "I've never thought of her sexually, nor, I would imagine, has she of me. We're not each other's types. We've talked it all out and we know that's one thing we'll never have to deal with."

If these comments are indicative of those who report that sex is not an issue in their extramarital friendships, then it seems safe to say that sex surfaces to some degree in all intimate relationships between men and women. Initially this would seem to verify what wives have believed all along about the relationships between their husbands and other women, but appearances might be misleading.

The attention given to thoughts of sex and the threat of sex between a man and an other woman by all parties—husband, wife, and other woman—tends to overshadow what is most important about these relationships. The significant finding here is that fully two out of every three men are in some important way as intimate with other women as they are with their wives. Of this number, half have disclosed things about themselves to other women that they have not disclosed to their wives. Reports from the men and women involved show that these are not casual or superficial revelations, but significant self-disclosures. Perhaps the evolution, nature, and consequences of these other relationships can best be illustrated by a comprehensive case, one that covers all sides; the story of Charlie, Polly, and Donna provides such an opportunity. First, Polly's side, the wife's view:

"Charlie and Donna are more than just friends, I know that. I'm afraid to think how much more than friends they may really be. What galls me most is that he talks to her about things that he doesn't talk to me about. Important things that a wife ought to know. I sometimes think that it's my fault because I let it get too far before I did anything about it. I mean I'd ask him what he and Donna found to talk about that took so much time, but he always said, 'Oh, just things, nothing important,' and shrugged it off. Then, too, most of the time they were together was at the church choir, and I thought to myself, 'How much can go on at a church, really?' I should have known they were up to something from the start, because she always called him Charles. No one has called him Charles since he was a teenager.

"It all came to a head over his car. I had been on Charlie for the longest time about selling his old sports car, which he's had ever since he got out of high school. It's a beautiful old Corvette convertible that's worth quite a bit of money, but it's definitely a teenager's car. It's completely useless for a family of four, and most of the time the weather here is so bad he won't drive it anyway. Plus, there are a lot of things we could use the money for. I've told him over and over again that we ought to sell it. He finally said that he would take out an ad in one of those car collector magazines, because that's where he could get the most money for it. It must have been almost two months and we hadn't had a single call, so I began to wonder if maybe he hadn't put the ad in after all, but he said sure he did.

"Along about that time I ran into Donna at the mall. We're not really close friends or anything like that, but we know each other well enough to say more than 'Hi, how are you?' Anyway, we were talking about this and that when out of the blue Donna says to me, 'You know, Charles just can't bring himself to sell that beautiful car of his. He feels as though it's all that's left of who he was when he was young.'

"Can you imagine hearing something like that from another woman? She as much as told me that she knew my husband better than I did. I was so flabbergasted that I didn't know what to say. That night I demanded to know from Charlie everything he had talked to Donna about. Of course he played innocent with me: 'Church stuff, the choir, nothing special.' Finally I confronted him with what Donna had said about the car. He couldn't deny that he had told her something that he hadn't told me but he said he really couldn't remember, and 'whatever it was, it wasn't important.' Right then and there I asked him if he was having an affair with Donna. He kept saying that they were 'just friends' and accused me of making a big deal out of nothing. He just couldn't understand how hurt I was. I thought, here I am practically begging him for some communication and hanging on every little shred of feeling or emotion that he leaks out and all the time he's confessing his whole life to this woman 'friend'! I'd almost rather he was having an affair with her. It's his sharing with her that really hurts.

"I can't very well stop him from seeing her, since we are

in the same church. But I have told him that if he doesn't put an end to their 'friendship,' I'm going to put an end to our marriage. For all I know, he's talked to her about that too, the bastard!"

Polly Leford's feelings are typical of wives who suspect their husbands of relationships with other women. Her frustration-turned-fury is characteristic of wives' response to confirmation of their suspicions, as is her statement that "it's his sharing with her that really hurts." In her more vehement moments, Polly was heard to describe Donna as a "hussy," a "homewrecker," "hot," and worse. Under the circumstances, her name-calling can be forgiven. Still, there is a certain image of "the other woman" that persists. Whatever your mind's eye conjures up for the other woman, the chances are that Donna Waltham does not match the picture. She is short, plump, given to dressing in nondescript shifts, and hardly looks like a man-stealing mistress. As she speaks, however, it is evident that here is an articulate woman whose attentive listening and animated responses make her very attractive:

"First of all, you should know that I am very happily married. I have been for sixteen years and I have every intention of staying happily married for a long time to come. I would no more want to be a source of problems in someone else's marriage than I would want some other woman to be a problem in mine. Second, I am truly sorry that Polly feels the way she does, but I don't feel the need to apologize for anything about my friendship with Charles. There's simply nothing to apologize for. That's the third thing. Regardless of what Polly thinks—or anyone else, for that matter—there is absolutely nothing sexual between Charles and me, nothing! It is really ridiculous to think that there is. I mean, look at me—I'm hardly the sort of woman that men see and immediately want to jump into bed with. Even if I was, I would never do something like that to my own marriage. Now that all of that is clear, I want to explain just what there is between me and Charles.

"Ever since I can remember, I have always been the sort of girl who was everybody's 'big sister,' especially guys. In grade school the boys used to ask me if I thought so-and-so liked them. In high school they'd come to me to make sure some girl would go out with them before they actually risked asking her. In college I was the one they asked to find a date for their friends. Of course, they'd never think to ask *me* out. I can't tell you how many times I was told, 'Oh, I couldn't go out with you, Donna, we're too good friends.' The point is, I have always had a lot of close friendships with men. Men have always confided in me, shared personal things with me, told me secrets. I don't know why, exactly. I'd like to think it's because I am a good listener and a good friend, but I'm smart enough to know that it's just as likely to be because men aren't trying to impress me. They don't want anything from me except my friendship.

"I would say that there are five or six men I know who would probably say that I am their best friend. Of course, they tell me things that they don't tell their wives. I know because I have asked them, 'Have you told your wife about this?' What the wives don't understand is that I always encourage the men who share personal things with me to share the same things with their wives. It's not my fault that they don't. They say things like 'She wouldn't understand,' 'I wanted to try it out on you first,' 'She'd just get all worried,' or even 'She isn't interested, she wouldn't care.' Wives who complain about their husbands being close to another woman need to take a hard and honest look at themselves, I think, before they get to blaming him or the other woman.

"The way I see it, the situation is not all bad. After all, how can any one person, no matter how loving they are or how long they've been married, expect to meet all the needs of any other person? We all need friends of the opposite sex just as much, maybe even more, than we need friends of the same sex. I am sure that my husband talks to both his male and his female friends about some things that he doesn't talk to me about. If I thought that he didn't communicate with me at all, I might be threatened by that, but we do talk, and whatever his reasons for talking to them, I know it doesn't mean that he loves me any less. Hey, if I can have friends and secrets with my friends, why can't he, too?"

Donna's testimony provides the answers to key questions about a common pattern in a man's extramarital relationships, specifically: (1) The relationship evolves naturally from a shared interest; (2) the man does reveal significant self-information that he does not share with his wife; (3) the woman frequently has no sexual designs on the man, nor is theirs a sexual relationship. Donna also suggests an answer to the most intriguing question: Why do men reveal dimensions of themselves to another woman that they do not reveal to their own wives? Donna's participant analysis, based on her own experience, says that the reasons can be found in the man's motives, the friend's methods, and the wife's manner. Polly did not understand the symbolic importance of the car to Charles, and he sought comfort from Donna. In Donna's experience, men seek someone who will listen empathetically without judging or jumping to conclusions. At one point she described what she offered that men sought and couldn't find at home: "hearing without a hassling." For Donna's part, Charles offers an important part of himself, affirmation of her self-image as a good listener and someone to whom others can turn, and a chance to be comforting.

It may be that the invitation to intimacy that other women present is the promise of response without responsibility, the idea that the man can receive some caring and concern without having to answer to any demands or exhibit any commitment. Charles's view of his relationship with Donna provides some additional clues:

"Donna is my closest friend. I have a lot of men friends that I spend time with at work, at church, wherever, but no one knows me as well as Donna does. It's probably true that that is because I haven't let anyone know me the way I have Donna, not even Polly. It sure didn't start out like that. At first Donna was just someone to talk to at choir; we joked, talked about nothing important, just to pass the time. Since we were choir officers, we got thrown together in a lot of meetings and such, so of course we got to know each other better as time went on.

"I can't think of any one time when I could say we went from being just casual friends to being really close. It just seemed that as time went on I found myself talking about more and more things to Donna, things that I didn't talk about to anybody else, not even to Polly—what I thought about things, how I felt about things, questions I had that, for whatever reason, I had never thought I could ask anyone else. I guess I first realized how important our friendship was to me when I started making time for us to be together to talk, instead of just seeing her at meetings or practice.

"I can talk to Donna about things that I don't talk to Polly about, but it's hard to say why. I'm not really sure. It's not that she is more intelligent or cares more about me or anything like that. There's nothing sexual, like you might think. I can truthfully say that sex has never been an issue between Donna and me; I've never thought about it, and I'm sure she hasn't, either. So what is there? Well, first of all, I'd have to say that one of the good things is that there is nothing at stake; I mean, if Donna and I disagree over something, like how to raise kids or what to do with money, it's no big deal, because we don't have to act on it. With Polly it's different because those disagreements have to be settled, we have to do something. Then, too, lots of the time they just open up old arguments that we've had time and again. Another thing is, Donna can listen to my wildest ideas without flying off the handle or overreacting. If I tell her I want to quit work and go live like a beachcomber on some island, we can talk about what that might be like and why I want to do it. If I said the same thing to Polly, she'd start worrying about the kids, our house, money. She'd act as though I was really going to do it, probably end up calling her parents and making arrangements to go live with them. Basically, my

113

fantasy would cause a fight and be destroyed before it ever got started.

"I guess what it boils down to is that I don't really risk anything by letting Donna in on who I really am and what goes on with me. A person needs someone like that. I even think it's good for my marriage. I can test a lot of things out on Donna, it takes a lot of pressure off my relationship with Polly. The kinds of things I'm talking about, you really can't talk to another guy about—there's too much competition, too much trying to be a 'real man.' Then, too, a lot of the stuff Donna and I talk about only a woman could answer, maybe even only a woman who is not your wife. For example, I really wonder if other women find me attractive. That's something that no wife can answer honestly, and that's just one of the things.

"The thing is, no matter how good your marriage is, you need friends, too. Sometimes you need a friend more than you need a wife—not all the time, but sometimes. It doesn't mean that you love your wife any less. I honestly feel that no matter how close Donna and I are or might be, it would never threaten my love for Polly. In fact, in a lot of ways Donna has helped me to see what a great woman Polly really is, and to love her even more. Still, I need Donna for a friend, too. Look at it this way—if I were married to Donna, I'd probably have Polly for a best friend!

"The really tough part of it is that I can talk about all of this with Donna, but not with Polly. It's a perfect example of what I was telling you about. I can tell Donna why I need her friendship, and she listens and helps me to see what it is about our friendship that is important to me. She accepts that part of me. I can't have the same conversation with Polly. I can't share that important part of me with her, because she can't understand that just because someone else knows something about me that she doesn't, it means that I love them more than I love her. Hell, it doesn't necessarily mean that I love them at all. It just means that I need to let somebody know me in ways that she doesn't or can't. Donna understands how I feel. I only wish that Polly did too."

It is difficult to understand how Charles feels. How can he not see that his relationship with Donna is threatening to his wife? It is difficult to understand what he wants from the two women in his life. What is most difficult to understand is how he can share some things with Donna that he cannot share with Polly. How is it that intimacy with an other woman comes more easily to some men than does intimacy with their own wives?

For Charles, the answer is that he needs a friend as well as a wife. In Chapter 2, men argued that they could not disclose themselves to their wives. Men have said it is because wives don't understand, are too close, overreact, don't deal with the here and now, shouldn't be burdened, or "can't do anything about it." In these explanations there is an implication that a man can be intimate with an other woman, more intimate than he may be with his wife, precisely because she is an *other* woman. That is to say, there is nothing about the other woman as an individual that makes intimacy with her more attractive than intimacy with a spouse; it is *what* she is, not *who* she is, that makes intimacy possible. This means that if from these relationships we are to learn anything about how men might be more intimate, more loving with their wives, we need to look more at the role the other woman plays in a man's life than at who the other woman is.

Reconstructed from the data and descriptions here, the structure of a man's relationship with an other woman is such that he can be revealing without risk, caring without commitment or loss of control, honest without being hassled. Men perceive that with the other woman they are free to be who they *are* rather than who they *must be*. No other relationship that a man has is perceived by him to afford this opportunity to be open; not in his relationships with his wife, his family, his friends, or in any other relationship will we see the same kind of intimacy that we find between a man and an other woman. Yet even in these relationships, men are not completely self-disclosing; something is always withheld so that the man remains less than completely intimate, less than fully loving. Few men reveal all of who they are even to those closest to them—wife or other woman. As a result, rarely does anyone *really* know a man, rarely does anyone know his love and feel loved by him.

A man's relationships present a mosaic of male intimacy. Some pieces of the man's self are revealed in his relationship with his wife. For many men, other dimensions of themselves are disclosed in their relationship with an other woman. Still other aspects of the man's self will define the special intimacies between a man and his family, and between a man and his friends. Only by knowing all the pieces can we know the man and how he loves.

4 Family Man or Phantom Man?

Madame Rosepettle—Life, Mr. Roseabove, is a husband hanging from a hook in the closet.

—Arthur L. Kopit, from *Oh Dad, Poor Dad, Mama's Hung You in the Closet and I'm Feeling So Sad*

"He doesn't talk to his parents except on holidays. He hasn't seen his brother in almost two years. He spends almost no time with the kids, and when he does, it's only to beat the pants off his son at some sport or show off his daughter on one of their 'dates'—and get this, he considers himself a real family man!"

Marsha Blick's description of her husband's relationships with the members of his family could apply equally to many men. Marriage and family come high on the priority lists of even the busiest of men in the most demanding of occupational, social, and political positions. We are quite accustomed to hearing everyone from movie stars and sports heroes to corporate executives and political leaders say, "My family comes first," or, "My favorite way to spend time is at home with my family." It is almost a required statement by any man in public or private life. The truth is that being a "family man" is more a way of talking about familial rela-

117

tionships than a description of how men behave with their families. The average man is barely familiar with his family, let alone intimate with its members.

There are some special intimacies that exist between a man and his children, parents, siblings. A man may share some portion of who he is in each of these family relationships, developing a certain conditional closeness that even, if it is not real intimacy, at least differentiates his family relationships from those he might have with a friend or work associate. Nonetheless, rarely is a man so intimate with the members of his family that they feel loved by him in the way that they love him. A closer examination of how men behave in their relationships with daughters, sons, parents, and siblings contributes to the developing picture of why men can't love.

DADDIES AND DAUGHTERS

I am from a family of all boys, and I have two boys of my own. I have never experienced firsthand the relationship between a father and his daughter. When my boys were younger, my friends would often say to me, "It's too bad you don't have a little girl, you're really missing out." Now, even though my boys are older, I still hear from other fathers, "There's something special about the relationship between a father and daughter that you don't get with boys." I've often wondered what this mysterious "something special" was. What is it that dads and daughters have that a father and son cannot? What exists between fathers and daughters is a special kind of intimacy that is, as often as not, built more on fiction than on fact.

The general disclosure pattern of men in familial relationships is for the man to reveal in some detail his public self and, in general terms, aspects of his private self. Apart from this norm, three distinct intimacy patterns can be discerned between fathers and daughters. The three patterns are here called The Loving Lie, The Distant Dad and Daugh-

118

ter, and The Daughter as the Other Woman. The first two of these are quite common; the third is less so, but each tells something about the ways in which men can and cannot love.

The Loving Lie: Deceitful Daddies and Dutiful Daughters

Most men are measurably more intimate with their daughters than they are with anyone else to whom they relate except their wives (or other women). They reveal more of themselves in every dimension—public, private, and personal—to their daughters than they do to their sons, parents, siblings, or closest friends. However, men also report that they misrepresent themselves in these dimensions more in their relationships with their daughters than in any other relationships. This means that men disclose a great deal of themselves to their daughters, thus developing intimacy. But what they disclose is as apt to be fiction as fact. They are close to their daughters, but when they are close they aren't real: the apparent intimacy is a loving lie.

As one father explained, "It's not that I really lie to my girls, I just sort of let them believe some things about me that aren't exactly true." The kinds of things that "aren't exactly true" of fathers run the gamut from the man's attitudes and opinions to his feelings about work and career and even to his self-image:

■ "I've told Carrie a lot of things about how a marriage should be, and I've given her the impression that her mom and I have that kind of marriage, when really nothing could be further from the truth. Not what I want in a marriage or what I have. Still, I think she ought to believe and look for something different in her marriage, something much better than I have—that's why I do it."

■ "It's important to me that my girls think I'm a success at work, and I'll go to any lengths necessary to give them that impression."

■ "I let on that I'm harder on myself than I really am,

119

because when I do she always goes on and on about how great I really am and that makes me feel good. It's an innocent enough little game that we play."

- "She has never seen me depressed, and she never will. No matter how down I may get, I've always got a smile for her. I try to be positive and upbeat whenever she's around. I don't want her to get the idea that I can't handle whatever comes along."

Implicit in these brief remarks are many motives for a father's misrepresentation of self: it's for her own good, it's protective, it makes him feel good, there's no harm in it. The motives for a dad's deceptive disclosure may be mixed, but the way in which such a pattern of intimacy comes about is much more predictable. Despite the changing patterns in parenting, still relatively few fathers take an active role in the early upbringing of a girl child. By the time she is involved in things he can use as a framework for relating to her—in grade school at the earliest, and for many, not until high school and dating—she has already formed an image of who he is and what he is about. A daughter's view of her father comes from what she has seen, what her mother has told her, and how he has been in her life until that point. "White knight" is the phrase that has been used to describe the daughter's perception of the father at this time, and the imagery captures much of how he is seen and how he sees himself as seen by his daughter. If he is to relate to this person at all, it seems to him as though he must be, or at least appear to be, the man she expects him to be. Therefore, he frequently feels the need to misrepresent himself to her.

One father, Andrew Reed, described the development of his relationship with his two daughters, Patti and Ann Marie, now twenty-four and twenty-two years old:

"I guess I wasn't really prepared to have kids when we did. I know I certainly never had any anticipation of what having kids would be like. When they were babies, I didn't have anything to do with them at all. I wasn't even all that comfortable around them, because I didn't know what to do with a baby. The first time I ever held a baby was when the nurse gave me Patti, and I was so nervous I gave her back as fast as I could. It wasn't much different later, when they were growing up. I wasn't around them all that much, because of work, and even when I was around, their mother took care of most of what they needed. There were always the three of them doing girl things. I didn't know where I fit in. In a way I didn't want to be included, and in a way I felt left out.

"I don't think it was till they got into high school that I realized I had these two beautiful young girls living in my house who were complete strangers to me. Partly out of guilt, I'm sure, and partly because I saw them involved in things I could get involved in, I decided I'd better get to know them and let them know me. To my surprise, they already had some pretty firm ideas about who I was. A lot of those ideas weren't quite right, but it was easier for me to let them go on thinking what they did than to try and be honest with them. With Ann Marie it's worked really well. I think we are as close now as we could have been if I'd been there all along. With Patti, the older one, it's different. We were close there for a while, but now we argue whenever we're together, so we stay away from each other."

As children mature, they inevitably come to see that their parents are less than perfect. Most adapt readily to this realization, experiencing a slight estrangement from the significant parent. But there are more extreme responses as well, and these are particularly evident where the father-daughter relationship has been built on illusion.

Andrew's daughters display two common responses to the deception of fathers. Ann Marie, the youngest, treats it as a harmless game she and her father play. Patti, the older of the two, has largely rejected any closeness with her father ever since she realized he wasn't the man she had always thought him to be. First, from Ann Marie:

"I've known all along that Daddy wasn't everything he

pretended to be, but it seemed harmless enough to let him think he was. Why should I hurt him? A good example is when he bought me my first car. Daddy likes to let on that he knows everybody in town; it's almost a joke with us in the family how, whatever we wanted or needed, Daddy always knew someone who could get it for us 'at cost.' It was the same way with my car; as long as I got a certain model, a certain color, Daddy could get me a real deal. He never thought that when you don't get what you really want, it's no deal at all. But I played along and *oohed* and *ahhed* over how fantastic Daddy was to be able to get this car for me.

"When things went wrong with the car right away, it was more of the same. 'Just tell them who you are when you take it in,' Daddy would say. It didn't make any difference who I was, except that I might have to wait a little longer to get my car done, 'cause Daddy was such a pain in the ass to them. I learned long ago that it was easier to let Daddy think he was the big shot, then go ahead and do it my own way; that way he's happy and so am I, and nobody is hurt. I don't know why Patti can't handle Daddy like that. Instead she cuts him down every chance she gets, and makes life miserable for both of them. I don't see why she doesn't realize that things would be so much easier on everybody if she would just play along."

Patti does not "play along" with her father's deception, and she is quite adamant about it:

"My father and I would get along just fine if he would be real with me, but instead he insists on being this 'big daddy' type that I know for a fact isn't real. He's just another small-time businessman in town. Why can't he admit that? I refuse to participate in his charade the way Mom and Annie do—why should I? How can you get close to someone who isn't honest with you? I won't go into all of it here, but there are some things I know about my father that are so far from the way he wants us to think he is that it's like two completely different people. Because he won't be straight with me about who he really is, I can never trust him. I'm not sure I'll ever be able to really trust any man, and I have my father to thank for that wonderful outlook."

Ann Marie's "playing along" is a common response of daughters to their fathers' misrepresentations of self. Most acknowledge that it is easier to relate that way than to try to discover who their fathers really are, with all of the turmoil that might involve. Ann Marie's choice is supported by many daughters who acknowledge that the "closeness" they have with their fathers is based on imagery and impression and is therefore not real intimacy, but a closeness born of convenience:

- "None of us knows what Daddy really is like, but we've all played along with him for so long that I think even Mom has stopped caring whether we know the real him or not. I don't think it matters much now. Maybe it would have, if we had got it all straightened out early on, but now we all know our roles too well to try to change."

- "Mother always told us how to relate to Father; anything we knew about him came from her. I guess in that sense it's less a matter of us catering to him than of us catering to her. We do what she tells us, because she says that's the way he wants it done. I never even thought to question whether or not he really wanted it done that way. He never said, and I certainly never would ask him!"

- "Papa's so easy to fool, if you just let him think you see him the way he wants you to. My sisters and I can get anything we want from him that way. The funny thing is, he thinks we have this super-honest relationship. It's a joke, really."

- "Maybe if I had been allowed to form my own opinions about my father from my own experience with him, we would have a more genuine closeness today. But my earliest impressions of my father were shaped by what my mother told me about him. By the time I got to know him on my own, we were already scripted for a certain sort of relationship, and frankly, now we're just living out the script. I don't think either one of us has the faintest idea who the other one really is. I think we're both a little afraid to try to find out this late in the game, so we just play along."

Unlike Ann Marie and other daughters who find reason to go along with their father's deceit, many challenge the father as he presents himself and demand that he be "real" if he wants a relationship at all. Like Patti, they argue that intimacy requires trust, and that there can be no trust if there is no honesty. For these daughters, the discovery that Daddy is not the man he led her to believe prompts rejection of any relationship at all:

- "Relationships with my father are a total sham. You can get along fine with him as long as you never ask him to be honest with you, as long as you let him play his little game. I refuse to play; I think it's insulting. And since I won't play it his way—meaning I won't pander to his ego— he won't have anything to do with me. That suits me just fine."

- "The real split between my dad and me came when I found out he was running around on my mom. I was fifteen and I had this image of him as super-dad, super-husband. When I learned he had been having an affair, it was like it was all a lie, everything I had ever believed about him. We've hardly talked since. If he would admit it, I might respect his honesty, but he goes on with his Mr. Good Guy act and it just makes me sick."

- "If what you know about a person is totally false, how can you have any kind of relationship at all with that person? That's true whether the person is your father or not. Only it's worse if the person is your father, because when you find out that someone you have totally believed in all your life has lied to you, it hurts more than if you've suspected someone all along. The way it is now, I wouldn't trust my father with anything, especially my love."

- "I never really knew my father until I went away to school and started doing the things I thought he had taught me to do, like being my own person and testing life and that sort of thing. Well, I soon learned that he didn't believe any of that stuff because he didn't approve at all of the person I wanted to be. He didn't want me to test life for myself, he wanted me to live my life for *him*, not for *me*. It was like he had been lying to me all along; he didn't really believe any of the things he had told me."

Not only do fathers frequently misrepresent themselves to their daughters, but they often compound this deceit by making little or no effort to find out who their daughters really are. They are fixed on the image of a little girl who worships her father, not realizing that the little girl grows up to become a person of her own. As she discovers her own identity, she wants to know his. No longer content with the "white knight" image that has been handed her, the daughter often wants to sort out her relationship with her father as, or before, she works out her relationships with the other men in her life. This inquiry inevitably uncovers deceit, for, whether they want to or not, few fathers can live up to all that a daughter has come to think of them. This discovery can be a shock for both father and daughter; with the end of idols comes the end of worship. "I search in vain for signs that he is the all-powerful, all-knowing daddy I've always thought he was, and I am disappointed time and time again as I realize he is not."

Some fathers and daughters seize this time of reality-testing to forge new relationships based on their true identities. Freed from the burden of being "all-powerful" and "all-knowing," a father can now be the person he really is, and discover who his daughter is. These relationships can become truly intimate and grow as the father and daughter grow. Others decide, for reasons of time, effort, or personal convenience, to let things go on as they have, the father continuing his deceit, the daughter dutifully conspiring.

On the surface, many of these deceits are quite innocent, bearing as they do upon the father's success, his status, his role in the family. But beneath this veneer lies a more serious deceit: "We both pretend that we understand each other; we in fact do not and can never understand each other because we've each got so much invested in pretending. No matter what we pretend, we never have been and never will be close." Not only does the father's behavior prevent any real intimacy and therefore any real expression of loving between the man and his daughter, but even more sinisterly, it sabotages the daughter's relationship with all other men. One woman of twenty-six was particularly eloquent as she wrote of the way in which her relationship with her father has affected her subsequent dealings with men:

"He was the first man in my life. I have been his girl from the beginning, and until I sort out my history with my father, I can't have a future with any other man. I am going back to him after a separation of many years to change our relationship. It is suffering that motivates this desire for change. A succession of unhappy love affairs, inability to enjoy sex, feelings of insecurity, repeated failures with weak men whom I wanted because I could dominate them, all of this pain has been because of the relationship I have with my father. I left because there was no relationship, only a routine, a meaningless pattern of talking and touching carried out since childhood, which I finally realized was a falsehood the whole family encouraged. I'm going back to force a real relationship with my father, because until he is real with me, I don't see how I can have a real relationship with any other man."

It may be that in their desire to protect their daughters through their promotion of relationships based on deceit and duty, fathers punish them for life. Less dramatically and more commonly, father and daughter withdraw from one another. Often the deceit doesn't lead to confrontation, and rarer still are the times when confrontation leads to intimacy. The more common pattern is for the father to become defensive and withdraw from the daughter, creating the distance that characterizes so many of a man's familial relationships.

The Distant Dad and Daughter

■ "There is no relationship with my father; for that matter, there never has been. He was always there when I was growing up, and we were civil enough to each other, but we never really talked. To this day I don't know much more about him than I do about some stranger on the street. I've always thought that it was like this because my father really wanted a son, and when he got me instead, he decided Mom could raise me."

■ "My dad was one of those 'absentee fathers.' He was simply never there. Every time there was something important to me, a school play, a big dance, even high-school graduation, he was away on business. Mom raised my brother and me virtually by herself. Dad did show up at my wedding, but by then it was too late; he had been gone so much, we had spent so little time together that it was almost like I was being given away by a stranger."

■ "Daddy has always done things with me. I guess I'm lucky that way, because a lot of girls I know never had any time with their fathers when they were growing up. The problem is that our time together didn't mean much because we didn't spend it getting to know each other better. We always spent it doing things. Plus, we usually did things where there would be other fathers, so Dad would have somebody to talk to and not be stuck with me. I remember way back to 'Indian Princesses,' the Y program for fathers and daughters. In our tribe, the dads always took us to this pizza place that had pinball machines. They'd give us girls lots of quarters and send us off to the machines while they drank beer and told jokes. When we went home, Mom would make a big deal over what a great father he was because he spent so much time with me. If he *had* spent time with me, he would have been a great dad."

■ "Dad and I are sort of at a standoff in our relationship; it's been that way for a long time now. He doesn't make any effort to get closer to me, and I don't make any effort to get closer to him. Everything we know about each other comes

127

through Mom. It's like we need her to translate for us. One on one, we just can't make it work. When she acts as go-between, at least we have some idea of what is going on with each other. I honestly don't know where we went wrong, 'cause I can't remember it ever being any other way. He's never been more than a presence, something, somebody 'out there' somewhere."

These stories of opportunities for intimacy between father and daughter having been lost or never having materialized are repeated in family after family. Little is shared between the two, there is little that each knows about the other, there is nothing that approaches intimacy. Once such a distance is created, it is very difficult to overcome, regardless of the good intentions of both parties. There needs to be a compelling reason for both father and daughter to make the effort required to establish intimacy. Curiously, divorce or the death of the wife/mother can be the catalyst for a closer father-daughter relationship.

One interesting characteristic of intimate father-daughter relationships is the mutuality of exchange of selves, with the daughter knowing as much about the father as the father knows about the daughter. This is different from the predominantly one-way exchanges in male intimate relationships with other women. The result is a loving relationship greatly valued by father and daughter alike:

- "A daughter's love is unconditional. There is a sense that whatever you have done or whatever you do, she will always love you, even more than a wife. Your daughter 'has' to love you. I guess that feeling of total acceptance is what frees me to feel that I can be totally honest with her, and I have been. There is nothing that I haven't discussed with her, almost no behavior of mine that she hasn't seen, the good and the bad. We have the best relationship any father could hope for, and it grows closer every day."

- "Daddy has really spoiled me, because I won't ever be satisfied with any relationship with a man who is not as loving as he is. I can't imagine what it would be like to live with someone who wasn't open with you, really told you what was going on with him all the time. My father is like that, he always has been. From my earliest memories of him, he didn't just ask me about me, he told me about him, even told me some things that I might not like. The point is, Daddy never hid anything from me, never tried to be someone he wasn't, and he always expected me to be the same way with him. It's easy to love him because he's so loving. It may be hard for me to find what I'm looking for in a man because I've set my standards so high, but Daddy has led me to expect the very best because he is!"

▪ "It doesn't always work out between a father and daughter, and I'm not sure I know why it does when it does, and why it doesn't when it doesn't. The two older girls I hardly know at all, but Kelly, the youngest, is my best friend. It probably has something to do with how old they were when their mother died. Kelly was just into her teens, and the other two had already graduated from high school. Maybe just like with everybody else, you hit it off with some people and not with others, even your own kids. You'd think you should be close to your own flesh and blood, but sometimes it just doesn't work out that way. As close as Kelly and I are, I wonder if I didn't miss out on the other two, but they have to take some of the blame, it wasn't all me. For whatever reason, I never felt I could open up with them the way I can with Kelly. It's just like marriage. You both have to really work at it, or it won't work. Fathers and daughters are so busy working on their own things that they don't work at being close to each other. We take each other for granted and it's great if it works out, and even if it doesn't work out, you love them anyway—though maybe not as much as you could or as much as you should."

There are many things going on between fathers and daughters that clearly require some mutual work if they are to become intimate and loving. Not the least of these things is that one is male and the other is female, and that differ-ence alone creates barriers to intimacy. The sexual issue in father-daughter relationships may account for an unusual but noteworthy intimacy pattern in which the father be-haves toward the daughter as he does toward the other woman.

The Daughter as the Other Woman

In some families an alliance is formed between the fa-ther and daughter against the wife/mother. Often in these relationships men use their daughters as the other woman, revealing to them things about themselves that they do not reveal to their wives. In any father-daughter relationship, there are likely to be some exclusive exchanges, some little secrets shared between dad and daughter, some activities that they do together without the wife/mother, some occa-sions when they "team up" against the wife/mother. These exclusive exchanges are a natural consequence of living to-gether and are, for the most part, quite innocent. But there are other disclosures by fathers to daughters that approxi-mate the intimacy a man has with an other woman:

■ "Dad and I do have a few secrets from Mom. Nothing evil or anything like that; it's just some little things that we've shared with each other and nobody else. It gives us a special kind of closeness. Sometimes I suppose that Mom might feel a little left out, but hey, sometimes I feel a little left out of the things she and Dad have together, so fair is fair."

■ "I confide a lot in her, in many ways much more than I confide in her mother. For one, she's a better listener and she can see both sides. She knows firsthand what I have to put up with from her mother, and I feel that she really under-stands what's going on. She's really very mature for her age [fourteen]."

■ "She's so much like her mom used to be when I first knew her, bright and funny, adventurous, open-minded.

She's just so much more responsive than her mother is, I find myself talking to her the way her mom and I used to talk, really opening up. And she really cares about what I have to say; I guess that's why we are so close."

■ "I don't know how he puts up with Mom. I mean, she is such a bitch! The things she does to him you just wouldn't believe! He tells me all about it, I guess because he doesn't really have anyone else to talk to. I feel a little funny about some of what he tells me, when he gets super-personal and all. At the same time I feel really good that he does tell me, because it brings us a lot closer and I can help him with some of what he has to put up with from her. I wish he would get a divorce so it could be just the two of us. We'd both be better off without her."

There are many dynamics at work in these relationships in which the daughter becomes the "other woman" for the father. The image of the father that is cherished by both the father and the daughter is often under attack by the mother, who wants the daughter to know what her father "is really like." Unwilling to give up their "game," father and daughter often form an alliance to ward off attacks of reality. Many fathers may find it easier to be revealing to someone who is continually accepting than to be challenged and confronted by a spouse. Also operating here is competition between the mother and daughter for the affections of the father. Total acceptance is the daughter's principal competitive advantage over her mother in vying for the time and attention of the father. Finally, there are hints here at the darker side of father-daughter relationships, sexual attraction.

Relationships between fathers and daughters cannot be discussed honestly without some attention to sexual dynamics, an area that is sufficiently complex as to be the subject of entire studies. We've yet to learn all there is to know about this dimension of familial relationships, and perhaps we never shall. So strong are the taboos against the behavior in question that it is spoken of only in the extreme. At one extreme, it has been established that the greatest incidence of incest is that committed by fathers upon daughters. Though the statistics are alarming (and even more so when we consider how few incidents of incest are actually reported), we must keep in mind the other extreme: in the overwhelming majority of father-daughter relationships, there is no sexual contact whatsover. This is not to say that there is no sexual dynamic operating between these fathers and daughters. Here is where the issue becomes difficult to track. So prevalent and powerful are the prohibitions against father-daughter sex that most feel that even to talk about the subject is taboo. Men and women, when approached on the subject, refuse comment or even take offense. At the least, they deny that it has ever been an issue: "I never thought of anything like that." "It simply has never entered my mind." "You're kidding, that's ridiculous!"

In the lives of most fathers and daughters, there is a time when the sexual tension between them is at a peak. Ideally this can occasion a discussion of what is happening in their relationship. If they talk about their feelings and what those feelings mean, they can develop a more intimate relationship. What more often occurs, however, is that father and daughter withdraw from each other as the result of a sexual incident. Kathy Waller describes one such incident with her father:

"During the spring semester I had really gotten involved with this guy, Jake. The last couple of weeks before summer we virtually lived together. Then summer came and we were apart for a couple of months. Toward the end of summer, Jake was flying through and had a couple of hours' layover at the airport. My folks and I went out to meet him and have dinner. I remember being really frustrated because I was really horny for Jake; the two months since we had last made love seemed like forever, but there in the airport, with my folks and all, there wasn't much I could do about it.

"Afterward, at home, Mom went to bed and Dad and I

stayed up to have a drink. We got to talking about me and Jake, and Dad started telling me stories about when he was my age and how different the whole sex thing was for young people then. I was sort of half listening to him and half thinking about Jake, still pretty much turned on from seeing him at the airport. Anyway, when I went to kiss Dad good night, I don't know what got into me, but I opened my mouth and started to tongue him a little. Well, he did the same thing and then put his hands up my top and touched my nipples. When he did that, I pulled away and ran upstairs. We never talked about it, though I've thought a lot about it since."

There need not be a climactic event for sex to come between a father and his daughter. Often there is a growing sense on the part of the father, the daughter, or both that they are playing a very dangerous game. As much as a man might value the intimacy that comes from treating his daughter as the other woman, ultimately guilt and fear drive them apart at the cost of whatever intimacy they have developed until now. It is as though they are repelled by their own feelings or don't trust themselves to be able to deal with their feelings in an acceptable manner. For the father, it is another example of the male confusion regarding sex and intimacy. In this instance, sex distances him from intimacy.

FATHERS AND SONS

Sexual attraction is the dark cloud that hangs over fathers and daughters, often making for stormy relationships. The persistent presence in father-son relationships is competition: competition for the attention of the wife/mother, territorial competition for supremacy in the household, even competition for the spoils of life in the world at large. Insight into the nature of intimate relationships between fathers and their sons comes from an examination of how they deal with competition.

From the research data, it is apparent that fathers are noticeably less intimate with their sons than they are with daughters or spouses. Fewer close relationships are reported, and those that are tend to be distinguished by the limited range of disclosure. Father-son relationships are focused almost entirely on externalities, the arenas of the public and private self, with little or no sharing of the more intimate personal self. Even though fathers and sons may know relatively little about one another, what they do know is usually accurate, without the pretense or posing so often seen in father-daughter relationships. Still, there are some familiar patterns.

Only Remotely Related

The "distant daddy," the "absentee father," the "part-time parent"—these phrases all describe the way in which many fathers are not in the lives of their daughters and are therefore not close to their daughters. In general, fathers are similarly remote from their sons and not intimate with them:

- "My father was a presence but he was never really present, if you know what I mean. Mom was forever saying, 'Your father this or your father that,' but my father himself never said this or that. When he wasn't away at work, he was off with his friends or with Mom. He was never off with me. I don't know whether he was really that busy or whether everything else was so important or whether he just didn't like me—I still don't know. He was never around enough for me to find out *why* he wasn't around. When you don't know someone, you don't know why they do or don't do things, do you?"

- "I'm treated more like an employee by my dad than like a son. He tells me things to do and how he wants them done. If I don't do them just the way he says, he lets me know. If I do them right, he never mentions it. Other than that, he doesn't talk to me at all. He never asks me about my life, what's going on with me, and he never tells me what's going on with him. Sometimes I feel more like his servant than his son. A lot of my friends feel the same way about their dads, too. Maybe that's just the way dads are, when you're a teenager."

■ "My dad was around all the time, but for all the communication I had with him, he might as well have been gone. He was there, but only in body; he didn't really have anything to do with me. I don't think it really mattered to him how things were for me, whether I was doing well in school or failing, and later, whether I was making money or not. If he ever did notice, he sure never mentioned it. Mom would always say how proud he was of this or that that I did, but he never said a word to me himself. I honestly don't think he ever gave much thought to me, let alone to our relationship."

■ "It was really pretty pathetic how my dad would go through these periods of trying to be a 'father of the year' type. He would be rolling along with his work and all, pretty much ignoring me, then all of a sudden he'd drop everything and be Super Dad for two or three days. He'd take me places, we'd do lots of things together, and he'd catch up on what I'd been doing. Then, as suddenly as it had started, it would be over. He wouldn't have anything to do with me again for four or five months. Then it'd start all over. When I was young I couldn't understand it at all. I thought it was my fault, that somehow, some way, I had failed some test when we were together, and that was why he stopped spending time with me. Mom would assure me that it was just because he was so busy with so many things. To this day I remember her saying, 'He's not *just* your dad, you know.' As I got older, I realized I was just another duty to him. When he got to feeling guilty about neglecting me, he'd give me a dose of fatherhood that he hoped would hold me so he could get back to doing whatever it was he really wanted to be doing. About then I stopped being a sucker for his Super Dad thing, because all it did was to set me up for a real letdown. He never realized that I didn't want a sometime Super Dad. What I wanted was a full-time *average* dad. As it is, I sort of feel like I ended up with no dad at all."

Where fathers were observed to be distant from their daughters, a common motive or rationale given was confusion and discomfort. Because they do not know how to be a father to a daughter, do not know what role they should play in her upbringing, many men choose not to play a role at all. By contrast, the distance and absence of intimacy that exists between most fathers and their sons seems to be the result of a conscious decision on the part of fathers that that is precisely the role they *should* play. They choose distance not in the absence of alternatives, but *over* the alternatives. Here are the comments of some fathers explaining why they are not more intimate in their relationships with their sons:

- "Now that he has a family of his own, I think he realizes that what I taught him was that a man's first responsibility is to provide for his family. Maybe I didn't spend as much time with him as he would have liked, but he sure liked the things my time spent at work allowed him to have. The best kind of learning is by experience, and the second best is by example. I think I gave my son a good experience and think I set a good example. We may not be all that close, but I was successful and I taught him how to be. There's no use in being a close family if you can't put food on the table or clothes on your back."

- "A man needs to be independent; he has to think and act for himself. I raised my boys so that they can take care of themselves. I never pampered them or protected them in any way. From the very beginning they've had to fend for themselves, because I let them know they weren't going to be able to depend on me or anybody else. That's how my father raised me. It worked for me, and it's working for them, too."

- "Right now I don't have a whole lot of time for my son, what with the demands on my time at work and all. He's pretty young for there to be many things that we can really do together, anyway. I'm sure that when things settle down at work and when he gets old enough that we can do stuff together, we'll become best buddies. I think the way for a father and son to become close is to do things together. I always wished that my dad and I had had more time to do stuff together, but he was pretty busy too. Now I can see what it was like for him, why he didn't have so much time for me, but as soon as my boy gets older, it's going to be different between him and me."

- "I don't want to be one of those pushy fathers who try to get their kids to do all the things they never did. Boy Scouts, Little League, all that stuff is for the fathers, not for the kids. I'm not going to try to live my life through my kid. He can make his own decisions about what he wants to do, without any pressure or guidance from me. He'll be much better off for it than all of the 'papa's boys' who have their dads to do it all for them."

- "As young as my boys are, their mother has more to offer them than I do. I'm sure there will come a time when it is the other way around and I'll take over the main parenting responsibility for them, but that probably won't be for some time. In the meantime, what is important is that they know I'm there if anything should go wrong and they need something more than what their mother can do."

These comments from fathers about their own behavior toward their sons convey a strong desire to "do what is right for the boy." Whether the right thing is to wait until "the boy is old enough," or "setting an example," or "letting him be his own man," the likely result is an emotional distancing between father and son, a closing-off rather than a drawing closer. The father watches his son's development from afar, neither sharing his own developmental struggle with him nor probing into how the boy is dealing with the same issues. For his part, the son must look to his mother for clues as to who his father is as a person, and how he should see him.

There is some very important modeling going on here,

for it is clearly a son's experience with his father that is most influential in shaping how he in turn will behave toward his own son. In explaining their behavior toward their sons, many fathers defended it by referring to the way their fathers treated them. Somewhat surprisingly, many sons acknowledged that they had lamented not being closer to their fathers, but nonetheless admitted repeating the same behavior toward their sons. It was as if they were saying, "I didn't like the way I was brought up, but it was the way I was brought up, so it is the way I'll raise my own." Many take some satisfaction in this, believing that they are better for it and that their sons will be, too. There is a tone of determinism about the distance between fathers and sons that is disturbing, as though fathers are fated to be at arm's length from their sons. Even though it always has been so, must it ever be? It is a question we shall consider in looking at the causes of male intimate behavior, in Chapter 7.

On all fronts, the evidence is clear that though they share a name, most fathers and sons are only remotely related. Where there is any degree of closeness at all between fathers and sons, it is a closeness born of time together, shared activities rather than shared selves.

Fathers and Sons: The Intimate Adversaries

Any activity in which father and son can compete is viewed by both parties as a shared activity and is typically cited as evidence of intimacy. In fact, father-son competition does result in certain very limited disclosures that account for whatever small measure of intimacy exists between fathers and sons.

Competition between fathers and sons offers at once the primary opportunity for them to develop intimacy, and the principal obstacle to it. To understand this complex dynamic, it is necessary to examine competition over the length of father-son relationships, to explore what competition means in the relationship, and to illustrate how competition is both a catalyst for intimacy and a constraint against it.

From the earliest months of the mother's pregnancy, the father finds himself in competition with the child-to-be for the attention and affection of the mother/wife. Freudian interpretations aside, the simple truth is that the pregnant mother alters her behavior vis-à-vis her husband; she has new concerns, diminished energy, and altered sexual interest. Often a father-in-waiting experiences these changes as a choice of the baby's needs over his own. All of this is exacerbated upon birth, as the baby's demands become more and more consuming of the mother/wife's attention, energy, and even affection at the (perceived) cost of the father's needs. It is quite natural for the father to become jealous of the newborn in much the same way that a young brother or sister becomes jealous of his or her new sibling. Few fathers acknowledge this jealousy and the ensuing competition, but their behavior reveals their emotion and is clearly seen by the wife/mother:

- "I thought I was having just one baby. As it turned out, I got two, my baby and my husband. There were times when I didn't know who was the more demanding. I was running from one to the other, trying to keep them both happy. The toll on my body alone damn near killed me. They each wanted their piece of me, and I mean that quite literally. I couldn't handle it at all. The baby came first for me, and I finally had to tell my husband that."

- "Something about a baby brings out the little boy in a man. I think it really is a competitive thing. They want some of the attention that goes to the baby, and they'll do some very strange things to get it. I remember my husband having one illness or injury after another during the baby's first year. He needed as much mothering as the baby did, sometimes even more."

- "When our first was born, it took a long time for me to bounce back, so my mother-in-law moved in with us to help out. I couldn't believe how jealous my husband was of the baby. Some of the things he did to get attention were so juvenile, and when I confronted him with this, he accused me of making it all up! I guess I can be thankful his mom was here. Between the two of us, we were able to take care of both the babies—the boy and his father! Even now I have to tell him to grow up."

A father's jealousy of a baby dissipates sooner when the baby is a girl than when it is a boy. Competition for the attention and affection of the wife/mother never completely disappears from father-son dynamics. In childhood, the son is likely to find himself pitted against his father's past achievements and/or aspirations. To define himself, to get approval, he must compete against standards imposed by the father, the famous "when I was your age" criteria. School, sports, hobbies, social life, all provide competitive contexts and evaluation experiences that mark many young men for years to come.

- "I never brought home a report card that my dad didn't tell me how much better he had done in that subject when he was in school. It was that way from grade school through college. No matter how well I did, it didn't matter, 'cause he had done better. I don't honestly know whether he really did do better or whether he just expected me to, it doesn't make any difference, 'cause after a while I just stopped trying to do better. When you can never win, it's better just to quit competing."

- "Dad never said anything about my getting into sports, but that actually made it worse. I felt that the reason he never said anything was that I wasn't good enough. I kept trying to be good enough at something that he would take notice. I was playing to get some reaction from him, not for me! I guess I never did get good enough, because he never did talk about it."

- "My father only allowed me to do those things that he did when he was my age, and he made it clear that I was to do as well as or better than he did, or else. I never got into any activity as a kid that I wasn't scared stiff of that 'or else' of his. I never really enjoyed anything I did as a kid for that same reason, but I've never told my dad that."

■ "Dad had a school story and a work story; they were sort of all-purpose 'this is what it was like' tales that he trotted out whenever we talked about how I was doing in school or at work. Of course, in his stories he was the hero, and in my growing-up years I never was. Looking back, I know that they were just stories, but at the time I thought they were like the Bible and that I could never be that good. I spent most of my youth going back and forth between hating him for being so great and hating myself for not being as great as he was. Now I know he wasn't so great and I wasn't so bad, but it's too late—there are too many years of hating in between."

During these important developmental years, competition—the son's present against the father's past—creates a difficult coach/judge role for the father. Fathers feel that they must teach a son how to compete, and at the same time judge the son's competitive effort. In attempting to juggle these often conflicting roles, most fathers come down hardest on the side of judge. Their criticism at a time when their sons are seeking approval makes it difficult for their teaching and coaching to make much of an impression on young boys. This marks the time when many sons reject the arenas of competition chosen for them by their fathers, believing it is better not to try than to try and always be found wanting. Others choose to stay and fight, forever seeking approval that may never come. The level of competition soon escalates for father and son into head-to-head encounters that will mark their relationship from early teens into late adulthood.

Until such time as the son can "hold his own" in the competitive arena against the father, he competes against the father's image and/or standards. Once he has proved himself

141

a worthy opponent, the contest is joined directly. From that time on it is man-to-man, father against son. They compete in sports, business, hobbies, social standing, or even for the favors of women (at this point it is usually the father flirting with his son's girlfriend or wife), always with a will to win that can be alarming to observers. More than one wife/ mother has had occasion to fear for the safety of her son at the hands of his father, and in later years to worry over the fate of her husband at the hands of her son. Whatever the contest and however bitterly fought, the issue for father and son alike is for the one to prove himself to the other, and in the proving to gain approval. All of this competition creates a certain amount of time together, hours spent at games or at the office or in the workshop, which is often passed off as intimacy:

- "Dad and I have played tennis together as long as I can remember, ever since I was able to lift a racket. No one else in the family plays. It's just between the two of us. Tennis has been a really good way for us to spend time together over the years, something each of us looks forward to, especially beating each other. We play for blood, always have."

- "A lot of people don't think of fishing as a competitive sport, but let me tell you, the way Daddy and I fish, it's competitive as hell! We keep track of the first fish, biggest fish, most fish, most pounds. We've got records that go way back to when I was little. Competing makes it just that much more fun. I think now that Daddy doesn't get around all that much because of his emphysema, the "big fish contest," as we call it, is all that much more important to him. Sometimes I think that the time we fish together is the only thing that keeps him going."

- "We work on the cars, my father and I, antique cars we own. I guess we do sort of compete at it, if you look at it that way. Each of us tries to get a better deal than the other one or know more about a certain year than the other. Mostly we just tinker. Even there we try to 'out-tinker' each other. It's just a healthy little bit of one-upmanship that gives a nice edge to working together. We've been at it for so long I don't think either one of us would let the other one stop if he wanted to."

■ "I went into business with Dad. We're partners, but the business itself—insurance—is competitive enough that we are always in a contest with each other. Dad always brags that we have to compete with each other because we're so good that there's nobody else to compete with. I do think that if we weren't after each other, it would get pretty boring because we do spend an awful lot of time together. That's one of the good things about the competition—I think it really does bring us closer together."

Competition between father and son does provide time together, time that might not otherwise be taken. However, the time is used for little more than competition. The regular golf or tennis game, the hours in the garage or at the office are spent almost entirely upon the task at hand, the game, the score, each participant bent on proving himself, neither seeking to *improve* the relationship. The events and externalities of competition control the time father and son spend together; little disclosure or sharing occurs. As a result, the time spent competing is just that: time spent as opposed to time invested in the development of intimacy through the sharing of self.

There is a kind of disclosure that occurs in competitive encounters that should not be overlooked. A professional competitor in any activity knows the importance of knowing his opponent, the better to exploit his weaknesses. Pros diagnose their opponents' strengths and weaknesses as thoroughly as they examine their own game. Competition does reveal strengths and weaknesses not only in play or strategy but in character as well. Competing against the same adversary time after time is certain to uncover dimensions of the other of which even he may be unaware. This is one reason why, in father-son relationships, what little knowledge sons have of their fathers' personal and private selves has not been voluntarily revealed but is very accurate. Fathers don't voluntarily reveal themselves to their sons, but in the course of competition they do disclose themselves so that what sons know of their fathers is close to the core of who the father is.

As important as it is to know your opponent, it is just as important, if not more so, to guard against your opponent's knowing what it is about him that you know and, most important of all, to keep him from knowing you. This strategic message is not lost on father-son competitors. Whatever self-disclosures occur between father and son in the course of competition are rarely acknowledged and never explored. Each may learn something of the other, but rather than using their knowledge to develop their relationship further, each typically keeps his discoveries of the other to himself, adding to the distance that must exist between all competitors. After all, how close can you afford to get to someone you are trying to beat?

The competitive relationship between father and son changes with age but rarely matures. In late adulthood, the all-out rivalry typically gives way to a kind of face-saving protection of the competition itself. Each makes concessions to the other to keep the competition alive, in almost subconscious acknowledgment that the contest is the only real link between them. The games of their younger days are continued, even though the times they are together may be the only times one or both of the parties play. As a father ages, a son will often make allowances in his own play to maintain the pretense of an even match, much as the father played down to the son's level when he was teaching him. The object of competition at this point in the relationship is no longer to win but simply to play together. Because it is all they have ever done together, their only way of relating to each other, father and son go to great lengths to protect this time they are competing together:

■ "You could say that Dad and I have come full circle. When I was little, of course, I wasn't much good but it didn't matter because the important thing to me was that I was playing with Dad. Lots of times I know he would let me get close to winning just to keep me interested in the game. As I got better and better, the competition got hotter and hotter. I would say that from the time I was in high school until about five years ago we played for blood, no quarter asked, no quarter given—beating the other guy was what it was all about. Then Dad had his heart attack and he pretty much stopped playing golf. He probably only gets out five or six times a year now, and most of those are with me. When we play now, winning isn't at all important anymore. It's the playing together that is the thing. I try to keep things going like there's been no change at all, like we're still competing just the way we used to. Sometimes now I'm the one who lets him win, just to keep him interested."

■ "When I came into the business, I absolutely could not have made it without Dad, no way. He taught me everything he knew about running a dealership. Of course, it was a lot simpler to sell cars then, but still there was a lot to learn and he taught it all to me. When he thought I was ready, he gave me the import side of the business to run. Those were the pre-OPEC days, so imports weren't such a big deal, but I saw it as a real chance to prove myself to Dad. From the beginning we compared sales and kept score of who was doing better. With him having the American cars and me the imports, sometimes we were competing for the same customers. It was mostly in fun, but we were pretty serious about it all the same. Anyway, the business sort of passed Dad by. Selling cars today is nothing like it used to be, and Dad is in over his head. I run the whole show now, both sides. I don't really need Dad, but I still try to make him feel like I do. I ask him to deal with some of the older customers. I ask him for advice. I'm not even above screwing up some little thing so he can set me straight and say, 'I can still teach you a thing or two.' It's worth it to me because working together is the only kind of together that we have."

- "Fishing is just not my thing. When I was a kid I went along with Pop because I had to, not because I liked it. Getting up at the crack of dawn, sitting in a boat for eight to ten hours in the hope that some poor fish will swim by and in a suicidal frenzy latch on to your hook is definitely not my idea of a good time. But my pop loves it, he lives to fish. Sometimes I think fishing is what keeps him alive. When I go to visit Pop, we go fishing. When we're not fishing, we're talking about fishing. All the time I let on that I love it as much as he does. I do it because I don't know any other way to spend time with my pop. If we weren't fishing, I don't know what we would do together—probably just sit there and stare at each other, thinking about how we really are strangers. Hell, anything is better than that, even fishing!"

One of the great values of competition for fathers and sons is that it provides time together. More than that, competition provides structured time together, a structure for proving oneself to the other, for socialization in the role of a man in society, and for relating to other males. Competition between father and son is thus a vehicle for contesting, for coaching, and, most importantly, for connecting. Competition would seem to provide a convenient and comfortable catalyst for the development of intimacy between a father and son. However, as much as competition provides the time together that invites intimacy, the very structure of competition constrains the development of intimacy. Competition, whether in games, in business, or in social relations, imposes a set of exchanges upon the competitors. There is no need to deal with one another as individuals because the interaction is dictated: rules regulate the relationship, time together substitutes for sharing, competing for communicating. Game after game after game makes for better players, but doesn't bring father and son closer together as people. Remove the competitive context, and the pair that spend comfortable hours together find themselves at a loss for words, speechless strangers without their sport. Whatever kernels of personal truth are revealed in the playing are unintended and unexplored. In some instances, self-disclosures are even exploited for the competitive advantage they afford. There is no caring or closeness in competition. The very thing that brings fathers and sons together in time and space simultaneously drives them apart in those important areas of self wherein lies intimacy. Still, were it not for competition and mothers, fathers and sons might never get together at all.

MOTHERS: THE LOVING LINK BETWEEN FATHER AND THE FAMILY

Some contemporary observers of the American family have described women as cultural go-betweens, interpreters for men and of men. It is an apt label for a role frequently described by fathers, sons, and mothers alike. In many families, relationships between father and children occur through the mother. It is the mother who defines for her children who their father is, inasmuch as he is rarely there to define himself. The mother absolves him of guilt and neglect and at the same time elevates his role in the eyes of the children. "He's really a very busy man." "He works very hard to give us the things we have." "A lot of people depend on your father." "Your father is very important/respected/successful/loving."

When the father is present, it is the mother who interprets what his presence means and does not mean to his children, what he really expects (never mind what he says). It is Mom who assures the children, "Your father really doesn't mean what he says." "Don't pay any attention to your father, he's not serious." Or, "Your father means what he says." Even when the father does not speak for himself, his wife speaks for him to his children. Dad may be silent as to his own feelings, but Mom makes it clear just how much he cares for his children: "You know how much your father loves you." "Your father wouldn't say this himself, but he loves you very much." "Your father doesn't always show it, but I know he loves you very much." Of course, the mother's representation of Dad may not always be accurate; sometimes she puts words in his mouth to her advantage.

All who are party to this interpersonal interpretation find it both convenient and comfortable: the father because it absolves him of responsibility to explain himself; the children because it is so much easier to deal with Dad through Mom than directly; and even the mother, who often seeks the interpreter role because the alternative is to suffer family discord:

■ A father of three acknowledges his dependence on his wife for communication with his children, both to understand them and to be understood by them: "I don't understand those kids at all. Sometimes it's hard for me to believe that they are my own flesh and blood. Maybe it's because I never have spent much time with them. Then again, whenever I do, it seems like we're at each other's throats. All in all, I figure it's better off left alone. Betty is the one who keeps everything on an even keel around here. She smooths over some of my rough spots with the kids and helps me try to see 'where they are coming from,' as they like to say. She even understands their language! Sometimes I envy her the relationship she has with the kids, but I don't see how I can ever be that way with them. I guess that's just one of those ways that fathers and mothers are different."

■ A teenaged boy talks about his relationship with his father and mother: "I'm really scared of Dad 'cause I never know what he's going to do. Sometimes I'll ask him for something and he goes all out to try to help me. Then other times when I ask he blows up at me. I never know what he's going to do, so I always fear the worst. Usually I'm right. Mom reads him a lot better than I do, so I go through her instead of going right to Dad. She either handles it herself or asks him for me, and she can usually get me what I want. When Dad comes down on me, Mom does what she can to soften the blow. Then she'll get us together and see to it that we sort of make up. I guess Dad and I both use Mom to get along because we don't deal too well with each other."

Even with age and maturity, little seems to change in the family's use of intermediaries to deal with Dad. Here a woman of forty-two describes her relationship with her father as conducted through her mother: "Even now, when I have a grown family of my own and I'm not dependent on Dad for anything at all, I still communicate with him only through Mom. Whenever I call home, I always talk to Mom. It's kind of awkward when she's out and Dad answers, because we just don't have anything to say to each other. It's usually 'Hello,' 'Your Mother's not here,' 'Tell her I called,' 'Goodbye.' Mom writes, but Dad never does. She fills me in on what's going on with him, how business is, and what's new at the lodge, and she tells him what the kids and I are up to. Every now and then she makes a point of saying something about how he reacted to something I did or one of the kids did, like 'Your father thinks you did the right thing about your job.' Or, 'He sure is proud of those grandkids.' But I never hear it from Dad himself. It must be that he needs Mom to talk to me as much as I need her to talk to him. It would be simpler if we could talk to each other, but we never have been able to, and at this date it's not likely that we are going to start. I imagine we'll just keep on talking through Mom. When she's not there anymore, we probably won't talk at all."

There are many motives behind the roles that mothers play as family interpreters. Some mothers desire to protect their children from the father and /or vice versa. Other mothers want simply to make things smooth and pleasant around the household. Still others want to facilitate the development of genuine caring communication between father and children. Three mothers described their own purposes in their go-between roles:

- "My husband is just flat-out insensitive to the children and their needs. It's not that he doesn't care about them, it's just that he has so many other things on his mind that he sometimes forgets he needs to deal with them differently than he does people at work or even me. The children just aren't strong enough to stand up to him on their own, and he doesn't take the time to listen to what they are really concerned about. He comes off as cold and not caring and they get hurt. They need to be protected from him, and where the children are concerned, he needs to be protected from himself. I try to step between him and the children as much as possible. That way I can make him seem not quite so harsh and uncaring in their eyes, so that they don't come to hate him when they are older. I wish that it didn't have to be that way, but the way he is, I don't see how else it can be."

- "As I see it, my choices are to listen to them fight or watch them seethe in silence. I don't know which is worse. At least when they're fighting they're talking to each other, sort of. The silences are like the calm before the storm, you know it's going to break, you just don't know when or how bad it's going to be. All I want is for things to be calm and easygoing among the three of us. The only way for that to happen is for me to get in the middle of them. They simply cannot relate to each other. Neither of them listens to the other or makes any effort to understand what the other one is saying. Sometimes I honestly think that without me they'd kill each other, it gets that bad. The only way I get any peace and quiet is to go from one to the other, explaining, placating, apologizing, just so we can have some semblance of normal family relations around here."

- "It pains me to see how much they love one another and what a hard time they have expressing that love. They can't even bring themselves to say 'I love you' to each other. I don't know if it's just that old male stubbornness or if they don't think that it's manly or if they really just don't know how, but there is so little affection between them that it worries me—especially when I know that they feel so much for each other. I think each of them depends on me to let him know how the other one feels. They can't say it to each other, but I can say it for them. I can tell family the things that the other one does to show how much they care, like when they brag about each other to their friends or when they talk to me about how they feel. Maybe I should be thankful that they do need me the way they do. Otherwise they'd probably spend all their time with each other and I'd be left out."

The motives underlying a mother's role as interpreter of family intimacy are in most instances mixed. Certainly there is a need to be filled, a need for communication, facilitation, protection, and more than one mother go-between mentioned the need to be needed. The positive aspect of this role is that the family's needs are met to some degree. What little closeness and communication exists between father and children is there in large part because of the mother's interpretative role. The other positive outcome of this triangle is that it typically strengthens a son's relationship with his mother and accounts for the fact that sons disclose far more to their mothers than they do to their fathers.

However, the mother-as-interpreter role is not played without cost. First, as long as the mother is willing to serve as go-between, there is little incentive for the father to change his behavior and become more directly disclosing and more intimate with his children. He doesn't need to express or explain himself because his wife will do it for him. Moreover, she will deal with whatever consequences are created by his absence, his lack of expression, or his misrepresentation. She cleans up after the father, repairing his damaged relationships. Viewed in this manner, it may be that the go-between role of wives/mothers frustrates the development of intimate behavior rather than facilitates it.

A second costly consequence of the mother's go-between role is the modeling impact it has on the children. In a family where the mother explains the father to the children, where they relate to him through her, children quickly perceive that this is the way it should be. Children learn that the responsibility for effective relationships lies with women. The son may perceive that he need not invest his energies in developing intimate relationships because a woman—first as mother, then as wife—will do that for him. She will interpret his emotions, intentions, and actions to others. A daughter learns that she must read the unexpressed intimate intentions of the men in her life—first her father, then her husband, then her own children. In this way, the mother's go-between role again perpetuates traditional role distinctions regarding intimate behavior. She may unwittingly prepare her children for the very conditions she laments in her own relationships with men. Evidence of these adaptations can be seen in the way men relate to their siblings.

THE BROTHERHOOD OF MAN

In his relationships with his brothers and sisters, a man has many opportunities to develop intimate familial relationships without some of the confounding factors that he faces in dealing with his father and mother or even with his own children. As it is, men rarely take advantage of these opportunities. The research indicates that in general men are no more likely to be loving and disclosing with brothers or sisters than they are with others who are not members of their families. With few exceptions, men relate to their siblings as they do to their friends—the latter being a label that covers a wide range of relationships from acquaintance to emotional ally. The most common exception is the relationship between a man and a sister where the sister is the "other woman" (see Chapter 3).

The sister as other woman was earlier seen to be a not

unusual role, and understandably so. The shared experiences in growing up together provide fertile ground for the growth of a genuine closeness between brother and sister. A large part of the reason that men find close relationships with sisters so comfortable is that little disclosure is required of them because so much has been revealed to the other through their time together. It is, as one man commented of his sister, "as though she knows what I'm thinking and feeling without my having to tell her. Sometimes she puts my feelings into words before I'm even fully aware of what I'm feeling. I'm closer to her than to anyone else, even my wife, and it's not something that I feel like I have to 'work' at. We are just naturally close, we use what's already there."

Many men share this feeling that they are naturally close to their sisters. There are certainly a great many loving and intimate brother-sister relationships, some so intimate that they must deal with the same sexual issues that occur between a man and an other woman who is not a sibling. For most brothers and sisters, however, little beyond a familial acquaintance comes naturally. They have public knowledge of one another, the kind that comes from living together, but know little of one another's private or personal selves. Moreover, what knowledge they do have of each other is often dated and their relationship bound by the past. Indeed, the most common pattern seen in male relationships with their siblings is one in which men report that they were once close during childhood but they grew apart as they grew older. Many men describe this evolution with a sense of loss:

- "When we were young we could talk about everything under the sun, and we did all the time. As we grew older it seemed like we talked less and less about less and less. Now it's to the point where I hardly know her at all. I guess that's just the way it is. We're both busy with our own families and we really don't have that much in common anymore. It's one of those situations where there is still a lot of love between us, but I don't think we know each other all that well."

■ "I remember us doing almost everything together. We were inseparable up until about high school. Then we just sort of went our different ways. Now we've been apart for so long that I don't think we could be close again, even if we tried. You just can't make up for all those years. To begin with, how do you explain why you haven't tried harder during that time? You can't go back."

■ "When we were real little we used to tell each other secrets. Then we got to the point where I guess we thought the secrets were a little too secret to be shared, so we backed off. We used to compete a lot when we were teenagers, and that may have had something to do with it. Today we know just enough about each other to compare how we are doing against each other in terms of work, income, kids—that sort of thing. I feel like we know each other pretty well, but we're not close anymore, like we used to be."

The different interests of brother and sister that emerge over time often come to separate first their time and then their knowledge of each other. Between brother and brother, competition often arises to keep them from being as close as they once were. In most cases, however, men who lament the loss of intimacy with either a sister or a brother may be projecting their feelings about what they don't have onto a remembrance of what they once had. Rather than that they have grown apart, it is more likely that they were never that close to begin with. Memories of time together as children may be distorted. What passes for closeness in youth seldom can sustain or suffice for an intimate relationship between adults. Perhaps one revealed one's deepest, darkest secrets to a sister or brother at age ten, but at that age secrets are not nearly so deep or so dark as are the secrets of adults, and therefore not nearly so damaging.

Adulthood raises the ante for intimacy, and few men are willing to play in a high-stakes game, even when it's all in the family. Family ties and time together may make siblings more eligible for intimate relationships with men, but very few men elect to pursue these possibilities.

This review of the relationships men have with the various members of their families has indicated that the average man is more "phantom man" than "family man." As a father he is largely absent. Even when he is present he is absent—there in body, but in every other respect removed from the family. Present or absent, the father is reliant on his spouse to relate to the children for him. Whatever closeness he has with his daughter is more likely to be based on imagery and illusion than on information about himself. His relationship with his son is circumscribed by competition, where proving oneself is more important than presenting oneself. As a son, the average man is likely to be closer to his mother than to his father, but he is also likely to reveal very little that is personal or private to either one; he is similarly distant from his brothers and sisters.

The family provides a context that seems to be conducive to the development of intimate relationships and the expression of loving behavior. Yet, by all accounts, men are even less loving in familial relationships than they are with their spouses. One might well ask at this point, "Is there anyone men *are* close to? What about their male friends?"

5 Man to Man

In our society it seems as if you've got to have a bosom to be a buddy.

—Elliot Engel

Whether male or female, you cannot be long in the company of the opposite sex without wondering just what their relationships with each other are like. If you grew up male, chances are you wondered what it was that kept your mother on the phone hour after hour with the same friends who had visited earlier in the day. As a teenaged boy, you probably were frustrated by the fact that girls always seemed to appear two by two; you could never talk to that special girl because she was never alone. In adulthood, men are struck by the way that women share with one another the major emotional events of their lives. Woman draw together in joy and in grief, making public what men feel to be the most private feelings.

For their part, women wonder at the friendships of men. As outsiders to their boyhood gangs and games, girls wonder why boys don't have "special friends" the way girls do. In the teenage years, it seems to young women as though the boys they are around are serious only about sex with girls and competing with other boys. These games continue into adulthood, where the time men spend on them gives women cause to wonder how men can spend so much time together and know so little about one another. How is it that they never talk about the things that are really important?

The differences in the intimate behavior of men and women are never more apparent than in the area of friendship. Research verifies what our individual experiences as men of women, and vice versa, have suggested: friendship means something very different to men than it does to women.

To say that men have no intimate friends seems on the surface too harsh, and it raises quick objections from most men. But the data indicate that it is not far from the truth. Even the most intimate of male friendships (of which there are very few) rarely approach the depth of disclosure a woman commonly has with many other women. We know that very few men reveal anything of their private and personal selves even to their spouses; fewer still make these intimate disclosures to other men. One man in ten has a friend with whom he discusses work, money, marriage; only one in more than *twenty* has a friendship where he discloses his feelings about himself or his sexual feelings.

The most common male friendship pattern is for a man to have many "friends," each of whom knows something of the man's public self and therefore a little about him, but not one of whom knows more than a small piece of the whole. These friendships are usually circumstantially contrived and constrained; most often, they are created in the context of common occupational or recreational interests and pursued very cautiously. Because of the lack of depth that comes from limited disclosure, these male friendships tend to be of the "fair weather" variety: men turn to them in neither celebration nor crisis, preferring at such times to be alone. In fact, men are rarely seen two by two unless the occasion is business or competition (some would argue convincingly that these are one and the same); most of the time, men are alone or in groups.

By contrast, women typically have many friends who know everything there is to know about them. Theirs is an open, fully disclosing interaction, not constrained by circumstance or content. A woman is just as likely to become fast friends with the women sitting next to her in the doctor's waiting room as she is with her neighbor of many years. The same could never be said of men, who are not nearly so quick to decide on the potential that acquaintances have to become close friends, and who are seen to exercise the utmost caution in disclosing themselves to other men even after years of interaction. Perhaps the most telling difference between the friendships of men and those of women lies in the uses of friendship. Whereas men are fair-weather friends, it is in times of celebration and crisis that women most often turn to their friends to share the joy and the sorrow they experience. Their intimacy enhances the highs and softens the lows.

The friendship of two women is true friendship. Women's friendships represent the extension into adult life of the "buddy system" of children's-camp partnerships for mutual help and protection. Women bare themselves to one another and bear one another, they are bosom buddies. Men, who neither bare themselves nor bear one another, are buddies in name only.

BEST BUDDIES

Every morning between nine-thirty and ten, a handful of West Coast businessmen meet in the garage of Bill Lang's Soft Water Service. There, amid trucks, dollies, salt tanks, and the constant sound of flushing filtered water, a banker, a mailman, the owner of the local laundromat, the liquor-store manager, a couple of routemen, and an insurance man sit on discarded office chairs, overturned crates, and assorted supplies and discuss the events of the day just as they have for almost twenty years. In a Midwestern town a similar group, though with noticeably more white-collar representation, meets afternoons in the card room of the Creek, a suburban country club. In padded Naugahyde armchairs, they sit around wood-toned Formica-topped tables, playing gin and talking as they have done every afternoon since the club opened twelve years ago. Near the Great Lakes the Mill Room is a second home to steelworkers. In good times, the Mill Room was a mandatory stop between the locker room and home. Now, with the mill closed down, the narrow, dark bar is still where millmen can be found if they're not at the union hall. They meet and talk almost as if they still had work, carrying out a pattern that was their fathers' before them and, for some, their grandfathers' as well.

Whether it is in a back room or a barroom, before work, during, or after, male gatherings like these take place all over America, at all hours of the day and night. This is where male friendships occur, where a man gets together with his "best buddies." In these settings, we can see the nature of what passes for intimacy between men.

What Do Male Friends Talk About?

In these exclusively male friendship groups, the teams may change but the topics remain the same. Sports dominate, both participant and spectator. If the buddies aren't telling stories of their own exploits, past and present, they are analyzing the performance of the local high school, college, and professional players. Among most buddy groups, the "Monday-morning quarterbacking" goes on all week. For younger, unmarried men, sex is almost as popular a topic as sports. Curiously, the two topics are discussed in much the same way, with anecdotes of past and present conquests and analyses of the players, but rarely a personal revelation. Among their buddies, men take a decidedly impersonal approach to even the most personal of topics.

Few would admit to it, but gossip is as common among

men as it is among women. There are some slight differences. Men tend to talk about other men in terms of compe-
tence, performance, and achievement, rather than character.
Men are more likely to discuss friends and enemies alike in
terms of what they do (or don't do) than who they are. But by
any definition it is still gossip. There is a fair amount of
what men would call "bitching" as well. (Men don't term
their own complaints "bitching," as this is viewed by men
as a woman's way.) One noticeable difference in male and
female gossip is that men say very little about their wives,
whereas husbands are frequently the topic between women
friends. This is further evidence of how little men disclose
of themselves to their best buddies.

Add business, politics, the weather, and events of the
day to sports, sex, and gossip, and you have the script for
conversations in male friendship groups. The focus is
almost always on externalities, things that happen "out
there." In the absence of any exchange of private and personal information, it is little wonder that these men who
spend so much time together scarcely know one another
at all.

Men's public knowledge of one another does afford
them the opportunity for the humor that is a unique characteristic of buddy relationships, a kind of exchange not typically found in women's friendships. The latest jokes are a
common conversational element among male friends, but
what sets these friendships apart from mere casual acquaintances (and from women's friendships) is the bantering of
buddies. In its simplest form it is an exchange of insults, "all
in good fun." This surface simplicity, however, belies a complex set of rules that are implicitly understood in male interactions. The personal attack can only deal with the target's
public self, information known to all—his looks, his performance or behavior, his speech. The jibe should have a
kernel of truth, be delivered in a light-hearted manner with
a smile or a laugh, and be received in the same spirit.

Women have a difficult time understanding both the manner and the meaning of this uniquely male kind of insult humor. It is not uncommon to hear the most scatological of nicknames exchanged among the best of male friends. Names that would be fighting words to strangers, such as "cocksucker" and "motherfucker," are only some of the derogatory terms commonly used by men to refer to a friend. All of this is quite acceptable, so long as the rules are followed. For example, it is acceptable for a friend to call his slightly overweight buddy a "lard ass." A woman would never make such a reference to a friend. Male rules dictate that such an insult should be taken with a laugh and returned in kind. Those men who take offense at such jibes or cannot make a retort soon find themselves excluded from friendship groups, as do those who go beyond a man's public self to a more intimate private or personal attack.

This sort of humor is an essential ingredient of male friendship patterns. It is learned at an early age, often in the home in the banter between father and son, and perpetuated in almost all interaction between male friends. It is frequently referred to by buddies as a badge of sorts—testimony to just how close they are: "We can say these things because we know each other so well." Casual friends or acquaintances rarely engage in such banter; it evolves through mutual testing as the relationship grows. As much as such banter may be a badge of closeness between buddies, it is also a barrier to their becoming truly intimate.

What Do Male Friends Mean?

Humor is used by men both as a guise for intimacy and as a guard against it. This is particularly evident in the reaction of men to any attempt to introduce more personal disclosures into a friendship group. Anyone who tries to deal with traditional male friendship topics in a manner that would lead to the development of genuine intimacy, either by disclosing something of his own private or personal self

161

or by probing for similar disclosures from others, is certain to be censured by his friends. Humor is the safest form of censure for males; the casual put-down of volunteered feelings or intimate disclosures saves the volunteer from embarrassment by acknowledging that surely he was joking. At the same time, the put-down reinforces male friendship norms that hold that personal subjects are not to be injected into the relationship. The man who persists in pushing for intimacy among his friends in the face of these sanctions is likely to be ostracized. Man to man, the message seems to be "If we can't joke about it, we can't talk about it."

Humor between male friends is one example of a more general observation: male friendships are never quite what they seem to be. It is important to look beyond what men say *about* their friends and what they say *to* their friends to discover what friendships mean to men.

Interviews with the friendship groups from across America reveal evidence of the dynamics of the buddy system as practiced by men. In the West, Tom Davidson, manager of the local Tommy's, home of "The World's Greatest Hamburgers" ("I'm not *the* Tommy, but everybody thinks I am"), has been taking his morning coffee at Lang's Soft Water for as long as he can remember:

"My first day at Tommy's, my boss brought me down here to Bill's for coffee. That was seventeen years ago, and I've been coming for coffee every morning ever since. Most everybody else has, too. Shit, outside of my family, I'm closer to these guys than to anybody else I know. Nowadays I'm closer to these guys than I am to my family! We've been through it all down here. The town has grown up and fallen down around us, the Rams have come and gone, the country's been to war and back, we even had one of the guys die. We've seen it all to where it seems like there ain't nothing new—same guys, same stories, same shitty coffee. Still, I wouldn't trade these guys for anything. When I retire, I'll still be coming down here for coffee. Where else are you going to find friends like these?

"Funny thing is, away from Bill's, I hardly know these guys at all. I know what they do for a living, of course, but that's about it. I couldn't tell you where more than two or three of them live. I don't know their wives or their kids or even if they have any. It's like we're really close here at Bill's, but when we're not here, we're just *not*. I'll tell you, one time I saw Charlie, the banker, at a wedding. I had to go right up to him before he knew who I was. He said he didn't recognize me without my apron and away from Bill's. It was kind of awkward. We couldn't very well talk to each other the way we do at Bill's, where he's "Charlie the Cock" since he got divorced, and they all call me "Burger Butt." Without all the other guys there, we didn't have much to say to each other, and yet we've been getting together every morning forever. I guess you can know somebody really well one place and then you put them someplace else and it's just not the same. When you look at it that way, I guess if it weren't for coffee at Bill's, I might not have any friends at all."

One of the things that has been found to be true about male disclosures is that they are often circumscribed by circumstance. By virtue of common occupation, recreational interest, or pure proximity, some public revelations are made and a kind of closeness is cautiously developed. The resulting relationships are constrained to these fragments of public information. So it is in male friendships that each knows a little bit about the other(s), but remove the circumstance, the reason for relating, and there is no adequate common knowledge of selves to sustain the relationship. This is one of the contributing factors to the fair-weather friendships so often seen between men. The relationships evolve cautiously in convenient circumstances. In the absence of any effort to get beyond circumstantial disclosures, there is no intimacy and no basis for conducting the relationship in times of crisis. What men mean by friendship is partial public knowledge of one another, without problems. If it is personal or problematical for a man, it doesn't have a place between friends.

The men who meet in the card room at the Creek have been coming together after work or golf almost every afternoon for twelve years. Theirs is but one of many such gin-game groups that can be found in the club's card room, where on any given afternoon as many as thirty or forty men can be found drinking, playing cards, and talking. The interactions here are loud and boisterous, the jokes and repartee flow as freely as the liquor. Everyone seems to know everyone else, but the serious cardplaying and conversation take place in well-defined small groups. According to one observer, these groups have been pretty much unchanged since the club first opened.

Judge James Lane is a onetime municipal court judge, now an attorney in private practice. The judge and his cronies are among the senior members of the club. Scarcely a day has gone by in twelve years that at least three or four of them have not met for gin:

"If I had to count, I'd say that our group is about eight guys. At one time there were an even dozen, but Bob Morris died, Travis Maggard sort of dropped out, and Keith Teal and Harry Saxon both left the club. So now there are just the eight of us left, and we're about as close as any eight guys could be. We're more than just golfing or cardplaying buddies, like a lot of the guys around here. We're real friends in all of the ways that friends should be friends. Maybe we're even a little too close. I say that because we haven't gone out of our way to make it easy for anybody else to join us. Then again, we had some bad experiences with Travis and Keith and Harry, so I guess we're a little gun-shy.

"Travis has been around here since the beginning of time. He was one of the charter members of the club and the first person that I met in the group. He was a great guy, funny and a hell of a competitor. Golf, tennis, gin—he played everything to win. When he got behind, he'd just laugh like hell and double the bet. Then, about three years ago he just changed overnight. He didn't come every day like he used to, and when he was here he was real quiet and wouldn't play cards, but would sit and watch and drink. A couple of us tried to draw him out of it, but he just seemed to lose interest in everything. He was really sort of depressing to be around, so we sort of stopped including him in things. He still comes around the club every now and then, but I don't think he has any real friends left here.

"With Keith and Harry it was different. Keith's wife had an affair with the tennis pro and it was just too embarrassing for him to be around, I guess. It was pretty embarrassing for us, too. I mean, everybody knew about it. What do you say to a guy in a situation like that? Especially when he is your friend. Harry couldn't afford us anymore. He must have had some business problems or something, because he got real slow paying up on his bets. At one time he was into me for over two hundred bucks. At first we all kidded him about it, but when it started to add up, it wasn't a laughing matter anymore. It wasn't the sort of situation where anyone could do anything except stop playing with him. What's the sense of 'double or nothing' when you know he's going to pay nothing even if you win?

"The eight of us get along just fine now. Everybody's pretty stable, the games don't get too rich for anybody. We've got some good, solid relationships going. Why should we mess with a good thing by bringing somebody else in? It could be a Travis or a Keith or a Harry all over again. That's not what friends are for."

What are friends for? It is a question that perplexes more than a few men. Men tend to view friendships as purposeful, a means to some end. So it is that a man may have his work friends, his sport/recreation friends, his church friends, his neighborhood friends. For each set of friends, he has a well-defined set of interactions and activities and he rarely mixes or matches sets. Men shy away from interactions that run contrary to the intended purpose of the friendship, such as seriousness in a frivolous atmosphere, or discussion of personal problems or crisis where superficial good times are the norm. Male friendships, which emerge cautiously over time in well-defined circumstances, typically have no way to deal with out-of-context behavior or experiences, the very good times or the very bad times, or very personal disclosures. Men do not think of going to their friends in times of crisis, and if a man were so inclined, his disclosures would more than likely be rejected by his friends. So what are friends for? For men, friends are for competing, for joking, for talking about common interests, but friends are not for help or solace in times of personal crisis.

At the Mill Room almost everyone is experiencing some measure of personal crisis brought on by the closing of the mill. Roger Nylander is twenty-eight, married, and the father of three. He went to work on the wire line of the mill right out of high school. Roger has been out of work now for nearly a year and a half:

"In the mill you get used to layoffs every now and then, but nobody has ever seen anything like this. Me, I say there's no way they're ever going to open her up again, so we might as well all move on. But here we are 'cause we can't move, can't do anything else but work in the mill. My whole family worked the wire line. My Uncle John, he pulled, I cut and stacked, and my cousin Barry drove the forklift. Now we're all out of work.

"If misery loves company, we've got plenty of it. Just about everybody at the Mill Room is out of work and broke or damn near. We don't talk about it a whole lot. Hell, it wouldn't do any good. Everybody is in the same boat, so who wants to listen to somebody else's sob story? Plus, you're talking about some pretty proud people up here, people who have always made a go of it on their own, without any help from anybody. Most of us wouldn't admit even to our best friends what we've had to do just to keep afloat. You always hear about how people come together when there's a disaster of some kind, a flood or a tornado or something like that. What's different is, in those situations everybody can do something. Here you got an economic disaster that is creating all kinds of personal problems for people. People are losing their homes, getting divorced, sending their kids away. I personally know of two guys who killed themselves. But who can do anything about that stuff? So nobody really talks about their personal situation.

"Even the ones who have managed somehow to get a job don't come in here to celebrate. You can see why. With everybody down and damn near out, we're not much in a mood to hear success stories, especially if it's one of our own. That's shitty, I know, but that's the way it is. You get pissed off at anyone who gets a job, 'cause you figure that could have been your job. I know if I got lucky I wouldn't go bragging about it. The other guys would think I was just rubbing it in. Even though we are all friends and we are all in this together, we're really not together, we are all in it alone, and that's how we're going to have to make it—alone."

There is a sense among men that to go to others in times of crisis is a sign of weakness. At the same time, to celebrate one's own success in the face of others' crises is unfair competition. Both of these dynamics are at work in the friendships in the Mill Room. When everyone is suffering, the heroes, to men, are those who suffer in silence. Roger and his friends do not reach out to each other for help with the personal crises spawned by unemployment, in part because they believe no one else can help, but in part also because they believe they should not ask for help, they should go it alone. Should they make it on their own, they will celebrate alone as well. Since no one else participated in their success, no one can share it with them. The ever-present competition between men further diminishes the joys of vicariously sharing in the success of a friend, but the rules of competition are such that you don't rub a friend's face in your success.

All of what has been discovered about male friendships—the caution, the circumstances, the constraints, the
conflict between competition and closeness—is aptly captured by Roger Nylander's statement that "we are all in it
alone." It is both a description of how male friendships are
and a prescription for how men feel that friendships ought
to be. Men believe that they should be able to go it alone,
independently, autonomously, without friends. Men believe
that they don't need friends, and when having friends becomes the slightest bit inconvenient or infringes on their
sense of self, they forgo friendship in favor of comfort, rationalizing that they have done the right and manly thing.

HOW DO MEN EXPLAIN THEIR
FRIENDSHIPS?

When questioned about the number and nature of their
friendships, many men take an extreme view. They argue
that men don't have close personal relationships because
they don't need them. More simply put, men don't need
friends:

- "I don't really belong to any groups at work or anywhere else. I would have to say that I don't have what you
would call close friends, not even one or two. Frankly, I just
don't see the need for them. I get along just fine on my own."

- "I have a lot of acquaintances, but no real buddies, so
to speak. I've never really taken the trouble to develop any
friendships, nor have I seen the need for them."

- "I don't have time for anybody but my family and my
employees. As far as I'm concerned, friends are more of a
burden than anything else. A close friendship is just not
worth the bother."

- "I don't have any real interests outside my work, so
there's not much opportunity for me to meet people. I don't
know what I'd do with friends, anyway. I'm plenty busy
with my job."

■ "The way I see it, if a man can't make it on his own, he's not much of a man. Hey, I'm the first one to get a group of guys together to go hunting or fishing, but that's where friendship stops for me. I don't need anything more from it. I don't *want* anything more from it. I don't have anything to do with anybody who does."

This male orientation to friendship is almost the antithesis of the way women view their friendships with other women. In light of this difference, it is not surprising that men cannot understand the time and attention women give to their friends, and women cannot understand why men do not give more time and attention to their friends. Men have many reactions to this noticeable difference. Most react with a defensive self-righteousness, arguing that the kind of friendships men have are all that men need. This reinforces the male view of friendships as purposeful, utilitarian, to be made as intimate as the situation requires (and we know that for men few situations require intimacy):

■ "I know several guys that I would feel perfectly comfortable talking to about whatever I wanted to. Just because we don't spend all of our time revealing our innermost personal feelings to each other doesn't mean that we couldn't or wouldn't talk about those things if the occasion demanded it. We can be as close as we need to be. Yes, even as close as women friends are, if we thought that was necessary. Though I can't really imagine when that would be necessary."

■ "Men don't talk about the same things with their friends that women do. On a day-to-day basis I would agree that men are not as close to each other as women are. But when men need to talk personally to each other, they can. At least I feel like my friends and I can. If we don't, it's only because we simply don't need to. I think that's the real difference between men and women friends. Women need to be close all the time. My wife is constantly with her friends, but I may only see my closest friends every now and then.

169

Still, I feel like if I really needed my friends, they'd be there."

There are some men who argue that the character of their friendships is equal to that of women's friendships in number, nature, and capability:

■ "I'm every bit as close to my friends as my wife is to hers. I don't see that there is any difference at all. We both spend a lot of time with our friends. We both talk about a lot of very personal things with our friends. We both have the same kind of friendships. I'm glad for that because I think it helps us understand each other's friendships. We aren't jealous of each other's friends the way some couples are."

■ "I don't see that my wife's friendships with women are any closer or more bonding than my friendships with men are. I don't know exactly what she talks to her friends about, but I imagine that it is much the same sort of thing that the guys and I talk about. Friendships are friendships. It doesn't make any difference whether they are male or female friendships."

■ "If anything, I'm closer to my friends than she is to hers. For one thing, we do more together. They just sit around and talk. Not that we don't talk too. We do, but it's just a part of the friendship. It's not the whole thing. My friendships are probably even better than hers, because they are more well-rounded, more complete."

There are certainly a number of individual instances of close, intimate relationships among men where the bonding is comparable to that commonly found in female friendships. Such intimacy among male friends, however, is the exception, not the rule. In our survey, men valued their friendships significantly less than did women, and did not have as many friends as did women. The friendships that men do have do not approach the depth or degree of self-disclosure that is common to women's friendships. Men are not intimate with one another in the ways that women are intimate. Any statements to the contrary by men indicate

170

their ignorance of the nature of true intimacy between friends, the kind of intimacy women friends share.

Aside from those few who argue from ignorance, isolation, or uniquely individual circumstances that male friendships are as intimate as female friendships, men cannot help but acknowledge that there is something in friendships between women that is very different from the interaction they know with their own friends. This realization hits hardest during times of personal trauma—death of a spouse, infidelity, or divorce—when men discover they have no one to talk it out with. But even casual observations of the superficial differences between male and female friendships can be the beginnings of a man's rethinking of what friendship has to offer. For example, husbands frequently express jealousy of the time and attention that their wives devote to their friends. The jealousy is often veiled by complaints, but there is an underlying tone suggesting an annoyance that the wife is so disclosing and that her attention is diverted from her husband:

- "I swear, I don't know what they find to talk about for hours on end, day after day. I'm sure there is nothing that goes on with my wife that she doesn't tell her friends. She knows everything that is going on with them, too. At times, I admit I'd like to eavesdrop on one of their sessions, just to hear what she's saying about me. Maybe I'm better off not knowing. It does seem like if she spent a little less time with her friends, she might have a little more time for things around here, like cooking and cleaning."

- "I don't like the idea that everything that happens in our marriage gets reported to her friends for analysis. And I know that's exactly what goes on. She'd rather talk to them about it than to me. When I'm trying to talk to her about something, I never know whether she's saying what she really believes or what her friends have decided she should say. I wish just once she'd discuss things first with me instead of rehearsing them with her friends. I guess I feel a little outmanned, or outwomaned, actually. Maybe I'm a little jealous that there's no one for me to rehearse my part with."

■ "We ought to come first—me and the kids. Instead, time with her friends seems to come first and we get the leftovers. I'm not kidding. I think she really prefers to spend time with her friends, instead of with her own family. If she'd try, she might find that we can do the same things for her that her friends can, whatever that is. I honestly don't know what her friends do for her, but it must be pretty special for her to spend so much of her time with them, when her family would prefer that she spend time with them."

These comments from men about the time and attention women devote to their friends deal only with the superficial aspects of women's friendships. One gets the impression that if men didn't perceive the demands of women's friendships as being met at the expense of attention to themselves, they might not be so concerned about what transpires between women friends. There is, however, a deeper side of the male response to women's friendships that has to do with the nature of those friendships.

WHAT ARE MALE FRIENDS MISSING?

Those few men who seem to understand the truly intimate character of women's friendships express envy that their own friendships with men lack this quality and the capability it affords women to deal with personal issues. The acknowledgment that women have something in their friendships that men lack and need or want typically comes when men and women face some shared personal crisis. At these times, men are made painfully aware of the absence of any aid and assistance from their own friendships. Confronted with the death of a parent, divorce, a problem with the children, men are left to their own devices, while women enjoy the company and solace of their friends. The intimacy of female friendships eases the suffering of women. The isolation of men intensifies their suffering. David Laster describes his traumatic introduction to the real limits of his buddy group:

"The four of us—Tom, Jim, Steve, and I—had been hunting buddies for ages. Every chance we got, we would go out for deer, ducks, birds; whatever the season, we hunted it, and almost always together. We had some great times together, the four of us, despite the difference in our ages. It didn't matter because we really hit it off well. I think each of us thought of the other three as our best friends. We often said how we felt—we could talk about anything we wanted to in the group. Even the wives got to know each other pretty well. Once or twice a year we'd get together as couples. But mainly it was just a good group of guys all the way around.

"I remember it was a Friday and we were all going to take off work at noon so we could drive out, set up camp, and be ready to go first thing in the morning. I had one of those four-wheel-drive trucks, so the plan was that I would pick everyone up. Steve lived farthest out, so we always picked him up last. As it turned out, I didn't get away from work as early as I had hoped, and by the time I got Tom and Jim, we were running about an hour late. We pulled up in front of Steve's place and honked a couple of times. Usually he would have come running out, yelling and swearing about us being 'slow old farts,' but this time there was no sight of him. I saw his gear back by the garage, and I thought maybe he didn't hear us. Tom and Jim stayed in the truck while I went around to get him. He was in the backyard and he was dead. He had taken his shotgun, put the muzzle in his mouth, and with a piece of wood pushed the trigger and blown the back of his head away. He left a note near his body: 'I'm sorry. There is no one to talk to.'

"At first I was just terribly angry. I was really pissed off at Steve. This was not some teenaged kid crazed out of his mind on drugs, or some guy down on his luck. He was thirty-one when he killed himself. He had a good job and a super wife. They weren't rich, but they didn't have any big

173

debts or anything. I just couldn't see that he had any reason for doing what he did. It seemed so selfish. I remember thinking, 'How could he do this to me? How could he say there was no one to talk to, when there was me?' I felt like I could have helped him, no matter what it was. We could talk about anything. At least I thought we could. Only later did it hit me that I didn't really know if we could talk about anything or not, because we never really talked about much that was personal.

"In the days following Steve's death, I transferred my anger from Steve to my wife and friends. I'm not saying that any of this was right or rational. I'm just saying it was how it was. I was pissed off at Steve's wife and my wife because at the funeral and all, it seemed like they could really let go of their grief with each other. They cried and hugged, they were really emotional in a way a man could never be. In the midst of it all, I had a sense that they were really helping each other. They were together, and being together helped them deal with Steve's death. As for me, I just had Tom and Jim. I knew that they were hurt by Steve's death, too, but for some reason we couldn't really share what we were feeling. While the women were together with each other, we men were together by ourselves, drinking, staring off into space, each of us full of grief. But for whatever reason, we chose to deal with it inside, each in his own way, instead of talking about what we were feeling. I was envious of the women's way with each other. I was angry that I couldn't be the same way, angry that my friends and I, who knew Steve best, didn't have the kind of friendship that we could draw on for help when we most needed it.

"After that I pretty much lost touch with Tom and Jim. We just sort of stopped doing things together. We never talked about why, but I think we all somehow realized that if our friendship couldn't help us through something as traumatic as Steve's suicide, then maybe it wasn't much of a friendship. I've spent a lot of time thinking about how much I was responsible for what Steve did because I wasn't the kind of friend he needed. I think I know now what Steve meant when he wrote, 'There is no one to talk to.' As close as I thought we were, I've come to see that we were never there for each other to talk to. Oh, we were there to do things with—hunt, fish, drink, play cards—but we were never there to talk about the things we were feeling, the things that might make you wonder whether or not life was worth living.

"I think now that what we called friendship wasn't really anything more than a casual and comfortable kind of 'acquaintanceship' where we shared certain things certain times, but we never shared ourselves. Maybe all male relationships are like that. Lately I've really tried to be more open with people, especially men. I've tried to build the kind of friendship Steve needed, because I believe I need that too. So far, it hasn't worked too well. Men get anxious when you talk about feelings, and it seems like the harder I try to get close, the faster guys pull away. Maybe I'm going too fast. But hell, if you go too slow, you may never get there, or when you do it's too late, like it was for Steve."

Judging by the reports from men who admit to an envy of women's friendships, it is when a man most needs friends that he is most likely to discover what his friendships lack. A common consequence of personal crisis for a man is his awareness of just how alone in the world he is. If he is not privy to the ways in which women use their friendships to deal with personal crises, he is likely to accept his aloneness as the male condition. He may even take some perverse pride in "going it alone." If he sees the way women cope with the same crisis, as David witnessed the women coping with Steve's suicide, a man is likely to be envious. Many men reported this kind of response to their own experiences of crisis:

- "When we got divorced, my wife's friends rallied around her like a flag. I'll bet she hardly spent a single moment alone, from the time I moved out to the time she got remarried. My friends hardly noticed the difference. When I was feeling pretty low, I sure could have used some time with the guys, but they were off with their own families as though nothing had changed. I guess for them nothing had. Still, you'd have thought that they would be a little more understanding of the changes I was going through. I know I will be, the next time I see a friend hurting."

- "She got over the death of our daughter much faster than I did. I think it was because she spent so much time talking about it with her friends. I didn't feel like it was something I could talk to anybody about. I still don't. Women are much better with each other over things like that than men are. I didn't know how to handle it, and it was obvious that my friends didn't either. In fact, I think it made them uncomfortable just to be around me, knowing that I was upset. To be truthful, things haven't been the same between my friends and me ever since."

- "The difference is that women talk their way through things and men think their way through things. Talking is something you do with somebody. Thinking is not. It stands to reason that women are going to spend more time with others when they have something important to deal with. Men, thinking alone, never really get at what is troubling them because they're not talking, not explaining, not asking questions, not using someone else to figure out their own feelings. Of course, they can't do that unless they are going to fully share all of what they are thinking. Men just don't do that with their friends."

- "Women lighten their load by sharing the weight. We men tend to think it's the manly thing to do to carry all the weight ourselves. That's why men get what I call 'emotional hernias.' We need to learn from women to share the load."

Walled off from other men, unable and/or unwilling to reach out to his wife, yet needing friendship in such times, we have seen (in Chapter 3) that a man will turn to another woman. Recall these comments:

- "I find it easier to talk to her [work associate] about the things that are really important to me than to talk to the guys. She knows a lot more about my work and how I feel about it than my wife does, but I think that's just because she works with me."

- "She [secretary] knows absolutely everything there is to know about me, because I tell her everything and she is completely trustworthy. In a lot of ways I am closer to her than I am to my wife, but then in some ways I'm not, too."

- "I go to her [boss] for help with everything from business to personal stuff, including how to handle my wife. She listens and asks questions that help me to see things I'd never look at as important, and she gives me advice."

It is one thing for men to recognize that they need more intimate friendships, but it is quite another thing for men to behave in the ways necessary to develop those relationships. All of the same dynamics that are operating to keep men at a distance from their wives and families are in high gear where friendships are concerned. The man who would develop intimacy with another man must first overcome societal prescriptions about what it is to be a man and a buddy. He must then overcome his own prohibitions against self-disclosure. Finally he must find a receptive and responsive friend. The era of "men's lib" has made it possible for men to at least consider alternative ways of relating to one another—although the focus of men's lib seems thus far to have been on marriage and family roles, with little being said about male relationships with other men. (Moreover, the language of men's lib, with its "consciousness-raising" and "support groups," is not likely to find quick favor in the hinterlands, where men meet over drinks and cards, and the very phrase "male support group" is a contradiction in terms. There, it is believed that males don't need support, and if they do, they aren't completely male.)

MEN: FRUSTRATED FRIENDS

Despite the unprecedented opportunity that modern times present for men to become close to other men, they are still constrained by conventional male inhibitions and prohibitions against self-disclosure. Those few men who do muster the courage to reach out to others by revealing themselves are more likely to be met with rebuke and even ridicule than with a responsive reception. Even in those circumstances, where the avowed purpose is for men to support one another and become closer, it is difficult for them to overcome all the barriers to interpersonal intimacy that they have erected over the years.

Marty Dodson has sought richer relationships with his male friends through involvement in his church. By his account, even a goal of "brotherhood" is not enough to bring men truly together:

"My church has a very active Men's Fellowship Program, which centers on the Wednesday morning Businessmen's Bible Breakfasts. The idea of the group is that Christian businessmen can come together one morning a week, early, before the business day begins, to share the Word, to witness, and to develop our fellowship. You would think that if there was anyplace where men could discuss personal concerns, the things that really gnaw at them, this would be it. Unfortunately, it hasn't worked out that way. To begin with, there is a lot of competition between the groups. It's not outright, but it's there. Ours is a very big church, and if all the men who were interested were put in one group, it would be more of a crowd than a group. Instead, there are about ten active groups of twenty-five to thirty men each. That in itself isn't so bad, except that there is a clear hierarchy among the groups. Membership is supposed to be open, but it is pretty obvious that the old-time 'power brokers' are in one group, the wealthiest members in another group, the young comers in their own group, and so on until you get down to the groups made up of guys who weren't invited into any other group. It's sort of like a little fraternity system within the church.

"In the groups themselves, it's not that much different.

In a normal meeting there will be a scripture reading. We discuss how the scripture applies in our daily lives, which usually evokes a lot of witnessing, men telling about their own religious experiences. Then we close with a prayer. There is a lot of what I call 'witnessing to win.' It's sort of a Christian one-upmanship, where everyone tries to outwitness everyone else or out-compassion everyone else in responding to witnesses. There is a lot of 'love talk' and references to 'brotherhood.' We're forever saying 'I love you, brother.' When you really look at it, though, there is very little loving, brotherly behavior. We don't reveal enough of the vulnerable parts of ourselves to be brothers in any sense of the word. Instead of using their Christian bond to further their fellowship, most of the 'breakfast boys,' as they call themselves, seem bent on using their fellowship to prove how Christian they are. The church should be a place where men can get close, but in our case it's become just another place for men to compete."

David Brann is a dentist who is very involved in dental education at the professional level. In addition to programs on the latest diagnostic and treatment techniques and on office finances and management, dentists can attend educational sessions on personal development. As a facilitator of many personal-development sessions, Dr. Brann is keenly aware of the difficulties men have in sharing, even when sharing is the agenda at hand. "It's no secret that dentistry is personally demanding work, but I don't think that the average patient has any idea of just how stressful the work is. First, there are the financial pressures. You can't start a practice without going into six-digit debt these days. The better your office and the newer your equipment, the bigger your debt. You have to fill a lot of teeth just to break even. Then there is the work itself. No one likes going to the dentist, so the dentist is constantly dealing with people who suspect that he is going to hurt them. It doesn't make for pleasant interpersonal interactions. Add to that the fact that after a

179

while the work can get pretty boring. The average dentist in general practice doesn't face a whole lot of challenges in his work. And the most important thing of all is that most dentists work alone. In the normal course of their jobs, they don't come into contact with their colleagues the way doctors do at a hospital. So here you have all of these guys with all of these problems, and most of them don't have any friends they can talk to. All of this contributes to the higher-than-average incidence of substance abuse—alcohol and drugs—among dentists, not to mention suicide. That is why I think the personal-development component of our educational programs is so important.

"What we try to do is to offer a format of a small, supportive group of professional peers where a guy can feel free to really open up, knowing that people will understand where he is coming from. I think we're pretty successful, but to tell you the truth, it's like pulling teeth to get these guys to open up. That's a poor pun. It's much harder than pulling teeth. They just have such a hard time admitting to others that they are having problems. The ones who volunteer first, sometimes the only ones who volunteer, are those who want to talk about the personal problems that come with being successful. 'I'm making so much money, it's causing me stress.' I don't mean to minimize the stresses of success, but it seems to me that that sort of combination boast and confession is not nearly so confidential as the admission that you abuse drugs or are sleeping with the technician or that you are bankrupt. It's the guy who is on the edge that most needs to reach out. The guy on top just wants everyone to look at him. The guy who has already fallen needs a safety net, real professional help. But the guy on the edge can be helped by his friends, if he'll just reach out. Even with all we do to encourage that, with the small peer groups and all, we probably get less than one percent of the guys who really need a friend. By the time they realize they really need a friend, they may be too far gone for a friend to help."

MEN AND MENTORS

One type of male bond that approaches intimacy and is found with some frequency is the mentor relationship. The biographies of successful men commonly point to the important role played by an older, more experienced individual in the development of the young man. In one study of corporate leaders, two-thirds of them reported that they had had mentors who helped them in the early stages of their careers. Top athletes frequently credit a coach they had in high school or college with helping them to realize their potential. In the entertainment field, stars feel a strong sense of indebtedness to those who gave them their starts.

A mentor may be a teacher or one who sets a good example. A mentor may be a protector or one who takes another along as he rises successfully. Mentors give challenges, publicize one's successes, and fight for opportunities. Any one or all of these activities can play a pivotal role in the development of a young man, and the relationship between a mentor and a protégé is one of the very few instances in which we regularly see a degree of intimacy between men.

Andy Markham has recently been promoted to divisional manager for a major Southwestern title company. At thirty-one, he is the youngest divisional manager in the company's history and is regarded by higher-ups as having the potential to go even higher. Reflecting on his rapid rise from entry level to just outside the executive suite in less than eight years, Andy points to the influence of his "sponsor," J.T.:

"J.T. hired me personally and he's always taken a strong interest in my career, influencing the job assignments I've been given, cluing me to company politics. He's even counseled with me when I've had problems—no matter what they were, business or personal. From the first, I have always felt as though he was someone I could go to with what-

181

ever concerned me, without feeling like he would take advantage of any weakness I showed or be put off by my approaching him. He's been both a friend and a father to me, without asking for anything in return. I know I wouldn't have gotten where I am without his help, and I know that I'll keep on relying on his help."

The Silver City Saddle Tramps are a country-and-western band that bounced around the backroads of Texas before getting their big break. After some moderate success as a club and recording band, the group split up, but their leader, Robin Morton, still speaks fondly of the man who took them under his wing:

"We were nobody going nowhere when Mr. Stiller became our angel. He got us bookings, hassled the studios, helped us with music. He became sort of a father figure to the whole band. We never had a contract with him or paid him any money—every time we offered, he said he was doing it just because he liked us, said we were like his family. To this day we keep track of each other through Mr. Stiller. I know for a fact that he's sobered up one of the guys, saved another one's marriage, and loaned out his own money to whichever one needed it. I love him like he was my dad, except that my dad never did do any of that stuff for me."

This strange combination of parent and peer seems to be the unique feature of these male mentor relationships. A mentor offers a man the guidance of a parent without the guilt that so often accompanies real parental guidance, the compassion of a peer without the competition. Men are capable of opening themselves to mentors in ways that they will not open themselves to others. Of course, mentor relationships are, like other male relationships, often constrained by the circumstances in which they arise. Much of the help is centered on work and career, but the closest of mentor-protégé relationships transcend work and move into private and personal areas.

In some mentor relationships, the sharing is primarily

one-way; the helper may reveal relatively little of himself to the one being helped. However, many mentors note that they value the opportunity to help as much as the protégé value being helped. This suggests that the opportunity to share of themselves is not lost upon the mentors. "I look after the younger guys around here because I like to do it. It gives me a new perspective on my own work and a chance to share some of what I think I have learned with someone who values it. Some of them you get closer to than others, but that's just natural. You find that with the ones you're closest to, you get at least as much from them as they get from you." Like James Cooke, a senior bank manager, most mentors do it because of the sense of personal reward they receive, not for any institutional rewards. (Many mentors mentioned, however, that they felt the development of young people was a responsibility that went with their position in the organization or their station in life.) The overwhelming response to the question of why a man became a mentor was, "I get more from it than they do." One elderly gentleman noted in his community for helping young businessman starting out on their own commented, "The best way for me to stay in touch with myself is for me to stay in touch with what's going on with those young people."

The absence of competition may be what allows for intimacy in mentor relationships:

- "He may be freer with me because we're not competing for the same job, but that doesn't have anything to do with my behavior. At my age I'm long past competing with anybody for anything."

- "I guess I sort of shame them into being open with me, 'cause I'm open with them. I tell them everything and they do the same. Now if I were fighting them for something, I sure as hell wouldn't be so open, but I'm just trying to help them. I think they have to know just where I am coming from in order to figure out just what kind of help I'm offering."

It is evident that in mentor relationships men engage in the kinds of self-disclosure that promote real intimacy, a tendency not seen in other male relationships. This compassion, the real understanding that can only come from someone who has been there, apparently removes many male inhibitions about disclosing. Moreover, the mentor relationship is not socially prohibited. It is okay for a man to have a "coach" in ways that it is not okay for him to have a close personal friend.

Men do not value friendship. Their relationships with other men are superficial, even shallow. "Best buddies" reveal so little of themselves to each other that they are little more than acquaintances. There is no intimacy in most male friendships and none of what intimacy offers: solace and support. Yet there is an identifiable man-to-man relationship—the mentor—that approaches the intimacy of true friends.

From the data revealed here, one might conclude that men can only be intimate with one another when institutional prohibitions are removed and individual inhibitions are overcome—for example, in mentor relationships, where all threats of competition are removed. This one instance in which men do participate in intimate relationships with other men, albeit a special circumstance, indicates that men *can* be intimate. It may be that we need to look more closely at the ways in which men claim to disclose themselves and their feelings to others, the ways in which men are intimate.

6 How Do Men Love?

If you don't understand my silence, you'll never understand what I say.

—Anonymous

Can it be that there are no men who are loving and affection-
ate husbands? Caring and demonstrative fathers? Close and
personal friends? That, of course, is not the case. There are
men who are disclosing of themselves in their relationships
with spouse, family, and friends in ways that allow them to
be truly intimate. The number of such men, however, is very
small. If you are fortunate enough to be such a man or to be
involved with one as spouse, father, or friend, yours is a rare
experience. The more common experience for most of us is
to be involved with a man without really knowing who he is
or how he cares. Perhaps this is why there is so much more
to be said about how men are not intimate than there is
about how they *are*.

Men have very limited views of what love is, and a correspondingly limited repertoire of loving behavior. So limited are male emotional expressions that those who love
men wonder if they are loved in return. In marriage, family,
and friendship, men share too little of themselves to give

185

any real indication of the extent of their loving. Yet, in each of these relationships, men persistently protest that they *do* love. Men say that they have intense feelings about their wives, family, friends—without, of course, revealing just what these feelings are. They attest to valuing these relationships and the exchanges that occur in them. Men argue that they are just as loving as women, it's just that they don't show it the same way. Men want to make the case that their level of loving is the same as women's, but the overt behavioral signals of their feelings in a relationship are different. Men assert that they express their feelings in subtle, often unseen ways. One husband angrily argued in defense of his own emotional reserve, "I love her plenty and I show it in my own way. She just doesn't see it. That's *her* problem, not mine!"

To many observers of male behavior, and especially to women, the argument that men show their love in subtle but significant ways is a suspicious if not altogether spurious one. They contend that love not expressed is love not experienced. Giving men the benefit of the doubt for the moment, it may be that if we sensitize ourselves to the ways in which men do communicate intimacy and involvement in their relationships, we can gain a new appreciation of male intimacy. If we learn more about how men love, we may discover more about how loving men are.

SURROGATES FOR SHARING

The measure of intimacy in a relationship is the amount and degree of mutual disclosure that occurs. The more two people reveal themselves in significant ways to each other, the closer they are. Sharing behavior is loving behavior. Against this definition of loving there is clear evidence from spouses, family, friends, and men themselves that they do not reveal their personal selves in overt ways in their relationships with others. But what about *covert* revelations? Could it be as men say, that they are subtly signaling their love through a number of surrogate sharing behaviors?

It is always striking to see the open display of emotion that athletes express upon winning a big game. Whatever the sport, whatever the age level, game's end brings the players rushing on to the playing surface, throwing their arms about one another, embracing, even crying in celebration of what they have achieved or lost. Nowhere else in male endeavors is there the same free behavioral expression of emotion, even though the stakes may be similar. Members of the sales group that lands a big account which may spell the difference between bankruptcy and a banner year for the company don't go around hugging and patting each other on the ass. When lawyers win a big case, they may have a celebratory round of drinks but they're not likely to shed tears of joy. When the mechanics at a paint and body shop painstakingly reconstruct a car that has been nearly totaled, they don't even pause for a "high five," the symbolic slapping of hands favored by athletes.

Why is emotional release acceptable behavior for men on the athletic field and unacceptable everywhere else? It may be because physical competition legitimizes touching, crying, caring. It may also be that, having proven they are men in the most manly of pursuits, sport, emotional expression is okay. Outside of sport, the prohibitions against open displays of emotion and personal self-disclosures are very strong. Here, in order to express what they feel, yet not violate what they see as prohibitions, men must rely on surrogates, substitutes for real sharing. Throughout these pages, stories of male relationships in marriage, family, and friendships have alluded to many of the most common male surrogates for sharing. Here we will examine these behaviors by which men claim they subtly signal themselves and their true feelings to others.

Sex
Our social customs do not so much change as accumulate. New values and forms of behavior do not replace older

187

ones, but are added to them. At any given time, all social standards from the most archaic to the most contemporary are operative, and any social act is subject to multiple interpretations, to be reviled by some and revered by others. Sex is one arena of human behavior in which the accumulation of customs has led to a considerable amount of confusion. It is difficult to know today just what sex means, simply because it does and could mean so many things.

For many men and women today, sex still represents the culmination of courtship, the consummation of the marriage, the physical expression of an emotional attachment. Side by side with these men and women are those who attribute little more meaning to sex than they might to a handshake. Indeed, so varied are the intentions and interpretations surrounding sex today that many have argued convincingly that sex has lost its meaning.

As with other behavior, it is helpful to look at the context of sex to discover what it means, much as we might read the remainder of a sentence or paragraph to decipher the meaning of a strange word. However, if there is no context, if sex is both the content and the context of behavior, then the meaning of sex is doubly obscured. So it is with men who substitute sex for sharing. In the absence of other kinds of intimacy, sex becomes very confusing. It is both the message and the medium, the means and the end. For men, sex is an expression of emotion and a substitute for emotion. With so many possible meanings and so little from men besides sex to guide them, women rightfully wonder just what sex does mean. From what we've learned of male and female intimacy patterns, there is every reason to believe that sex is used very differently by men and women in loving relationships. Sherry Stam describes the many meanings of sex for her husband:

"I think being close means sharing. He thinks being close means screwing! That's the difference in the way we love. Maybe it's the same for other couples.

"The whole idea of having an intimate relationship with someone, as far as I'm concerned, is being able to really share your innermost feelings and emotions, not screw them away. When I'm anxious or insecure, I want to talk about it with someone who will listen—not just to what I'm saying, but to how I'm feeling, too. When he's anxious or insecure, he wants sex; it reassures him.

"When I come home tired and tensed up from all that's gone on in the day, I want to talk about it and let go of whatever emotional baggage I've brought from work. Talking about what has got me so tense releases it for me. When he comes home tired and tense, he wants me to 'do him'—you can guess what that means. Getting off is his tension release.

"When I've accomplished something that's really neat or something super has happened to me, I want to find everybody I know and tell them how happy I am. I want to share it with everybody, make a real celebration out of it. When he has something to celebrate, he wants some 'special' sex, he acts like it's his reward.

"When I'm sad, the only thing that consoles me is a shoulder to cry on and an empathetic ear to hear me out. When he's sad, he wants to be seduced out of his sadness, then left alone. When I'm mad—and I get mad a lot—I want to get it all out in the open right now, let him know just how I feel and why. When I'm mad, I want to fight! When he's mad, he wants to fuck! He thinks that will take care of everything, make up for whatever's wrong.

"That's why I say the difference between me and my husband is that I want to share and he wants to screw. Don't think that I don't want sex, too. I have physical needs that are just as strong as his. I get horny and there are plenty of times when I'm the one who wants to screw. The difference is that for me sex is just *one* way of being close. It's not even the only way to be close physically. Sometimes just holding each other is enough. I need to feel close emotionally, too, I need some emotional intimacy to satisfy my needs. For him, sex is his only way of satisfying every need! It's his one and only way to be intimate. How close can you get to someone who only communicates with his cock?

"That's probably not fair. I get a little worked up when I get into this. What really bothers me is that he never talks about his feelings, so I can't ever get closer to him. I have to guess at what he's feeling from the kind of sex he wants! He seems to think that if he's sharing his body, he's sharing himself. He doesn't understand that there are other ways to be loving without making love, or if he does understand, he doesn't do anything about it. Maybe he can't, maybe no man can."

"Well, as far as I'm concerned, you can see right there the difference between us, in fact the difference between men and women in general," Tom Stam responds. "Women have this need to make everything into a big emotional deal, and men just take things as they are. Look at this whole sex thing between Sherry and me. She wants to think there's some deep emotional meaning behind the kinds of sex I want. The simple truth is, I like to make love to my wife all kinds of ways. Sometimes one way feels better than another just because it does, not because of anything psychological. You'd think she would be thankful I still like sex with her as much as I do after eleven years of marriage. But no, now she wants to know what it all means. When I tell her that it doesn't *mean* anything—because it doesn't—she accuses me of not being intimate.

"I think women have this need to analyze everything, talk it through down to every little detail, no matter how private it might be. What's more, if you don't do the same thing, they accuse you of not loving them enough. Just because I come home and don't immediately start spilling my guts about everything that happened at work doesn't mean I don't love her. If I don't talk about my feelings, it may be because I'm not feeling anything. Do you think she'll accept that? Not for a minute. She gets all over me for not being 'feeling,' whatever that means. It's one of those areas where you just can't win with a woman. You're damned if you do and damned if you don't.

"The simple truth is that this is the main difference between men and women. No matter how good it is between a man and a woman—it really is pretty good for us most of the time—they're going to have problems when it comes to this. Men don't need the same things from women that women need from men. And it's not just that 'men want to screw and women want to share,' like she says. Hell, it goes way beyond that. Men and women want different things from people in general, from family, friends, you name it. Women need all this feeling, emotional stuff from relationships. Men don't—at least not as much or in the same ways. Does this mean that women are right and men are wrong? Not by me, it doesn't. It just means that men are different from women and need different things. Maybe the real difference between men and women is that men understand the difference and accept it, whereas women don't understand it and want men to change."

Tom and Sherry Stam candidly portray the issues that surround men's use of sex as a substitute for sharing of themselves. Among most couples, these sexual issues are rarely brought out of the bedroom, but they run as an undercurrent to all exchanges between the man and the woman. Speaking for women, Sherry Stam says that whether or not Tom consciously means anything by his sexual preferences, in the absence of any other, more direct evidence of his feelings, she has to interpret what he is feeling from how he wants sex. For his part, Tom argues that sex is the ultimate sharing. He says that Sherry ought to need no more than his desire for sex as evidence of his love.

Throughout the many relationships men have, there is a tendency to confuse sex with intimacy and loving. Many men do believe that sex can substitute for all other types of exchanges in an intimate relationship. Sex becomes equal to—if not greater than—all public, private, and personal disclosures. It is both a measure of intimacy and a means to intimacy. Men seem to be saying to women, "You know I love you because I make love to you."

Women view sex as only one dimension of a relationship—at that, a dimension that certainly contributes no more to the development of closeness than do private and personal disclosures. For women, sex is but one means and a very poor measure of intimacy. This sharp contrast between views of sex in relationships between men and women is seen in the following statements.

On sex *as* love:

• From a once-divorced man of thirty-eight: "My first wife divorced me because she said we never 'communicated.' She was always after me about talking to her more. We got along great in bed, but that wasn't enough for her. I've told my current wife that if she needs a lot of conversation to know she's loved, she's got the wrong guy. I don't feel that I have to prove my love to her any way except by making love to her. If I don't talk to her or tell her everything she wants to hear, it doesn't mean a thing. If I don't want to make love to her, that means I don't love her. That's what she ought to worry about."

• Married young, at seventeen, this twenty-nine-year-old housewife is now beginning to question how she is loved: "I suppose I should be happy that he still wants me as much as he does. I know a lot of my friends complain that their husbands don't show much interest in sex at all. Even so, looking back, sex is really the only kind of love he's shown me. There's never been any tenderness, any real togetherness. We don't even talk all that much. I worry that there is nothing more to our loving than making love. Then I get to feeling guilty, feeling like I ought to be satisfied with what I have. It's all so confusing. And it's not something I can talk about with my husband at all."

On sex *and* love:

• A self-avowed "swinging single" writes: "The best way to show a woman that you really care for her is to make

192

love to her as well as you know how. That means you take care of her sexual needs as well as your own. No woman is going to think you are very loving if you're only interested in your own satisfaction. Women today don't want to be used, they want to be loved. The way to give yourself to a woman is to give her what she wants. Then she'll know that you love her."

- For this housewife, sex at home is fine, but she wants something more from her lover. "I have a husband who is a great lover. I think that's really why I married him. He does things to my body that no other man ever did. When we make love, it's like he is totally dedicated to giving me pleasure, and he does. At the same time he's not really there, if you know what I mean. He's making love to me and I'm loving it, but all the while he is sort of detached. I feel like it's a performance for him. He's going to make the audience happy, but he's not really into it himself. I never feel like he's really giving himself to me, even though I love what he does to me. On the other hand, I have a lover who is terrible in bed, but he talks to me. He talks about himself, about us, we even talk about sex. Because he's so open with me, I have the feeling that he's giving much more of himself to me than my husband does, and in a lot of ways I love him more. Believe me, sex is great but it's no substitute for real love."

- A man in his early twenties has some strong views on what women really want: "Supposedly, women today are attracted to 'vulnerable' men, like the ones they see in the movies and on TV. You know, the guys who talk about their feelings all the time and always look like they are about to cry. Well, one thing I've noticed about those vulnerable guys is that they're still pretty studly in the sack. Seems to me that all that vulnerable stuff don't mean shit to a girl if you can't get it up."

- An experienced female executive puts the issue in business terms: "Men would realize that real communication is more valuable than sex to a woman if they just took more of a businesslike view. It's a simple supply-demand problem. You can always find a man who wants to screw you, but there are hardly any men at all who want to talk to you."

On sex as a *substitute*:

▪ A twice-divorced man of thirty-three acknowledges his use of sex as a surrogate: "I guess I do use sex a lot to substitute for my feelings, or at least to substitute for talking about my feelings. There are a lot of reasons. You have to start with the fact that sex is a lot more fun than anything else I can think of. It sure is easier than trying to talk things through. Then, too, it gets to be sort of a habit. You get used to using sex to make up after a fight or to make you feel good when you're depressed or to celebrate when there's something to celebrate. What it really comes down to is that I guess I'm not very comfortable with expressing my emotions—I don't think that many men are—but I am pretty comfortable with sex, so I just sort of let sex speak for me."

▪ Finally, from a forty-one-year-old wife: "It's probably as much my fault as it is his. I let him get away with it. I let him use sex to deal with his feelings rather than really getting them out in the open and talking about them. Sex has become sort of a crutch for us. We can't seem to communicate any other way. When I say it is my fault, I mean that because I think my sexual appetite is larger than his right now, I want it more often than he does. I may be too eager to suggest that we take our problems to bed, so to speak. Maybe if I forced him to talk it out, he would. Instead I suggest that a quick roll in the hay will solve everything, because it's what I want. Naturally, it doesn't solve anything except my horniness. It sure doesn't bring us closer together. I keep saying I'm going to try to help him open up, but my body gets in the way of my good intentions."

What message is there in these many meanings and methods of sex? For every wife who complains that her husband *only* thinks of sex, there is a wife who complains that her husband *never* thinks of sex. For every man who insists that his sexual intentions are nothing more than sexual, there is a man who says that he expresses his emotions sexually. Clearly, the meaning of sex in any relationship can be determined only contextually, in concert with the other behaviors exchanged. This, of course, reinforces the very point women make. In the absence of other indicators of intimacy, they have only their men's sexual behavior to know how they are loved. Thus, whether intentional or not, a man's sexual behavior becomes a substitute for loving. It is a clue that women must read to know who men are. Sex is, as one woman said, "The only part of himself he gives to me. Even then, when I'm done using it, I have to give it back."

Giving

The phrase "generous to a fault" is one of those anomalies that sets you to thinking. Generosity is typically a virtue. Is it wrong to be too generous? Where men are concerned, the fault in being generous lies not in how much is given, but in what the giving means. Jayne Bishop is a twenty-nine-year-old woman who, on her first birthday following her father's death, reflected on her father's giving:

"When we were little, we all thought Daddy was just the most wonderful father anybody could have, because he was always giving us presents. On holidays and of course birthdays there were always so many gifts they would take your breath away. On not-so-special days, too, there were presents. Report-card days, sick days, or when he came home from trips. On any occasion at all, Daddy would have his 'little surprises' for us. And for each of us he had his own little ritual. When I would *ooh* and *aah* over my presents, he would always say, 'It's 'cause I love you, Princess,' and then we would hug. Those were the only times I can ever remember him saying 'I love you.' When there were presents.

"As I got older, the presents got more expensive but they came just as frequently. I went from dolls to clothes to cars

195

to jewelry. After I turned twenty-one it was always jewelry, on every occasion. I don't think Daddy ever even noticed that I didn't wear much jewelry. The gifts weren't exactly right for anybody else, either. The older we got, the less he knew what we really wanted, because the less he knew about us. We were pretty much strangers to each other, but still he kept up his 'little surprises.'

"I remember one birthday Daddy had given me a terribly expensive but absolutely ghastly necklace. I asked Mother, 'Why does he do it, why doesn't he just give me the money and let me buy what I really want?' She said, 'Dear, your father's gifts are his way of telling you he loves you. He's been giving me things I don't want or need for almost thirty years. It's the only way he has to show his love.' I know now that Mom was right. Daddy was always so uncomfortable with any kind of emotion or affection. It was only the presents that made it okay for him to say 'I love you.' I'm sorry I didn't let him know that it was *him*, not his presents, that I loved. I guess that's one of those things that you don't realize when you are young, and when you do realize it, it is too late."

Jayne's father, Stephen Bishop, is dead, and there is only her interpretation of why he gave to the family as he did. But what she perceives as his motivation is consistent with what other men have implied, if not said outright, about their giving:

- "I consider myself to be pretty generous. I hardly ever miss an important date—birthdays, anniversaries, and the like. I always give a card with some money inside. That way I don't have to worry about getting the right thing. They can pick something out for themselves. Then, too, it saves the time of shopping, which nobody likes to do. All around, giving money is easier than actually buying gifts, and there's no doubt about the value."

- "I have everybody make a list of what presents they want, and that's what they get. It saves me the trouble of looking around for the right thing and they get exactly what they want. It works out for everyone. Sometimes if I can't get out to the stores I'll just give them the money and they pick up the gift for themselves. Or maybe I'll have one of the girls do it for their mom. Still, it's a gift from me. That's the important thing, not how they get it."

■ "I probably do go a little overboard on gifts. Christmas and birthdays especially tend to get out of hand. Sometimes there are so many presents that even I can't keep track of them all. I don't really know why I do it. I guess the occasion sort of makes it okay to give in to your feelings. Maybe there is even guilt working—to make up for not showing them more how I feel about them from day to day. Whatever, it's a harmless sort of indulgence. I can afford it, they enjoy it, and I think I get my message across."

■ "I'm just like the guy in the commercials; it's a lot easier to show her how I feel with presents than it is to tell her how I feel. You can say 'I love you' with a gift, or 'I'm sorry,' or 'Thanks,' or 'What about it?' or anything at all, without any of the awkwardness that I have when I try to tell her how I feel. So you could say I give because it's easier than talking."

■ "There's nothing special about giving. With me, it's more of a habit than anything else. There's a regular routine I follow. Flowers for our anniversary, candy for her birthday, perfume at Christmas. Nothing fancy or expensive, but, hey, it's the thought that counts. Isn't that what they say?"

■ "Giving is just a normal part of relating. It's almost like a duty, one of those things you have to do if you're going to be involved with someone."

These men are "givers." At the other extreme are those men who do not give, whatever the occasion. Their position is captured by the man who said, "Why should I give her presents? If she needs anything, she can go buy it. If she doesn't need it, there's no sense in giving it to her." Whether intentionally or through benign neglect, the men who do not give far outnumber those who do. Somewhere in between are the money-giving and routinized giving that most men engage in. For women, the Christmas perfume is as pervasive as the Christmas tie is for men. One curious aside is that men rarely exchange gifts or even cards with one another, even on the most obvious of occasions, such as birthdays. Women friends commonly exchange thoughtful, if small, birthday or holiday presents. Perhaps giving between men is seen as too intimate a gesture.

Giving means different things to different men. For some it is dutiful recognition of an event or relationship. For others it is a show of wealth. Still others use gifts as bribes, apologies, or an award. Men use gifts as vehicles for expressing their feelings. Whatever the means and meaning, a particular man may attach to his gifting, women are quick to point out a common pattern in a man's presents: he rarely gives of himself.

- "He is definitely saying something to all of us when he gives money instead of a gift. He's saying he can't be bothered to shop for something personal. He hopes that if he gives enough money we won't raise a fuss over it. For years the children thought that he bought me presents. Actually, I bought presents for myself, wrapped them, then pretended to be surprised when I opened them. I even thanked him as though he had done it all himself. But of course he would never make the effort. He doesn't understand that giving money, I don't care how much it is, is not really giving, because there is nothing of him in it."

- "Giving, with him, is like a charity. He figures that if he gives presents at all the appropriate times of the year he doesn't have to engage in any other sentiment for the rest of the year. A present is his way of saying 'I care.' In his mind, if he says that on birthdays, anniversaries, Valentines, and all the rest, he doesn't have to say it on just your average nothing day. The problem is, it's on your average nothing day that I most need to hear that he cares."

■ "Of course, men use presents to keep from dealing with the real issues. When the children ask their father if he loves them, he'll say, 'I gave you a bike, didn't I?' Or, 'I gave you that doll, didn't I?' The present takes the place of showing some real emotion. Why can't he just say 'I love you'? He's no different with me. Any emotional issue between us is closed off when he starts in recounting all he's given me. What he leaves out is that he's never given me what I most want, and that is some honest emotional statement from him."

■ "There's lots of gifts but there's no real giving because there is no thought in them. He doesn't get close enough to me or the kids to find out what would really be a good gift. There is none of him in his giving. It's just another duty to him."

■ "I think that lots of men use money and gifts, which are, after all, just another form of money, like some sort of emotional currency, legal tender for emotional debts. It's almost as though it's a big board game and men are always drawing the card that says, 'Express your feelings or pay two hundred dollars.' Whenever they land on that space, men always choose to pay. Maybe it's not intentional. I suppose we have to give them the benefit of the doubt. But they certainly act like a gift means we can't probe for their true feelings. It really puts a woman in a tough spot, I think. If you say that you'd rather have something of them instead of a gift, it sounds ungrateful. Yet if you don't say anything, you'll keep getting gifts when what you really want is for him to give something of himself to the relationship, not something of his wallet."

A unique perspective on the meaning that men attach to giving was provided by a woman who has been surrounded by men all her life. With three brothers and three sons of her own, Darlene Newsome has had a lifetime of experience with men and their gifts:

"I long ago got used to the way men give. If it wasn't for

me and my mother, no one would ever have gotten any presents in our family. We bought all the gifts, then made it look like they were giving to each other and to us at birthdays, Christmas, even anniversaries. It's the same way now in my own family, much as I would like it to be different. You get used to it. What I haven't gotten used to is the way men *receive* gifts. They don't know how to receive graciously. Most of the time they don't even bother to say 'Thank you.' More than anything else, I think it is the way that men receive gifts that says how they view them. Even when you go out of your way to find just the perfect thing, not only for that person but as the perfect expression of how you feel about that person, they take it with all of the emotion that they take a birthday card from the dentist reminding them their next checkup is due. If they don't see the feeling in others' gifts, how can they put any meaning in their own giving? It's simple—they don't."

Again, as with sex, it may not be so much that men intend their gifts as a substitute for sharing of themselves as it is that in the absence of any other kind of sharing, gifts are interpreted as a substitute by the recipients. There are many men who sincerely believe that giving gifts is an honest and adequate expression of feeling and that nothing more should be required of them. There are others who hope by their giving to be excused from revealing their feelings. Others view giving as a duty, a requirement of the relationship, but little more, and still others give not at all. One man, when confronted with the perception of women that giving is a compensation for not expressing feelings, said, "Fine, if she doesn't appreciate it, I won't give her anything. It's a pain in the ass anyway. Let's see what she has to say about that honest feeling!"

The point is not that a man's gifts are not appreciated. Where giving expresses some knowledge of the recipient and/or sentiment on the part of the giver, then giving is a manifestation of intimacy and is appreciated as such. If giving is just one of a number of acts of disclosure, and thus occurs in a caring context, it enables the recipient to use the giving as loving. Giving that reveals no giving of oneself, giving that is habitual, dutiful, giving that is used to defuse emotional issues, however lavish and expensive the gifts may be, is no substitute for giving of one's self. It is that giving—intimate giving—which is so often missing from men.

Touch

Earlier in this chapter, the ease with which athletes touch one another in celebrating their common efforts was contrasted against the difficulty men have with touch outside of athletic contexts. The prohibition against touch is one of the most prevalent taboos in male behavior. Men simply do not touch one another except in aggression or competition. Men rarely touch women except in sexual ways. These prohibitions are so persistent and powerful that anytime a man voluntarily violates them he may be said to be reaching out, trying to establish intimacy. Most men never make outright disclosures in these taboo areas. They typically engage in any of a number of "testing" behaviors— actions that might be interpreted as an invitation to intimacy but might just as easily be taken as innocent, even accidental. An excellent example is the roughhousing that is a staple of father-son interaction.

"I swear, sometimes Daryl gets so rough with the boys I'm just certain that one of them is going to be hurt. They've been doing it since the boys were babies, so I guess it's just one of the ways they have of getting along. They roll around on the floor, wrestling for hours, and they all just love it. The boys will even beg for Daryl to roughhouse with them. I think they just like the excuse to hug their dad, and I'm sure it is the same with him. None of them would ever think of hugging or admit that's what they want. It's only okay for them if it happens in one of their wrestling matches."

Outside the family, the same forms of male touching can be seen in organized competitions and in the physical games men play informally—arm-wrestling or punching each other or shadowboxing. For reasons explored fully in the next chapter, few men would admit to enjoying these games for the opportunity they provide to violate a taboo and touch another man, yet it is an important way for men to test their relationships. Leigh Searles tells a fascinating story of what happened when she challenged this touch taboo:

"My senior year in college I had an apartment off campus. Upstairs from me lived these two guys, Charlie and Kevin. They had graduated a couple of years earlier and were working as house painters because they couldn't find anything else. We all got to be really good friends. Charlie and Kevin had been together since diaperhood and were as thick as thieves. After we sorted out that there wasn't going to be a romance between me and either one of them, they sort of took me in like a sister. Anyway, like I said, Charlie and Kevin had done everything together since as long as either of them could remember. They grew up in the same town, went to the same schools, dated the same girls. I don't think I've ever seen any two guys who were closer than they were.

"They were always hitting and punching each other, but then that's just the way guys are. One night I came home late from a date and there were these terrible noises from upstairs. I mean, I thought the ceiling was going to cave in on me. I ran upstairs and went in and there were Charlie and Kevin wrestling on the floor. I could tell that it wasn't for fun. Lamps had been knocked over, there was a broken chair and table, and they were calling each other names and fighting like they were out for blood. I tried to stop them, but they wouldn't pay any attention to me. It went on for the longest time until Kevin knocked Charlie out against the leg of a table. Next, Kevin had Charlie's head in his arms, kind of cradling him, and they were both crying and telling each other how much they loved each other. There wasn't anything at all sexual about it. It was just two friends finally admitting that they loved each other. I spent the night staying up with them, listening to them talk about all they'd been through and how much they meant to each other.

"The point of the story is, about two or three days after this happened, I was with them again. I started talking about how neat it was for me to see how much they loved each other. How I had never seen guys be like that before. Well, I could tell that it really embarrassed them. They just clammed up and wouldn't talk about it. In fact, after that they didn't have much to do with me at all. Three months later they moved out without a word. I was really hurt. I guess they just couldn't handle the fact that I had seen how they feel. I don't know why it should have been such a big deal to them. I mean, it wasn't like they were gay or anything. They were just two guys who really loved each other. You'd think that they'd be proud of that. I would if I felt that way about someone."

The rejection that Leigh experienced when she faced her friends with their love is different in degree but not in kind from the rejection that mothers, sisters, wives, and friends experience when they ask men, "Why are you so rough with each other?" Many men honestly don't know why, because it has become such a ritualized way for them to relate. Those who do know are reluctant to say.

If aggressive, "testing," physical contact among men is commonplace, nonsexual contact of any kind between men and women is relatively rare. Moreover, such contact cannot be externally distinguished in many respects from sexual contact.

- As one woman said: "I can't tell you how, but I can tell you that a woman knows when a man hugs you 'cause he wants a friend and when he hugs you 'cause he wants a fuck!"

- "You just can tell when they want something more."

- "I get a feeling, that's all. So far, I have never been wrong."
- "Somehow you just know when it's sexual. It's an instinct more than anything else."

For their part, men are somewhat confused, not by their own intentions but by how their actions are received:

- "Sometimes I just want to hold and to be held, but she always takes it as something sexual, and that takes over."
- "I guess I'm just a little afraid to hug a woman or put my arm around her friendly-like. They always take it the wrong way and I'm left feeling like a fool."
- "What with the sexual harassment stuff and all today, I think that the best rule of thumb is just not to touch anybody. Every now and then I sort of feel like a brotherly hug with a woman, but there's no such thing anymore. It can only get you in trouble, so it's better off left alone."

The sexual dynamics between men and women are such that it is not possible to distinguish physical behavior that is clearly intended as sexual from that which is not. Nor is it possible to predict how touching will be received. Certainly not all of a man's touching of others is sexual, nor is it all an invitation to further intimacy. But violation of the taboos against touching is often a man's way of testing what exists in the relationship and what more there might be. As such, it may be a small act of courage on the part of a man, but it is no substitute for self-disclosure as a building block of intimacy.

Intellectualizing

There is considerable conflict between men and women over just what constitutes sharing and self-disclosure. Nowhere is this conflict more evident than when men and women talk about the disclosure issues that are important to intimacy. Consider the following exchange between a husband and wife:

"My wife says that I never talk to her about the things

that she thinks are important. I would gladly talk to her if I could. The thing is, she gets all emotional every time we talk. There is no such thing as having a rational conversation with her, so there is no possibility of a real discussion. If talking is what she wants, fine, but if it just means a lot of crying and ranting and raving, I can do without it."

"Oh, he's happy enough talking about things, as long as you don't press him for any kind of personal statement about what he feels. As long as the discussion is very logical and rational and completely impersonal, he'll talk till he's blue in the face. Ask him for some emotion, some feeling, and you might as well be talking to the wall. To make it worse, he tries to make me feel childish for getting emotional. How can you talk about a loving relationship without getting emotional? I keep telling him, 'This is our life, not some goddamn TV documentary!'"

There is a marked tendency among men to intellectualize emotional issues, to depersonalize the very personal. This tendency manifests itself in many forms: a focus on logic and rationality; a debatelike demeanor, which values form over substance; the need for time to think. Not only do men discuss emotional issues in this manner, but they demand that women deal with them in the same way. If not, men reserve the right not to discuss them at all. ("These are the rules. I'll play this way or not at all.") Men seem to think that discussing disclosure issues in this manner is both responsive to women's needs and a safe and comfortable way to deal with personal dimensions:

■ "I understand her need to talk about us and our relationship. I happen to think that there is a right and a wrong way to talk about those things. If you're not careful, the whole thing can get out of hand. It's best to be as rational as possible. If you let it get too emotional, you never can make any good decisions, and if it gets too personal, someone could get hurt. A little bit of distance goes a long way where a lot of these things are concerned."

■ "It's important first to set out clearly what the issues are. I don't think that women do this very well. They latch on to the first thing that comes to mind, get totally emotionally wrapped up in it. The next thing you know, you're arguing about everything under the sun, and no one is happy. I believe in a clear definition of the problem at the outset. If she can tell me exactly what is bothering her, we can deal with it logically. If she can't do that, then there is no sense even talking about it."

■ "She expects me to have all these reactions right at my fingertips and be able to call them up on the spot. Well, I can't do that. I don't operate the way she does. I need a little more time to think things through. I don't want to say something I'm going to regret later on. Somehow she has the idea that wanting time to think is not being open and honest with her. That's ridiculous. I'm not trying to hide anything, I'm just trying to be sure in my own mind before I talk to her about it. What's wrong with that?"

■ "Men are just more rational than women. We prefer to deal with things in a thoughtful, rational way. Women are emotional, and that's the way they want to deal with things. Just because a man prefers to discuss things logically doesn't mean that he is any less involved than a women who wears her emotions on her sleeve. Women could profit a lot from thinking things through instead of just reacting off the top of their hearts all the time."

Men seem to understand clearly that their intellectualizing is a substitute for another way of dealing with disclosure, what they call the "woman's way." This belief itself underscores men's misunderstanding of what it is to be disclosing. The self-disclosure that is required for intimacy is not achieved by talking abstractly and impersonally *about* the concept of private and personal self. Intimacy requires talking of and from one's private and personal self. There is a vast difference between talking about work and money as socioeconomic issues and talking about how you as an individual feel about your own work, how you deal with money. The difference is even more apparent in discussions of feelings about oneself and the other in a relationship. Talking *about* self-esteem is no substitute for revealing one's own sense of self-esteem. Women argue that men's way of intellectualizing both the content and the form of personal discussions makes any *real* disclosure impossible:

- "Thinking, rationalizing, intellectualizing, debating —that's all I ever get from him! What I want are some real feelings. I want to know that he cares about me. I want to know what's going on with us. Instead I get his 'businesslike approach.' Well, damn it, our relationship is not a business to me. Just once I would like to see him get really carried away with some emotion. I don't care whether it's anger or joy or what it is, so long as it's not logical. So long as there is something of him and not just his head."

- "He always has to define everything. It's like trying to talk to a dictionary. Whatever I say, he says, 'What do you mean?' If I can't tell him in what he calls 'facts' instead of in feelings, he refuses to talk about it further. He'll say, 'I don't see how I can talk about it if you don't even know what you mean.' I know very well what I mean, but it's all feeling. Since he refuses to consider feelings as real, I can't discuss them with him."

- "My boyfriend is a lawyer and he uses the same methods on me that he does in the courtroom. Whenever I want to talk about him and me, I get cross-examined. He makes points of order and he even objects to my way of expressing myself. He claims that he's been trained not to get personally involved. He thinks we have great discussions. Actually, they are more like debates. The only thing great about them is the size of the headaches they give me."

- "Men simply can't see the difference between talking about something 'out there' and talking about themselves. When I want to know a man, I want to know *him*, not his opinions or his analysis. I want to know his feelings, who he is deep down. Too many men come on like textbooks. They think that they are being open. But what women want are novels. Maybe there is less substance, but it comes across with a lot more soul."

- "Why is it that men have to think about how they feel? Don't they know how they feel? You can't talk to a man about his feelings without him saying, 'I'll have to think about that.' What is it that he has to think about? Either he feels something or he doesn't. I guess men think that if they seem to be considering emotions we'll give them credit for their emotions, but it doesn't work that way. Once you let them think about their emotions, you're playing by their rules. You're right back into logic and all that rational shit they try to pass off as honesty. I say, if they don't know their own feelings right off the bat, thinking about them isn't going to help."

- "The worst thing that men do is to try to put you down because maybe you are a little emotional. Their calm, cold, rational way is not better. It's not even the same thing. It's just their way, and we've let them get away with it for too long."

There is more to disclosure than *what* is disclosed. There is the *how* of disclosure as well. As long as men treat the private and personal self as impersonal issues devoid of involvement and emotion, they will fall short of the disclosure demands of intimacy. Women are saying that discussion and debate are no substitute for real sharing. In real sharing, there is a mutual level of emotional involvement. In intimate conversation, the rules of conduct are consistent with the content, and the heart is as much in evidence as the head. One of the respondents put it best when she said, "He gives his body, and I can have his mind if I ask. But his heart is his alone. I really want his heart. Nothing else will do."

Listening
There is one substitute for sharing that was pointed out by only a small number of men and women, but it is inter-

esting enough to deserve mention: listening. A divorced woman, back into dating after seven years of marriage, had this to say about the men she was meeting:

"One reason that I left my husband was that he never listened to me. He never once showed the slightest interest in what I was doing or how I was feeling. He just really didn't seem to care much about me. I suppose that was what made me such a sucker for any man who would listen to me. Not that there are a lot of them out there, but there are some, and I think I've been to bed with every one of them. It was just so good to be with someone who asked me questions about myself and listened to my answers, someone who seemed genuinely interested in me. So I would fall for a listener and go to bed with him. Things would always go along fine until I wanted to hear about him, and then—nothing. All of a sudden I would realize that I didn't really know the first thing about this man who listened, because he never said anything about himself. He gave me nothing to listen to. Every time I tried to get him to open up, he would just turn it around and ask me about myself again. It got to where it was like talking to a mirror. I finally realized that he didn't care enough about me to tell me about himself; his listening was just a line.

"I wish I could say I saw all of this the first time around, but it wasn't until about the fourth guy that it hit me why none of these relationships with these guys who seemed so attentive ever went anywhere besides bed. Now my advice to all my single friends is, 'Beware of the listeners, it's only a line.'"

Is listening the new "line"? Most women would welcome a man who demonstrates his interest in them by questioning and listening. A common complaint among women is that men don't listen. However, listening can be a disguise for not revealing and a substitute for sharing. Gloria Factor found it to be so, and others have as well:

- "Most men want to talk about themselves. Oh, not who they are as people, of course, but what they've done. It's boring but basically harmless. The ones to watch out for are the ones who want to talk about you, because you can get seduced by their interest. The real test is whether they are willing to answer the same questions they ask you. If they are, then you've got a winner; if they're not, then look out."

■ "What could be as flattering as a man who wants to know about you? I was totally charmed and more than a little in love before I even thought to ask about him. When I didn't get any answers, just more questions in return, it began to feel more like the 'third degree' than the 'real thing.' I don't think he ever did understand that real sharing is two-way communication, asking and answering. Luckily I got out before I gave him all of the answers."

Private and personal disclosures are difficult for men. They are noticeably uncomfortable with these topics in relationships. At the same time, many men realize that women expect some valued exchanges if there is to be a relationship. A way for some men to meet the exchange demands of women and ease their way into intimate disclosures is through expressed attention to a women, the kind of attention that is manifest in personal questions. Real interest in the other is seen as a way to forestall if not put off completely the need for one's own disclosure. One man acknowledged his use of listening to get close without, in his words, "getting too close."

"Women today do want more than a lot of boasting and posturing from men, but I'm not comfortable with getting quite as personal as a lot of them seem to want. I've found that I can be a pretty good conversationalist and not have to offer a lot on my own, if I am just attentive to what a woman says about herself. I ask a lot of questions, I follow up on things, I genuinely am interested, and it keeps me from having to volunteer a lot. It's not just a line; I genuinely am interested in what they have to say. I just don't want to have to say a lot about my personal life. Plus, it does work better than any line I've ever tried."

It may be that as women become more and more demanding of disclosures toward intimacy in their relationships with men, more men will seek refuge in listening. At present, men do so little listening to anyone but themselves that the appearance of a caring conversationalist is almost sure to be perceived initially as charming and disarming. It is only later that women see that men who listen without revealing are no more intimate than the majority of men, who don't listen at all.

It is always difficult to gauge intention. Is every sex act, logical argument, gift, touch, or question from a man intended to be a substitute for sharing something of himself with another? Probably not. Yet many men acknowledge that they use these devices because they believe them to be intimate or because they intend them to take the place of being intimate. In the absence of other intimate types of behavior that might create a context for proper evaluation, these acts are perceived by women as male substitutes for intimacy. In no way do these or any other actions take the place of the private and personal self-disclosures, the giving of one's self that intimacy requires. When confronted, even men will admit that these forms of behavior are not truly intimate, yet they persist in them. Women are led to ask, "Why are men not more intimate?"

7 Why Aren't Men More Loving?

"A personal friend?" inquired the Vogon, who had heard
the expression somewhere once and decided
to try it out.
"Ah, no," said Halfrunt, "in my profession [psychiatry],
you know, we do not make personal friends."
"Ah," grunted the Vogon, "professional detachment."
"No," said Halfrunt cheerfully. "We just don't have
the knack."

—Douglas Adams, from *The Restaurant at the End of*
the Universe

At this point, the case is clear: In all significant interpersonal relationships, save those with each other, men get more than they give of love and intimacy. The evidence from their own relationships has not been lost on men. Most are fully aware that they do not love as they are loved. The majority of men argue that the issue need not be taken further. Some men do admit to a desire to be more loving, if for no other reason than to accommodate the needs of wives, families, and friends who increasingly demand of them that they be more demonstrative of their feelings. A very few men would like to be able to be more loving for themselves, more expressive of the emotional bonding they feel. Yet, even among those who want to, men don't express their love. Why?

Why aren't men more loving? Are men constitutionally incapable of intimacy, or do they consciously choose not to be close? Is the lack of loving a kind of "professional detachment," or is it that men simply "don't have the knack" for intimacy? These are important questions. The answers may suggest what loving can realistically be expected from men, and how men can be helped to be more loving.

IT'S NOT THAT MEN DON'T FEEL LOVE

Reports of relationships with men are rife with accusations by women, in their roles as wives, lovers, daughters, friends, that men do not love them. These accusations are countered by male protestations that they do love. The battle of the sexes rages on. How can such conflicting perceptions exist in the same relationship? How can a wife claim she is not loved at the same time that her husband claims he loves her? Don't men know their own feelings? Don't they show their feelings to those they love? The answer is both yes and no. Yes, men do know their own feelings. No, men do not show what they feel to others. The reason men are not more loving is *not* that they don't feel love.

Women see feelings and behavior as one and the same. They act on the basis of what they feel, and their feelings are evident in their actions. There is little doubt for women as to how they should behave and little doubt for others as to what women are feeling. When a woman is angry, she behaves angrily. When she's concerned, she behaves anxiously. When a woman is in love, she behaves lovingly. A woman's behavior is an open window to her feelings. Her actions fully disclose her emotions, and she expects the same to be true of others. To women, the absence of such behavior suggests the absence of feeling. When a woman sees no loving behavior, she assumes no loving. It is a presumption and perspective that is fully consistent with her own orientation to emotion and action.

213

Men do not view feelings and behavior in the same way. For a man, emotion and action are not inextricably linked. At times they may even be quite unrelated. At other times a man's behavior may be a blind, distorting or obscuring his true feelings. As a result, it is not always possible to tell what a man is feeling from observations of how he is behaving. The presence or absence of behavior on the part of a man may bear little or no relation to his emotions. A man who is angry or enraged may appear to be calm and controlled. A concerned or worried man may put forward a confident, secure face to others. A man in love may seem to be detached, even indifferent. For a man, the presence or absence of a particular type of behavior does not signal the presence or absence or a corresponding emotion or feeling. The fact that a man does not behave in loving ways does not mean that the man does not feel love.

So it is that women can correctly accuse men of not loving in the same moment that men can correctly protest that they do indeed feel love. This rational explanation of conflicting views of the relationship between feeling and action is little solace to anyone who wants to know how a man truly feels. The words of one woman capture the sentiments of many: "It's typical of men to define the problem so that they always win. How can I know what he feels if I can't *see* what he feels? Am I just supposed to take his word for it? Words aren't enough. I want *proof* that he loves me."

Given that men do not always behave in ways that fully disclose their feelings, the dilemma for anyone involved with a man is how to know what a man really feels. Are we to take men at their word and acknowledge that they do feel love? Or are we to assume, as most women do, that the reason men aren't more loving is that they really don't feel love?

Men do not conceive of love in the same way that women do. Love means many more things to women. Love has many more roots and covers a richer, fuller emotional

range for women than it does for men. Women see love
in time spent together, in the variety of what is exchanged
in a relationship, in the value and exclusivity of those exchanges, and in the degree of collective concern expressed
in a relationship. Men often confuse love and intimacy with
sex. Their view of love tends to be solely romantic, their
relationships time-bound and topic-specific, with little or
no collective concern. Not seeing the many dimensions of
love that women do, they don't use these dimensions to
build intimacy and loving relationships.

Because love does not mean to men what it does to
women, men do not feel love in the same ways that women
do. It does not necessarily follow from this that men do not
feel love. There is much in the reports of men about themselves to suggest that they do feel love, but there are other
signs of a man's feeling as well.

The subtle behavioral signs of a man's loving (Chapter
6) give considerable benefit of the doubt to a man's behavioral intentions. A much more telling measure of a man's
true feelings is to be found in comparing his statements of
love with his relative loving behavior. Recognizing that men
disclose very little to anyone, it remains that they ought to
disclose relatively more in those relationships they value
most highly than they do in relationships that are not so
important to them. Even though there is not a one-to-one
connection between feelings and behavior for men in their
most significant relationships, there ought to be some cor-
relation. In the majority of cases, this is true. Where men
asserted love and ranked the relationship correspondingly
high in value, they disclosed more of themselves than in
relationships they reported as not being important.

This is one proof beyond their word that men do love.
The man who says in response to his wife's complaint, "I
may not tell her much, but I tell her a damn sight more than I
tell anyone else," is in fact offering a kind of proof of his
love. Is such proof adequate for a woman to feel loved by a

man? Not really. Since we can rarely know what is disclosed to others, it is difficult to assess the exclusivity of what is disclosed to us. Moreover, no amount of self-disclosure in the public or even in the private arena can substitute for the personal disclosures that are required for real loving and genuine intimacy. It may be true that men do feel love, but that only makes the fact that men are not loving more paradoxical. If men feel love, why don't they show it?

IT'S THE WAY MEN ARE

Wherever men have been criticized for not being more loving, they have been quick with explanations as to why:

- "That's just not the way men are. Women may not like it, but that's the way it is for men."
- "Men don't know how to love any way but the way that they do. Sure, it may not be the best way, but it is all that most men know."
- "It's good enough for men. It ought to be good enough for women, too."
- "Show me a man who is loving the way women say they want men to be, and I'll show you a flaming fag!"
- "If I truly showed my feelings, the other guys would eat me alive. It's too dog-eat-dog out there to be honest about the things that really count to you. You can't leave yourself wide open like that."

Men aren't the only ones who find ways to explain away their absence of intimacy. Women, too, have been heard to explain away male behavior. The argument that men are not intimate because "that's the way they are" is the single most frequently heard excuse from men and women alike. This excuse actually takes three popular forms: (1) Real men aren't intimate; (2) men don't know any other way to behave; and (3) men can't afford to be intimate.

Perhaps the most pervasive stereotype in American society is the American man as the strong, silent type. Immortalized in our literature, films, and television—indeed, in every aspect of our popular culture—is the American hero as cool, capable, autonomous. For years, men have measured themselves against this social standard, which places a premium on being unemotional and independent. The liberated male of recent years notwithstanding, the majority of American men today believe that real men do not show their feelings. This is particularly the case where those feel-ings imply some degree of dependency, as love does. This is more than a *description* of how men are; it is a strongly held and widely subscribed-to *prescription* of how men should be:

- "No man I know cares a whit about whether this woman knows he loves her or not. He shouldn't, either. Men don't have any business being all lovey-dovey. That sort of thing is for women and queers. A real man doesn't need to show anybody anything; just the way he is shows plenty."

- "A man has to learn that he can't count on anybody but himself. He has to be independent because that's the only way he's going to make it, when you get right down to it. He should not be dependent on anyone or anything but himself. If that means he comes off as being sort of aloof and alone, well, so be it. So much the better, if you ask me."

- "Nobody wants to be thought of as less than a complete man. I think it's pretty clear to everybody just what a man is. A man doesn't show a lot of emotion, including love. If that does lead to some doubts on the part of women, that's too bad, but that's just men being men. A woman who wants something else has got a tough row to hoe, because men have a whole lot of years of being the way they are."

There is an implicit homophobia in these defenses and rationalizations that should not go unexplored. Homophobia, the fear of homosexuality, is an active agent in the behavior of many men. Whenever someone asserts what a "real man" is or does, there is a concomitant, though often unstated, assertion that the contrary behavior is not male.

217

Hence, loving behavior is not the behavior of a real man; it is the behavior of a homosexual. It is impossible to say precisely how many men act as they do because they are fearful of being labeled homosexuals. The number of instances in which men speak of loving and intimate behavior as feminine suggests that a great many men reject behaving in more expressive, loving ways because they fear that those forms of behavior would be seen as homosexual:

- "These days you don't know who's gay and who's not. Everybody is a little more sensitive to the slightest little thing that might give you a clue to how a guy swings. Maybe I'm too sensitive to it, but I don't like to see a guy that's always talking about how he feels. Or how important relationships are to him. Guys that are too emotional get me the same way. Like I said, you can't ever know for sure these days, but the soft guys are usually pretty light on their feet, too, know what I mean?"

- "No self-respecting guy would ever tell another guy that he cared about him. He might as well offer to kiss his ass, and he probably would, too! You've got to be suspicious of guys who are friends with women, too, because everybody knows how well gays get along with women. They can 'relate' to them, whatever that means. Any guy who gets along too well with women maybe speaks their language too much for his own good."

- "I don't care how somebody else gets his kicks. I just don't want anybody to get the wrong idea about me. That's enough of a reason to keep a harness on your emotions, as far as I'm concerned. I don't want to give anybody a reason to talk."

- "You have to be wary of the guys who want to get a little too friendly. It's sad, but there is a lot of guilt by association where gays are concerned. Maybe that's why we men aren't any closer to each other than we are; we're all afraid that everybody else will think we're gay. That, of course, shouldn't have anything to do with the way we are with women, but it does. I think that a lot of us go overboard these days to be manly and macho, just so there won't be any doubts."

■ "You want to be the way your woman wants you to be, but at the same time you've got to watch out for your reputation among the guys. If you're too much the way she wants, you're not going to be man enough for the guys. You know what that means. Since you are with the guys most of the time, that's the way you are going to be most of the time."

The fear of homosexuality keeps men from each other. It also keeps men from behaving in the intimate, loving ways that women would like. There is a fear that not behaving "like a man" is an admission of homosexuality even when that behavior is directed toward a woman. Men have a pervasive and powerful sense of what a man is, and it excludes a man from being any other way. Men argue that even if a man desires to be more intimate, more loving, he will not be, for fear of what it might mean to others.

Yet another defense commonly used by men is that they don't know any other way to behave. The popular images to which men have been exposed over the years in society at large have been accompanied by persuasive role models in the immediate experience of men. The upbringing of men at the hands of fathers and mothers reinforces the notion of males as unemotional, undemonstrative, unloving. Any number of men commented that they had never heard their fathers say "I love you"; couldn't remember the last time their fathers had touched them; had never seen their fathers cry. Deprived of experiencing firsthand these emotional behaviors with their most significant role models, their fathers, men have a ready defense when their own emotional expressiveness is challenged: "I never knew anything else":

■ "I don't think my experience was all that different from most boys'. The only emotion I ever saw my father express was anger. I never saw him be loving or vulnerable or caring or any of the things my wife wants from me now.

219

How am I supposed to do things that I've never seen done? I can't do them her way, because she's a woman. I never learned a man's way. I'm left on my own, and I can't do it on my own."

■ "There really are no role models for a man who would like to be more demonstrative. Not that I really would, understand, but I can see where if a guy did want to open up, he might have trouble getting a handle on just how to behave."

■ "I can't really relate to the movie and TV heroes who are macho but vulnerable too. My dad was Mr. Macho all the way, and that's how he raised me. I guess I don't know any better. I don't know how I'd go about learning now."

■ "As a father, you face a hell of a responsibility. You need to teach a son how to get along for himself in the world and you need to teach him how to get along with others, too. I guess since the beginning of time most fathers have felt that making it was more important than getting along. My dad believed that, and his dad believed that, and so on. Now, when it looks like getting along may be as important as mak- ing it alone, we don't know how to teach it. Since none of us have ever known anything else, in a way we are trapped by what we have been."

There is no question that most men have had few or no models from which to learn loving and intimate behaviors. The absence of intimacy is for them a product of their up- bringing. There is some truth to the statement that men are not more loving because they don't know how to be more loving and have no role models from which to learn.

Some men claim that even if a man did desire to be more loving, and if he could learn how, he still would not because of the costs. Competition is a theme that runs throughout male relationships; it explains in part why men relate to one another as they do. There are those who point to competition to explain why men are not more loving. The rationale here is that men are so imbued with the ways and means of competition as a necessary condition of survival that there is a spill-over effect into all their relationships. Men cannot afford to let their guard down in loving relationships for fear that that vulnerability might somehow slip over into their competitive relationships. In this way, men argue that the cost of being as loving as they feel is too high:

- "You have to understand that there are people out there just waiting for you to make a mistake. If you let your guard down even a little, they will nail you to the wall. You can't wear your heart on your sleeve, because some SOB will rip it off, and your arm with it! I think that makes any man a little harder than he really would like to be with the people he loves, but that's just part of the price you pay for being a man."

- "We are all, men and women alike, afraid of losing advantage. The way it is today, if you let up, you lose. It would be great if we could all be free and open and honest with each other, but that's not the way the world is. You have to cover up and protect yourself, just to get by. After a while, it gets to be a habit. You do it without even thinking about it. You get to where you cover up even when you don't need to, maybe even when you don't want to."

Most men would have us believe that the reason they are not more loving is that that's the way they are; the way they've been brought up to be; the way their experience dictates that they must be. The argument is a convincing one. A great many women quote the same reasons for their men's lack of loving behavior. Women rationalize that "He can't help the way he is, he's just being a man." This argument has won widespread approval today. Everyone from academics to popular columnists to the man and woman in the street has focused on socialization, the process whereby we acquire and learn social roles, as the *real* reason for the differences between men and women. It is widely believed that men and women grow up differently. Men are taught as boys to be unemotional, undemonstrative, independent. Women are taught as girls to be expressive, caring, nurturing. When they do come together as men and women, they experience relationships differently and they express their relational feelings differently. It may be true that men are not more loving because they are men and products of male socialization, but this is only a partial truth.

Upon closer examination, it becomes evident that the popularity of socialization as a given reason for male intimacy behavior may be more because it is convenient than because it is convincing. Socialization does account for how men come to be as they are, but it does not adequately explain why men do not change. Individual histories are replete with examples of the ways in which men have overcome socialization to make major, even radical, changes in their work practices, religious beliefs, health and exercise habits and so on. Often, men have gone against family, friends, and society to make these changes. Why have men not similarly rebuffed their male socialization and become more loving? Some say that the real reason men are not more loving has less to do with the way men are than with the way women are.

IT'S THE WAY WOMEN ARE

Few men or women get much beyond socialization in their search for an explanation as to why men are not more intimate. Most seem satisfied with the simplicity and face validity of the socialization explanation. Moreover, socialization is a "safe" explanation; it allows us to admit that something is wrong, but it doesn't demand that we place any blame. It's not the fault of men or women, it's just the way things are. Most importantly, from a man's point of view, if the cause is socialization, little can be done about it. The way things are is the way things are. The causal agent is impersonal and impenetrable. We, men and women alike, have to live with what our upbringing has wrought. Another way that men avoid responsibility for their own behavior and for changing is to put the blame on women. There are men who say, "Maybe we are unloving, but it's not our fault. Women are to blame." Among the arguments to be found here is that women don't recognize a man's loving behavior. Almost universally, men respond to challenges that they do not show love with claims that they do, but not in the same ways as women. Women, so the argument goes, do not recognize or appreciate the ways in which men are loving. This is the most frequent way that women are blamed for the fact that men are not more loving.

One variant on this theme is mentioned infrequently but is nonetheless strongly felt by many men, particularly those who feel they have made an effort to be more demonstrative, to open up to women. Such men assert that women discourage disclosure by setting themselves up as arbiters of what is a true expression of feeling, and what is not. According to these men, women set the rules for what they will or will not accept as intimate behavior, and the rules are unfair:

- "I honestly try to do what she says she wants. I really do. But I swear there must be some book of rules somewhere that only women read, which tells what's a feeling and what's not and how to show what you are feeling. According to her, I never get it right. I'm 'not really feeling.' Or I'm 'not really being honest,' or, get this, I'm not 'really being real.' What a crock! I've decided I'll be me and the hell with the way she wants me to be."

- "When I try to be sweet and attentive, she says I'm only doing it because I feel guilty. Then she starts to grill me on what I've done to feel guilty about. When I show concern about work, she says I just want attention—it goes on and on. I've told her if she knows so goddamn much about how I feel, she shouldn't need me to tell her!"

- "Women seem to think that if you are both present for the same event or experience or whatever, you must both experience it the same way. You know, it ought to mean the

223

THE McGILL REPORT ON MALE INTIMACY

same thing to both of you. More to the point, she believes it ought to mean to you what it means to her. Her feelings are the 'right' feelings, and if you don't feel what she feels, you're wrong. I just can't accept that. Nobody can tell somebody else how to feel. As long as women think that their feelings are the only right feelings and only they know the right way to express feelings, men are never going to be able to satisfy them. I know my feelings, and they're right for me. Any rules for relating that allow somebody else to judge my feelings are going to mean no relating at all for me."

It may be that men, inexperienced as they are with the kinds of personal disclosure that lead to intimacy, are overly sensitive to the ways in which their disclosures are received. Perhaps they take the questioning and probing that constitute a woman's attempts to go deeper into the man's self as judgments registering approval or disapproval. Perhaps women unfairly expect from men the same sorts of disclosures and loving behavior that they themselves engage in. Whatever the case, and it is probably some of each, some men do react negatively to the idea that the standards for intimate behavior are both established and judged by women. These men argue that their loving behavior ought to be held to a different standard than that for women; as long as their loving is judged against the standard of women, they can never be more loving.

Women Don't Really Want Men to Behave Differently

Is what a woman says she wants from a man what she really wants, or does a woman say one thing and mean another? There are any number of men who take the position that women don't really want men to be more disclosing, more intimate. These men argue that they are not more disclosing because they know that women don't really want them to be.

- "Women *say* all sorts of things. What you have to look at is what they *do*. What women do is fall in love with guys who are unemotional, who don't fawn all over them, who keep themselves to themselves. So what do women want? They want men to be like men, not like women. There is a reason for the difference between the sexes. The difference is what makes it work."

- "Women may say they want men to be more open and honest, to show their feelings more, and the whole bit. But when men are that way, women can't handle it. They don't know what to do. Nine times out of ten, they end up falling apart. The guy has to hang in there till she gets it back together, just like always. At least I know what to do when she gets all emotional on me. She doesn't have the slightest idea how to handle my emotions. No woman does, and if they don't know that, they find out. I guarantee you that once a woman has been with a guy who has really been honest, has really opened himself up to her, she'll never want him to do it again."

- "I think that what women really want is someone who is strong and dependable, someone they can lean on, someone who can take care of himself and them too. I don't think the 'vulnerable man' is nearly as desirable to women as they say he is. If he were, you can bet there would be a whole lot more vulnerable men out there. We men are not totally oblivious to what women want. I believe that men are the way they are because it is the way most women want men to be."

The point to be made here is not that men know what women want from them, or that men do not know what women want. That is another subject for another time. What is apparent is that many men defend their absence of disclosure by claiming that it is what women really want and expect of men.

Women Don't Give Men a Chance
The wife/mother frequently plays the role of emotional go-between in the family, interpreting the father's feelings and behavior for the children, and theirs for him. Wives

225

comment that they perform this interpretative function out of necessity. Men, too, note the role and the need for it. There is, among men, the claim that when women act as emotional intermediaries they obviate the need for men to express themselves. Some even go as far as to say women usurp their sincere attempts to be loving:

- "I never get the opportunity to deal with my feelings toward her or the kids, because she is always dealing with them for me. Including my feelings for her. She tells the kids how I feel about them and what they do. She does the same thing where my feelings for her are concerned. She loves them and herself *for* me. I couldn't do it better if I tried. It's a moot point, though, since she won't let me try anyway."

- "I could handle all the loving she wants for herself and for the kids, but she does it. She says she can do it better than I can, so why should I try? They're all taking care of each other and sort of leaving me to fend for myself, so I do. I'm not complaining, and she shouldn't, either, because she's the one who makes me the way I am."

In many families, men feel as though they are never given the chance to be demonstrative and loving because of the wife's role as interpreter. The role is a common one (see Chapter 4); most men would acknowledge that their spouse eases the emotional interaction between family members. The usual male reaction is to see this as a blessing. It relieves men of the responsibility to express themselves. If it is true that men are not more loving because women don't give them the chance, it is true only for a very, very few men.

Women Will Hurt You

"If women really want to know why men aren't more loving, all they have to do is to look in the mirror. Or better yet, they should listen in on their own conversations with other women. The reason men aren't more open with women is because they know that just like in the cop shows, 'anything you say can and will be used against you.'"

Most men give very little thought to why they are not more loving. When pressed for an explanation, they are likely to point to socialization and/or training and upbringing. Even those who blame women for the way men are do so in an offhand manner. With few exceptions, men give only the most casual and cursory of thought to why they are as they are. In the survey, most responded as though the question were not even worthy of consideration. The most common exception to this general pattern came from those men who believed that women would use a man's self-disclosure against him. To a man, those who gave this explanation illustrated their point with a detailed story of just how they personally had been victimized at the hands of a woman. The stories were told with a vehemence, a vengefulness, not heard from other men. One gets the strong impression that these men feel that being open with a woman is tantamount to inviting an assault. In the minds of these men, they are not more loving for good reason:

- "The difference between men and women is that women are vicious. They aren't satisfied with just winning. They want to destroy you. A woman will take your weakest point and use it against you. Fair play doesn't mean a thing to them. A friend of mine got divorced. He got taken to the cleaners because his 'ex' used his love for his daughter to blackmail him. He agreed to everything she wanted just so long as he could continue to see his daughter. Anyway, she was about fifteen or so, I think, just beginning to think about dating, and he was as proud as could be of her. He was always telling us how he talked to her about everything and how much she worshiped him. One night we're at the club for drinks, four or five couples of us, when his ex comes in. She walks right over to our table and says to my friend, in front of everyone, 'I just wanted to tell you that your daughter had her first date tonight. She said she wanted someone special for her first date, "someone who is nothing at all like my father."' Well, my buddy was devastated. He couldn't

227

even think of a comeback. He's never mentioned his daughter to any of us since that night."

■ "I'm very wary about what I tell my wife, because I honestly believe that if I ever did anything to cross her, she'd use everything she could against me. I've been hurt by her when I know she didn't even mean to hurt me. She shared something with her friends that I thought was just between us. It may have seemed kind of inconsequential to her, but it was important to me and I didn't want it blabbed all over the place. Now there's no telling who knows. Can you imagine what she might do if she really had it in for me? Women simply can't be trusted."

■ "Women just don't use good judgment where private things are concerned. I don't want our financial situation to be the subject of coffee klatches all over the neighborhood, I don't want my sister-in-law to know how we did it last night. Those are only the things that I *know* she's told others about. There's no telling what I've revealed to her that she's passed on without my knowing."

■ "I learned my lesson the hard way where loving women is concerned. I have always been a little anxious about my performance in bed because I was totally inexperienced before I got married. My wife and I did talk about it. She assured me that I was doing fine and she would teach me everything I needed to know to please her. I thought our sex life was okay, but I learned differently, to my humiliation. One night at a party the conversation somehow got around to abnormal sex behavior. I said some things about what I thought was unnatural. My wife and I had been fighting earlier in the day, and I guess it was her way of getting back at me. Right there, with our friends and everything, she said, 'Grady, you wouldn't know natural from a hole in the wall. You knew so little about sex when we got married that I could have told you to put it in the wall and you would have thought that was normal!' I couldn't believe she would say something like that! She didn't even stop there, she went on and on. Finally I just got up and left. Later she said she was sorry. She said she hadn't meant all those things and she certainly hadn't meant to hurt me. The point is, she did say them and she did hurt me. Our relationship has never been the same since. You can't take back those kinds of things, once you've said them. And women are always saying them."

It is true that there are men who have had bad experiences as a result of disclosing themselves to women. There are vengeful women (and vengeful men, as well). One can well imagine a vicious, self-perpetuating cycle in which women, hurt because they don't feel loved, punish men who, in turn, point to the punishment as reason for not loving and withhold themselves from women, who are further hurt, and on and on. Each can point to the other and say, "You started it!"

At issue here is trust. Who can be trusted, with what, and when? It is the position of some men that women can never be trusted with any private or personal information. Others argue that time is needed before trust is established, and women want too much, too soon. Still others point to the differences in perception that lead a woman to treat as public what a man believes to be deeply personal information. These are important considerations.

It is true that, generally speaking, the longer the duration of a relationship, the greater the disclosure, although there are abundant examples of significant disclosures in relatively new relationships, which suggests that time alone is not the sole cause of trust. For trust to develop, there must be disclosures; for disclosures, there must be trust. When men claim that they avoid intimacy because women can't be trusted, they are avoiding responsibility for their own behavior. On reading of these explanations, one women commented, "Leave it to men to figure out a way to blame us for what is wrong with them."

The many rationalizations that men offer for their behavior—blaming heredity, socialization, and women—are testimony to the fear men have of intimacy. This fear is not

229

confined to a few men or a few relationships. The fear of getting close is apparent in the way men interact with wives, family, friends. It is implied, too, in the way they defend their behavior. In some instances, it is voiced outright. Why is it that men fear self-disclosure? The answer might enable men and women to go beyond excuses and learn why men are not more loving. Most important, knowing why men fear intimacy may suggest how men can change.

POWER AND PERSONAL KNOWLEDGE

Upon closer examination, what have been presented by men and women alike as explanations for men's behavior are seen to be little more than convenient excuses. True, for a particular man in a particular relationship, these reasons may explain in part why he is as he is. But they do not adequately explain why he has not changed. Each excuse— socialization, ignorance, women's behavior—is clearly something that could be overcome if men wanted to. Even men admit, in their own way, that these "obstacles" to intimacy could be overcome:

- "I'm sure I could be as loving as she wants me to be, if I put my mind to it. There's really nothing stopping me. It would mean a big change, of course, but I've made big changes before. When you come right down to it, I'm not sure why I don't do it. I guess it just doesn't feel right to me."

- "I'm not afraid to get close to people. Maybe a little anxious, but not afraid. You don't fear something like that, because there's nothing to be afraid of. It's just that I'm not sure I really want to, you know? When I really want to, I'll go full speed ahead. Until then, I think it's best that I just stay the way I am."

- "Just because you don't do something doesn't mean you are afraid of it. Maybe some men are, but not me. I just don't want to show my insides to everybody. I could if I wanted to; I just don't especially want to."

■ "A man does two things. First, he does what he *has* to; second, he does what he *wants* to. If he doesn't have to do it, he won't. If he doesn't want to, he won't. Now you figure it out. A man doesn't *have* to love, so if he doesn't do it, it must be because he doesn't want to. Right? Right!"

The real question is not "Why aren't men more loving?" but rather "Why don't men want to become more loving?" The answer has to do with power and self-knowledge.

Intimacy requires self-disclosure. The reason men do not behave in more loving (self-disclosing) ways has to do with what self-disclosure means to men.

When you give information about yourself to another, you are giving that person influence and control over you. The other can use the information (1) for your welfare; (2) against your welfare; or (3) to give you back information about yourself. Suppose, for example, that I tell you I really pride myself on being a good father. It is an important part of my self-esteem. With that information about me, you might: (1) tell my boys how important the father role is to me, i.e., use the information in my behalf; (2) use my role to black-mail me into doing something I don't want to do "because all the other fathers are doing it," i.e., use the information against me; or (3) challenge my self-image by pointing out how much time I spend away from the boys, i.e., give me back information about myself. You could use the information I have given you about myself to influence and control my behavior. In this way, when I give you information about me, I give you power over me. The more you know about me, the more intimate we are and the greater the potential for you to control and influence. This is true not just in a quantitative sense, but in a qualitative sense as well. You may, for example, know very little of my public self, but if I reveal to you something of my private or personal self, you would be a potentially powerful force in my life. In personal relationships, information is power.

By withholding information from our relationship, I not

231

only retain power over my own actions, I also gain power over your actions. This is so because my use of information about myself in our relationship determines what you know and thus what you can do. One often hears of people working to "hidden agendas," pursuing goals that are not disclosed to others. This is information. If I act in our relationship on the basis of information known to me but not to you, such as information about myself, I have a decided advantage. This is especially true if you have been open with me.

The reason men are not more loving is that they want to retain power over themselves and attain power over others. The research data and interviews with relational others indicate that men make of themselves a *mystery*. Men withhold information about themselves, they mislead and even misrepresent themselves to others. It is now apparent that they promote this mystery in order to gain *mastery*. This mystery-mastery behavior, identified by sociologists some years ago, discourages the sharing of feelings, motives, and goals with others. The logic of mystery-mastery behavior is familiar to many women:

- "He won't let me into him. Never is there the slightest clue as to what he's thinking or feeling. It's so frustrating, because he knows everything there is about me. That's just my way—to be completely open. His way is just the opposite—completely closed. That gives him all the control in our relationship, because he can use what he knows about me and there's nothing I know about him that I can use."

- "They learn it as little boys. As a mother, you lose them as soon as things start to go on with them that they don't tell you about. The older they get, the worse it gets. By the time you marry a man, his whole life is a secret. He tells you only what he wants you to know, and it's never very much. I think it gives them a sense of power to know so much about themselves and know that you want to know so much about them. They use it like a bribe or a weapon:

'You want to know how I feel? Do this and I'll tell you.' As women, we're powerless. We just have to play along."

The mystery presented by men is a path to mastery of others. But not all of this is intentionally manipulative. Many men treat their own feelings as a mystery. How frequently have the men in these pages seemed to treat what goes on within themselves as mysterious, inaccessible, irrelevant, or inappropriate in relationships, making such statements as:

- "I don't really know how I feel."
- "Who knows why I do it, I just do it."
- "That's the way I am, I guess."
- "I don't know how to react."
- "I need to think about how I feel."
- "What am I supposed to feel?"

By treating his own feelings, perceptions, and purposes as a mystery, a man forces others to deal with whatever information is at hand, on the pretense that other information is unknown or unknowable. Treating himself as a mystery serves another important purpose for a man: it protects him from learning about himself.

Our most important source of information about who we are comes from others. As others give us confirming or denying information, we learn about the accuracy or inaccuracy of our self-perceptions. When a man withholds information about himself from others, he avoids facing up to his own incongruities and inadequacies, which might otherwise be apparent in others' feedback to him. The man who never reveals his feelings is never confronted with the inconsistencies in his own behavior. The man who withholds his values from others can never be held to judgment. The man who does not disclose his goals is never seen to fail.

This controlling behavior, which is the absence of intimacy, thus serves two purposes for a man: it gives him the power he associates with success in life, and it protects him from feedback that might reveal his inadequacies. So much do men fear both losing power and facing who they really are that they withhold and distort themselves in their relationships with others. Intimacy is feared for what it requires, i.e., disclosure, and for what it brings, i.e., true self-awareness. Power and his own self-image are important enough to a man that whatever the urging from loved ones that he be more open, more disclosing, more loving, he is likely to resist.

Does this mean that men cannot be more loving, that they will not change? So long as men see mystery-mastery behavior as the path to power, it is unlikely that they will be disclosing in the ways that loving relationships require. The paradox is that a man's lack of intimacy is self-defeating. Without disclosure to others and the feedback that disclosure invites, men can never know themselves; they cannot be clear about their own feelings, emotions, and priorities. In the absence of this kind of self-knowledge, power is purposeless. No man can be truly powerful unless he knows himself. Since no man can know himself unless he discloses himself to others, intimacy is the path to power. When men see that personal knowledge and personal power come from the disclosure of self in loving relationships, they will be as loving as women would like them to be. But first, men must be made to see why they need to be more loving.

Why Should Men Be Loving: What's in It for Men?

8

I have learned this: it is not what one does that is wrong, but what one becomes as a consequence of it.

—Oscar Wilde, *De Profundis*

Where men are concerned, intimacy is a "hard sell." The majority of men do not see the need to be more disclosing, more loving either for their own sakes or for the sakes of their wives and loved ones. Men are quite satisfied with their relationships as they are, so why change? For others? ("That's her problem, not mine.") For themselves? ("Why? What's in it for me?") What indeed? Men might be well advised to look at the results of some current research.

Research studies with animals shed some light. They have disclosed, for example, inappropriate sexual behavior in insects, birds, rats, and dogs that have been reared in social isolation. Regardless of species, the subjects exhibited immature sex play, failure to respond to other members of the species, and an inability to discriminate sexually relevant cues. And animals living in isolation have been shown to be less effective when stressed. For example, they develop gastric ulcers more rapidly if they experience stress alone than if they do so in the company of others. There is no doubt that social isolation has a marked impact on the behavior of animals. Might this same research not have some relevance for humans?

On the human front, seriously ill patients and those in long-term care facilities, such as nursing homes, have shown improved response to treatment when they were allowed small pets as companions. More to the point, social isolation has been demonstrated to be a contributing factor in depression, paranoia, schizophrenia, and a wide variety of diseases. Recent investigations into stress and its management have suggested two important findings. First, low social support is a source of stress to the extent that the absence of a close intimate relationship is related to psychiatric impairment. Second, among people exposed to high stress, those with social supports have much lower levels of symptomatology than those without social supports.

Does this suggest that if men do not become more intimate, more loving, they will be afflicted with high stress and any number of physical and mental diseases? Before drawing conclusions, we should be mindful of the many distant, withdrawn, unloving men who have enjoyed good health well into their nineties. Nonetheless, there is a growing body of evidence to suggest that social relations have a profound effect on the physical and mental health of individuals. These studies are supported by the related observation that in the United States elderly men have the highest suicide rate, over forty per one hundred thousand. Among men, suicide is the third major cause of death, following only heart disease and cancer, both of which have been tied to stress. Is this coincidence, or cause and effect? Could it be that the man who is not loving may be the cause of his own infirmities?

These findings should at least provoke a man's curiosity, if not convince him outright that there is something tangible to be gained from his being more loving.

INTIMACY AS A PATH TO IMPROVED
MENTAL AND PHYSICAL HEALTH

It would be pure chicanery to imply from disparate and disjointed researches that men can ward off mental and physical illnesses and live longer, happier lives by being more loving and intimate. It is not too farfetched, however, to say that if men become more self-disclosing and expressive of themselves in their relationships with others, they will be better able to deal with the stressors that are associated with disease. In this way, intimacy can be a path to improved mental and physical well-being.

There is no such thing as a stress-free life. Although stress has been made out to be a villain in the etiology of contemporary illness, we should be thankful that our lives are not stress-free. Positive stress, or "eustress," as it is termed, accounts for much of our peak efforts, those times when we are at our best, when we reach our potential. When we say of ourselves, "I always do best under pressure," we are acknowledging the benefits of stress. When we are overwhelmed by conditions and events and stretched beyond our limits to adapt, we experience "distress." Distress debilitates and incapacitates. Stressors, which can be anybody or anything, are neither positive nor negative. Stressors produce eustress or distress as a result of one's response to them. Prolonged stress, either eustress or distress, has been linked to heart disease, depression, ulcers, headaches, insomnia, irritability, weight loss and gain, loss of sex drive, impotence, and suicide. The key to living with stress lies in the ways we deal with and adapt to stress. This is popularly called stress management. One of the central components in effective stress management is social support—that is, participation in close, caring relationships.

Gerald Printman is a fifty-three-year-old electronics executive who has resided for the last six weeks in the mental health unit of a California community hospital. As Gerald now describes what happened to him, he "flipped out at work":

"One day I was given this choice assignment as director of our international group, and the next day I was hiding in my office in a semicatatonic state. I was unable to answer the phone, unable to get up and leave. I just sat there, afraid that someone would come in and ask me for a decision. In talking to the doctors about it, I found that it was a case of my wanting the job and not really wanting it at the same time. I knew I had to take it—for the money, the prestige, because they'd never offer it again—and at the same time I knew I couldn't do it. I had nobody I could confide my fears to, so they just bottled up inside me until my whole system called it quits and checked out on me. I'm hoping I can get well enough to go back and do it right, but I'm not so sure. At work, they think I had a heart attack. I haven't told them any different. The doctors say that until I can tell them at the office what really happened, I can't kid myself that I have made any progress."

Gerald Printman is not unlike most of the men we have met in these pages. A successful businessman, he was without friends and not close enough to his family that he could share even with them his own feelings of inadequacy. What does make Gerald different is that through his breakdown he may have discovered an additional source of stress and an important way to manage the stresses he experiences.

Low social support, the absence of close, caring relationships, is itself a source of distress for men. Additionally, low social support diminishes a man's ability to adapt to the other stresses in his life. Intimate self-disclosures and the closeness they create between people give a sense of perspective and keep emotional reactions within bounds. In an intimate relationship, the meaning of a stressful experience can be neutralized and balanced by a caring other. And the man's self-esteem can be maintained. Intimacy can even modify the conditions that produce stress. Indeed, being in-

timate with someone, by definition, removes a stressful circumstance.

Gerald is now a member of a support group composed
of men who, like himself, have come to recognize that they
need to reach out to one another in order to save themselves.
These men cognitively know the value of intimate relationships, the importance of relationships to their own health
and well-being, but it is still a struggle for them to behave intimately:

- "You know you need to get close to people, but it's
like you can't make your legs move. I try to tell myself that
every step makes the next one that much easier, and I can
already feel it helping."

- "The hardest part is to overcome all of that shit that
glorifies 'going it alone.' Hell, going it alone was why I was
going crazy!"

- "All of us are here because we hurt badly enough to
try anything, even loving someone. To think that we did the
things we did to ourselves—some of us half-dead from heart
attacks or booze or drugs, the rest of us half-crazy—and all
the time we could have handled it, if we'd just talked to
somebody about what was going on. Our motto here in the
group is 'Talk or die,' and when you've been where we've
been, you believe it."

The members of this men's support group have come to
intimacy as a last resort. Many of them feel that the next step
in their personal breakdown would have been the last
step—suicide. It speaks to the intransigence of men in the
face of self-disclosure that such dramatic events are required
before they will even consider change. As evidence mounts
in support of the role that close relationships can play in
helping one to adapt to the stresses that bring on mental and
physical impairments, men may come to see that loving
truly is a matter of life and death.

INTIMACY: A MEANS TO MORE
EFFECTIVE ACTION

The threat of physical and mental impairment may persuade some men to explore loving behavior, but the cases to date suggest that men may come to this point not as a preventative measure but only after they have been afflicted. For all too many men, disease of any kind is a sign of weakness. The use of preventative or curative measures is an admission of weakness. It is part of the macho image to "play hurt," to continue on, even though injured. Indeed, the threat of stress-related illness may make a man take increased pride in the fact he can go it alone in a stressful world. A more direct and convincing way to a man's heart, then, is to show him that by being more disclosing and more intimate, he will be able to act more effectively in those arenas that are important to him.

One of the distinguishing characteristics of male relationships, whatever their nature, is that (save for mentors) they are rarely "helping" relationships. Men seldom turn to others for advice, counsel, or an extra hand, no matter how complex the problem or weighty the task. A man will stew over a difficult work problem, spending untold hours trying to comprehend something that might be very simply explained, if only he would ask. The same man may struggle to the point of exhaustion with a heavy home-improvement project rather than ask his neighbor for a helping hand. In part, this solitary behavior derives from the belief that a real man can and should handle his own affairs. In part, it is because the shallow relationships men have with others do not provide a context for asking for help. In part, it is because men do not ask for help due to uncertainty about what they might be obligating themselves to do in return. Any one or all of these reasons may keep a man from reaching out to others when he is confronted with problems. Because he does not disclose or demonstrate his need for help, he is less effective than he might be.

240

The fact that men do not avail themselves of social support in the form of intimate relationships seriously hampers their problem-solving effectiveness. Problem-solving is here used in the broadest possible sense to convey situations that require a decision to act. These situations may range from how to move a refrigerator to what short of computer system to buy for the business, to how to handle a teenaged daughter. When a man "goes it alone," eschewing the help he needs, his problem-solving process is prone to many deficiencies.

An individual acting alone will seldom see all aspects of a problem. He brings only one perspective and therefore has a limited view. This usually results in an inadequate definition of precisely what the problem is. If we share our problems with those who know us well enough to have some sense of our own priorities, yet who bring a different perspective to the situation, we improve our grasp of the full nature of the problem and why it is that we find it problematical. This can only happen when a man discloses enough about himself to another that that other can appreciate his priorities and aims. The commonly heard complaint from men, "You're no help at all," might be appropriately answered, "How can you help someone you don't know?"

The same limited perspective that results for many men in poor problem definition is responsible for both the limited review of alternatives and the constrained consideration of consequences that is evident in their problem-solving patterns. Because they do not share their problems with others, men do not see the many ways they might solve their problems. Nor do they see the consequences of alternatives, particularly where those consequences affect others more dramatically than they do themselves. Women are especially sensitive to this ineffectiveness, because it is often they who must clean up after the man.

- "I can't begin to tell you the number of things that I've had to have redone after he has supposedly done them. It always turns out to be twice as expensive than if we had had

241

it done professionally in the first place. But, oh no, he had to do it himself. He just barged in without thinking about what he was getting into and left me to clean it up when it was beyond repair."

- "He does what he thinks is best for himself, without so much as a thought for the rest of us. Then he wonders why we're not excited by what he has in mind. He just doesn't have any clue to the problems he causes for us when he solves his problems. If only he would ask us what we think, we'd all be a lot happier with the result."

- "He insists on doing things his way, whether it's the best way or not. You can't make suggestions or ask questions or, God forbid, say he's wrong, because he gives you no chance to do it. It makes absolutely no difference that most of the time he *is* wrong. You'd think, when he's blown it time after time, he'd be willing to consider some other approaches or someone else's advice, but not him."

Another way in which the absence of intimate relationships limits the effectiveness of men's problem-solving is that it makes it difficult for them to commit themselves to a decision. Close, caring relationships provide a certain sense of security, a predictability, a certainty that facilitates commitment to a course of action. With someone who loves you, you know that whatever may go wrong, you will always be loved. Because men do not have these emotional backstops, the accuracy of a course of action becomes all the more important. A man feels that he is accepted only so long as he does "the right thing." The heightened importance of "doing right" creates anxieties that are frequently manifested in men taking unreasonable amounts of time to make decisions. They vacillate and backtrack and do what is widely known in management circles as CYA—"covering your ass." The decisions they do make are made in such a way that they cannot be held accountable. If things go wrong, they are not at fault. This gives rise to commitments that are slow to be forthcoming and, if and when they are made, are at best conditional. Such a decision-making process is hardly the basis for effective action:

- "My boss prides himself on making the tough decisions, but as far as I can tell, he never makes any decisions at all. He doesn't consult with anyone or talk with anybody. He just studies things on his own until people forget what the problem was or somebody else solves it or it just goes away. I think he's just so afraid of doing something wrong that he has decided it's safer not to do anything at all."

- "First he's going one way, then he turns around and does just the opposite. I never know what he's really going to do from one minute to the next. I've told him I think it would be better for him to talk things all the way through, instead of going off in one direction for a while, then changing his mind and heading off the opposite way. He doesn't feel like he needs to share his thinking with anybody, so he doesn't. He is decisive, but it never lasts very long."

Men value action. They pride themselves on being clear-thinking, decisive, consistent. The way that men relate to others around problem-solving results in indecision, vacillation, and an unwillingness to commit themselves to a course of action. If a man could bring himself to share his problems and priorities with another in ways that were truly self-revealing, he would be able to sort out his own anxieties and insecurities *before* he took action, rather than *as* he acted. He would also have a base for acceptance of himself as a person. The foundation of a loving relationship can give a man the freedom to commit himself to a course of action without the immobilizing fear of failure.

Because men think and act alone in their personal and social problem-solving, one might expect that they are prepared to take full responsibility when things go wrong. Such is not the case. In fact, what usually occurs is that men look for external forces to blame, and they typically blame others:

- "What I don't understand is how it can be my fault when he's done it all. It doesn't make any difference what it is or why it has gone wrong, it's never his fault. It's always because someone else fouled up—usually me, even when I've had nothing at all to do with it. If he can't blame me for anything else, he blames me for not making him see what was going to happen. Can you believe that? It's my fault that he didn't listen to me!"

■ "Whenever things go wrong for him, he starts in on all the other people and things that were responsible. It's either his boss, or the poor or the rich or the government, or the Communists or acid rain. Really, sometimes it's quite funny what he comes up with. Most of the time it is pretty sad. He pretends he's in complete control of everything, never asking for any help or anyone else's opinion, until something goes wrong. Then all the people he didn't ask are in control, and it's their fault, not his. The saddest thing of all is that he doesn't learn from one time to the next."

Men who are encapsulated in their own experience because they don't share themselves with others rarely do learn from one experience to the next. Learning to act more effectively in personal and social situations comes from two sources: first, from listening to others, and second, from examining where one has gone wrong. Men don't listen to others in defining their problems, searching for solutions, or committing themselves to a course of action. Even if they did, the listening would be for naught unless the man had shared enough of himself in the relationship that the other could give some personally relevant advice. It is also true that men do not take responsibility for their own failures. Reluctant as they are to share their failures and insecurities with others, they can never learn from their mistakes, but are, instead, doomed to repeat them.

One way that men can act more effectively and learn more from their actions is through disclosing more of themselves, their priorities and thought processes. Men can act more effectively if they will first act more intimately. This is particularly true in dealing with personal problems, where men are most likely to suffer the inadequacies of going it alone.

Evan Packard is a director of personnel for a large bank. He describes the way a splinter group from a professional association has turned into a helpful forum for sharing and personal problem-solving:

"The larger association has people from companies of every size and description. It's fine for the once-a-month meetings, but for those of us who are more or less on our own in financial institutions, it wasn't really meeting our needs. Five or six of us decided to get together informally, on our own, to talk about issues that specifically affected us. The beauty of the group is that there is no real competition; everybody is as high as they can go in his own company, and nobody is out for anyone else's job. We all need the group because none of us has anybody else in his organization who is interested in what we are interested in.

"At first, we just talked about business things. Even then, it was not so much particular problems as issues. You know, unemployment, inflation, that sort of thing. I guess we were sort of testing each other out. As we gradually got to feel more comfortable, we started talking about problems at work. From there we just sort of opened up to each other and got into some pretty personal areas. Now it's 'anything goes.' I think we all feel that the group has made us better at work and at home. I know for myself that now that I've got these friends whom I can go to with any problem at all, I wonder how I got along on my own, really alone for so long. For that matter, I wonder why I did it alone when it was so obvious that I could have used some help. Foolish pride, I guess. Thank God, pride went before I fell."

Through a number of avenues—professional groups, church groups, hobby clubs, and one-on-one relationships with those closest to them—men are awakening to the realization that they can benefit in tangible ways from sharing themselves and their problems with others. When they let others know who they are and what concerns them, they can use the caring context that is created to define problems better, to explore alternatives and their consequences more fully, to be more secure in their commitments, to accept their own responsibility and to learn from their experience. The more a man discloses of himself in a relationship, the greater these benefits will be and the broader the range of application, from work problems to family to dilemmas of the most personal sort. Intimacy is a means to more effective action.

INTIMACY AND INCREASED SELF-AWARENESS

One of the most devastating effects of the absence of intimacy in the life of a man is not so much that he is alone but that his aloneness leads to alienation of the most damaging type, alienation from himself. The man who is alone—and in the absence of intimate relationships, most men are— does not know who he is. Alienation literally means separation. To alienate is to make something foreign, strange. Men today suffer from many forms of alienation, and each can be traced to the failure of men to be disclosing of themselves in relationships. They are estranged from themselves by their inability to be loving.

Self-estrangement is that form of alienation in which the individual does not know who he is. It is most commonly seen in men who feel compelled to play a variety of roles in their lives: husband, father, businessman, church member, community servant, and so on. These roles become so all-consuming, and the man moves from one to another so quickly, in such a short time, that he loses sight of who he is. He begins to see himself as nothing more than a role-player. Without the roles, he is nothing. His way of relating to others has made him a stranger to himself:

- "At work I have to be one way, at home I have to be

another. Then there's coaching the kid's teams, work with the Lions, the church. I could go on and on, it never seems to end. Everywhere I turn, there is somebody else wanting something else from me. There's no time for me. Christ, if there were time for me, I don't know what I'd do with it. I've been doing these 'shoulds' for so long now that I've lost sight of whatever I might have *wanted*. If you took away all of the things I have to do, I'm not sure what you would find. I've pretty much lost track of who I am."

- "It wouldn't be so bad, being involved in so many different things, if I could be *me* in each of them. Instead, each person I have to be forces me into being something different. At work, I have to be a son of a bitch because that's my job. At home, I'm supposed to be in control, on top of everything, and at the same time supportive and helpful. At the Sunday school, I'm supposed to be a teacher and a guide to stuff I don't even understand. With the guys, I have to be a hard drinker and a hell-raiser. When do I get to be who I want to be? Who *do* I want to be, anyway?"

- "You have to be so many different things to so many different people that it's easy to lose sight of the fact that you have to be somebody to yourself, too."

- "What if you're really not sure that you want to be all of the things that a man is supposed to be? Is that okay? I don't think so, but I don't know. Who knows what they want to be? These days, who has the time to figure it out?"

In the impersonal world in which most men live, roles provide a convenient escape from the need to get close to others. The dictated social interaction that is the substance of roles removes the need to deal with people and situations as individuals. The appropriate role behavior dictates what the man needs to say and do. He can move through required interactions in a perfectly acceptable way without ever revealing who he is as a person. He can be husband, father, worker, citizen, without ever having to be himself. A lifetime of role-playing, however, can erode one's sense of self.

247

The line between who one is and who one *plays at being* becomes more and more obscure, until, finally, the self is completely consumed by the roles. The role-player is left estranged, literally a stranger to himself. The only way a man can discover himself is to reveal himself to others. To escape roles and be real, he must be intimate.

Another contemporary form of male alienation is powerlessness. Powerlessness, or impotence, is the feeling that a man's actions have no impact or influence on his world. Certainly there are times when we all feel somewhat adrift, times when it seems as if OPEC and Washington and the changing jet streams are pulling us in ways over which we have no control. But for many men, this feeling of inefficacy is not a sometime thing. It is a perspective that pervades their outlook on themselves and on their lives. In large part, powerlessness is a problem of scale. Without the immediacy of intimate relationships in which the impact and influence of their actions might be more clearly seen, men project their own behavior against a panoramic screen and are devastated when they scarcely cast a shadow. Imbued with the sense that a man should control his own destiny, many men are frustrated that they cannot:

▪ "I think we just have to accept the fact that the individual doesn't count for a hell of a lot these days. Any one man is absolutely powerless to control his own life. Right now, today, there are things being done by people somewhere out there that are going to have more of an impact on me than anything I can do myself. What's scary is, I don't even know who those people are, or where they are, or what they're doing. All I know is that I don't count for shit!"

▪ "You think you are doing the right things to make it, and then something comes along from out of the blue and wham! you're right back where you started. That's when you start to wonder if you can ever make a difference in your life. Maybe it's all luck. I don't know. Maybe there is somebody out there somewhere who is in charge, controlling everything. Whatever, the bottom line is still the same for us average guys. We are totally powerless to do anything about our lives."

What a different perspective these men might have on their own power and influence if they would only narrow their scope and look closely at their personal relationships! The average man cannot act to alter the course of world affairs, but any man can influence the direction of his relationships with others. Through this interpersonal influence, a man can have a powerful and profound effect on his life and lives of others. There is, of course, a certain safety in having as one's point of reference events larger and more remote than one can reasonably hope to affect. The very size and distance of the field means that few will hold a man accountable for his efforts against the price of oil, or for peace in the Middle East. On the other hand, if a man selects as his arena of activity relationships close at hand, it's very likely that some performance will be expected of him, something approaching intimacy.

It is a frustrating and complex world we live in. Millions of people feel powerless in the face of world affairs, but they don't conclude from that that they are powerless. They find personal power in the relationships they participate in:

- "If he would give me and the kids the same kind of time and attention that he gives to the headlines and the sports page, I don't think he would feel quite so impotent. He's certainly not without power where our lives are concerned. The problem is, he doesn't pay enough attention to us to see just how much he influences us. Maybe he doesn't care as much about us as he does about world affairs. I try not to think about that, because that's what really saddens me, the thought that we don't count."

- "I don't know whether it is power or not. Somehow the word *power* seems negative when you're talking about the family. Perhaps what I'm really talking about is the feeling that what I do makes a difference. I think that the closer I get to my wife and children, the more in touch I get with my own ability to make a difference in the things that are really important to me. In my case, it took a bleeding ulcer to persuade me to give up on the world and give in to the things that really count."

- "I can make my son smile. I can make my wife feel my love for her. I'm trying very hard to learn that those accomplishments are more important than work or anything else I could do in the world. What I can do ought to be enough for any man. That's what I keep telling myself."

There are many ways to measure a man, but too many of them have to do with the world "out there," beyond his influence. Too few of the measures of man have to do with those things closest to him. Closer at hand are the intimate relationships where any man might feel a sense of efficacy. There his emotional efforts might be appropriately rewarded. Even those men who do find power in their performance in the world at large cannot escape feelings of estrangement. Without the close, caring relationships that give our individual actions a sense of perspective, even the most successful of men has occasion to wonder what it all means.

Meaninglessness

Among middle-aged men today, there is often a malaise, a despairing detachment that comes from the feeling that their lives are without purpose, without direction. The alienation that afflicts these men is "meaninglessness":

- "I spend half a day at the office debating with other vice-presidents the merits of plastic wood-grained faces on the new phones versus plain faces. When I get home, the wife and I fight about whether or not the kitchen linoleum needs replacing. After that, it's my daughter's soccer team, where the other coaches and I argue about script or print for the team name on the jerseys. And that's a good day! On my tombstone they're going to put, 'Here lies a man who spent his entire life doing totally meaningless things.'"

■ "There's just nothing worth getting excited about these days. That doesn't keep me from getting excited, of course, but it is all negative energy. I get pissed off about everything and positively enthusiastic about nothing at all. Even when I'm ranting and raving, I know deep down it just isn't worth it. What is there that's worth getting excited about these days? You tell me. I can't think of one damned thing."

■ "It simply doesn't mean anything—none of it does. Not my work, my family, my mistress, or my friends—none of it. I worked like hell to get all of the things I have, and they don't mean anything at all to me. Maybe it's me, maybe I don't mean anything."

■ "Nothing seems worth the effort anymore. I just go through the motions. I'm not really involved with anything I'm doing, or with anybody. The worst part of it is that I don't care enough about it to try to change."

In and of themselves, things do not have meaning; they assume value only as we give it to them. The reason that so many men experience a sense of meaninglessness is that they do not have loving connections with others who would give meaning to their lives and their actions. In the absence of a caring relational context, a man behaves in a vacuum. He doesn't care about his behavior because he doesn't care enough about others to value their caring. He collects achievements in life, but there is no caring context to give his efforts meaning. It's not unlike those family hand-me-downs, the bric-a-brac that litter our homes. An old tin cup, a cracked pickle dish, a faded photograph—they are unattractive, don't really fit in with the decor of a room. They have no value to anyone else, but they are priceless to us. Their meaning lies in the fact that they meant something to those who owned them before us. Without loving relationships, a man's life resembles bric-a-brac that has no history, no caring context, and hence no value.

Another source of the feeling of meaninglessness that is

so prevalent among men today is that many sincerely do not know what they themselves value. When so many things vie for our attention, it is impossible to treat all things equally. No man can give equal time and attention to all of the demands upon him. One response to these conflicting demands is to say that since not everything can be equally important, nothing can be important at all. Another response is for a man to determine what is important to him and devote his efforts to those things, ignoring all others. This is a risky alternative. It requires that a man expose his priorities to others. He must share his goals in order to sift among them for the things that really count. Discovery requires disclosure. It is far safer and saner from a traditional male point of view to treat all things as equally unimportant and therefore uninspiring.

A man cannot know what he wants to do, what will be important to him, without testing his priorities against those held by others. This testing requires more disclosure than most men are comfortable with. But even were he to know what was important to him, a man might still confront alienation in the form of anomie, the absence of rules.

Anomie

Anomie is a condition of normlessness. The anomic individual feels that there are no rules to govern behavior, no guides for his life. Anomie describes the way individuals relate to society that is most often associated with suicides. The social isolation in which most men live gives rise to this condition. Unconnected to others in any significant ways, men question the rules for relating. Many conclude that there are no rules. This is a situation that has the appearance of freedom, but more likely leads to frustration and ultimately to a sense of the futility of life:

■ "I don't know what the rules are these days. Who does? When Presidents lie and women want to behave like men and children can sue their parents for the way they were raised, who can say what the rules are? I guess any-thing goes."

- "He is completely without morals. He has absolutely no scruples whatsoever. He will do anything to get what he wants, without a thought to what is fair or who gets hurt. It's of absolutely no concern to him that others believe in a sense of right and wrong. Maybe society doesn't know the difference, but two people living together ought to be able to work out what is going to be acceptable behavior for them and what's not going to be acceptable. We don't have to play by society's rules, but that doesn't mean that we can't have some rules of our own, does it?"

- "Whatever happened to the traditional values around God, country, and family? Have we just thrown all that out the window? It sure seems like it. Today it's every man for himself. Everybody is out to get as much as he can, any way that he can. It's all so senseless, and I'm just as guilty as the next guy."

It is true that societal values and norms are undergoing dramatic changes today. The rules for acceptable behavior have been challenged and changed in every aspect of so-ciety. Those who would look to society for some indication of what is morally right or even socially acceptable are bom-barded instead with alternatives and contradictions. Most of these challenges and changes have hit men hard, for it is primarily men who have defined traditional mores and have profited by them. Told that the old ways are no longer right, and confronted by confusing and conflicting new ways not of their own choosing, many men believe that there are no longer any rules at all. The absence of consensual social norms is seen by some as a license to behave in thoroughly selfish and irresponsible ways: "It's not me, it's the way so-ciety is." For others, the absence of rules immobilizes them. With no sense of social direction, they cannot act. They, too, say, "It's not me, it's society."

The anomic man is doubly alienated. He feels cut off

from a society in which there are no clear prescriptions for behavior, no cues as to how he should act. When he does act, he feels cut off from himself. Those who are closely connected to others can look to their relationships for definitions of acceptable behavior. The intimacy they have with another enables them to construct within that relationship norms and values to guide their behavior. Men who are isolated from these intimate relationships don't have this important avenue available to them to resolve their feelings of anomie. When they bring their amoral anomic behavior into relationships, they are rejected. This only confirms their sense that society is confused and confusing. These men do not see that the way to connect with society is to connect with a caring other. Such a connection can only be brought about through self-disclosure and an exploration of what is right and wrong in an intimate relationship.

The dilemma that confronts a man facing self-awareness is that he cannot really know himself without revealing himself to another. The more he withholds of himself, the more estranged he becomes. The more he discloses of himself, his meaning and methods, the more he learns who he is.

WHY SHOULD MEN BE MORE INTIMATE?

Should men be more intimate because their wives and families want it? Yes. Should men be more intimate, more loving because it will improve their mental and physical health? Yes. Should men be more intimate because they will be able to act more effectively? Yes. Should men be more loving because it will make them more self-aware? Yes. Will men change their intimate behavior for these reasons? Probably not.

The reason that men are not more loving is that they believe they have more power and control by withholding themselves from relationships. They believe that mystery is mastery and that disclosure makes one vulnerable. The apparent advantages of intimate behavior described in the preceding pages are likely to have an impact on a man's behavior only if he sees that by disclosing himself to others in loving relationships, he is *empowered* rather than *emasculated*. A man will get close if he believes that getting closer means getting control.

The use of the language of power and control in talking about relationships may be offensive to some. But these concepts are important because they describe what men aspire to in relationships. Men desire not so much a sense of power over others as individual power, self-power, having the ability to act or to produce. It is important that men see that their lack of intimacy, their inability to love, limits their ability to act powerfully in relationships.

Consider the following: Is a man who is physically and/or mentally impaired by stressful events capable of acting to his full potential? Is a man with diminished problem-solving skills capable of being fully effective? Is a man riddled with self-doubt, who questions who he is and what he wants, able to realize his full potential? The answer in every case is a resounding "No!" The limits to a man's realization of his own potential are the limits he sets on his loving. A man *should* be more loving so that he might be all he can be. The remaining question is, "How can a man be more loving?"

9

How Men Can Be More Intimate

Men must be taught as if you taught them not,
And things unknown proposed as things forgot.

—Alexander Pope

"Look, I really do want to be more intimate. I'm finally convinced that I'm missing out on a lot in my marriage, my family, and my friendships because I really am not at all close to them. I'll even go so far as to say that it is probably my fault. I'm the one who hasn't wanted to get closer in the past. Now I do. Whether it's the time I spent in the hospital with the heart attack or just that time of my life, I have finally realized that I need to reach out to others. But wanting to is not enough. I mean, wanting alone doesn't make it happen, does it? That's where I have problems. I really don't know how to make it happen. I don't know how to get close to people.

"I don't think that it's the sort of thing where you can just step in and start being intimate with people. I really don't know where to start. My wife wants too much, too fast. I'm just not ready to reveal everything, even to her. I get the idea that she won't settle for anything else, so that's not a

256

good place to start in. I think my kids would be shocked out of their minds if I started to come on real personal with them. They're not used to that kind of a relationship with me, and I'd be scared that I would do or say the wrong thing. As for my friends, there's no chance at all there for getting close. At the very least, they'd laugh at me. At the worst, they'd think I was gay.

"So what do I do? Where do I go to get what I want? I don't know. I'm like the guy who is all dressed up with no place to go. I'm ready for something more from my relationships, but I honestly don't have the slightest idea of how to go about getting it. I can't go back and I don't know how to go ahead. Where do I go from here? How do I get the closeness I want? Help!"

Jack York is one of an increasing number of men who recognize the need for intimacy. Some men are responding to the growing numbers of women who are demanding more open, honest behavior from men. For other men, the desire to be more intimate can be traced to the increasing freedom they feel to explore new roles and forms of behavior. For still others, the motivation to change lies in the pain they have come to feel over the absence of intimacy in their lives. The numbers are by no means large, but there are more and more men who admit to a desire to be more loving. As varied as their motives may be, all these men share one thing in common: they don't know how to become more intimate. They need help.

A man's plea for help to become more loving rarely gets a receptive hearing from the women in his life. It is difficult for many women to understand that what comes so naturally to them must be learned by men. To women, a man's statement that "I want to be more loving but I don't know how" is commonly viewed as just another in a long line of excuses. For women, knowing what they feel and expressing their feelings freely comes easily and effortlessly. Women assume that it is the same for men. They are often impatient with men's learning to love, intolerant of their ignorance in matters of intimacy. In this frame of mind, women are not inclined to *help* men be more loving. There is a dual agenda here. Men do need help in learning how to be intimate, and women need help in learning how to help them.

In the context of our research, we met a great many men who were making genuine efforts to be more expressive of their love and to develop more intimate relationships. From the experiences of these men, we can comment on the issues involved as men attempt to become more intimate, and identify some of the actions by men and women that lead to greater intimacy. These comments are not intended to be a "how-to" or "cookbook" approach to increased intimacy. Our research has revealed that the motives and methods of men's loving behavior are too complex to be changed by simple prescriptions. The intent here is to provide a cognitive map of the territory, identifying the issues that lie ahead and the initiatives that must be taken by men and women who pursue a more loving relationship.

"I WANT TO BE MORE LOVING"

There is no change without the desire to change. No man can be made to be more intimate unless he wants to be more intimate, but there are many things that can lead a man to want to change. For Jack York, a near-fatal heart attack brought on the realization that his connections with the people who counted most in his life—his wife, children, and friends—were shallow. He had any number of socially acceptable relationships, but none of the sort of ties he could draw upon during his crisis. Personal crisis often leads men to a desire to make something more of their relationships. Illness, divorce, or the death of a loved one creates emotional needs for men that can only be met by intimates who know a man's pain. Few men allow themselves to be known in those ways. It is this unresolved personal pain that causes these men to want to reach out to others and become more intimate with them.

Other men want to change their intimate behavior as a kind of repayment for the love they have received. For these men, there is usually an event in their lives that brings about an outpouring of love and caring from others, which in turn spurs a man's own desire to be more loving. Terry Minderman describes his reaction to the support he received while he was out of work:

"You don't really know how much people mean to you until something happens and all of a sudden you are overwhelmed with just how much other people care. When I was laid off, I thought I'd just have to deal with it on my own. I never imagined so many people cared so much about me. And it wasn't just my family that pitched in and helped. Neighbors, people at church, people I hardly knew, all did what they could. It made me feel a little guilty. I couldn't help but ask myself what I had done to deserve all of this. I was pretty embarrassed by the answer: nothing. I hadn't done one thing to let those people know that I cared as much for them as they did for me. I wasn't even close enough to them to know that they cared that much! I'm telling you, that's never going to happen again. I'm on a one-man crusade to show people just how much they mean to me as soon as I can. I just have to figure out the best way to go about it."

Like Terry, many men who genuinely want to be more expressive of their love and affection have come to that position out of a sense of guilt, a felt need to repay others for the love they have shown. There need not be a traumatic event in a man's life for him to get in touch with this guilt. Often men, particularly middle-aged men, reported a gradual but growing sense that they had been greatly loved by their wives or children without having shown much love in return. This became the driving force in their desire to change.

For other men, the desire to be more intimate begins with the recognition that they cannot fully know themselves and their own potential unless they disclose themselves to another. Larry Parker wrote of his need for increased self-awareness:

"At forty-one I found myself doing some pretty bizarre things. I would leave my job in the middle of the day and just drive around aimlessly. I stopped having any sexual relations with my wife, but I couldn't have sex with anybody else, either, even though I sure tried. I wanted my kids to be constantly loving, but I didn't really want to be around them. The worst thing about all of it was that I didn't know why I was doing any of these things. I didn't know what I really wanted. I didn't know *me*. The reason I didn't know me was because I hadn't let anybody else know me. It's a funny paradox. I somehow finally realized you can't discover yourself by yourself—you can only discover yourself through others. Now I'm trying to reach out. I admit my reasons are completely selfish. I want to know what I really want."

Men avoid intimacy in the mistaken belief that mystery equals mastery. Men fear that if they are no longer a mystery to others, they can no longer master others. A few men are realizing that until they know themselves, they can never be in control. They have learned through their estrangement that they can only know themselves through their intimate involvement with others. It is this enlightened view of self that is spurring men to be more disclosing of themselves as a means to being more intimate.

The varied reasons that men give for wanting to be more intimate suggest that the desire for change is motivated by one or more of four conditions: reward/punishment (coercion); guilt/anxiety; disconfirmation; psychological safety. As seen in the self-reports of individual men, events of a man's life may make him aware of these conditions and motivate him to be more loving. But these same conditions and the consequent motivation to change can also be created by others.

Reward/Punishment (Coercion)

Very seldom are we physically forced to change our behavior. More often we change because we are seeking a reward that someone else offers, or we're seeking to avoid punishment at the hands of another. You cannot force a man to be more loving, but you can create conditions in which he will want to be more intimate in order to receive a promised reward or avoid a promised punishment. This is a subtle but potentially powerful form of coercion that can result in creating in a man the desire to change and be more loving.

Realistically, a man is more likely to want to change in order to avoid being punished than because he is pursuing a reward. This is true because typically the man in a relationship is already receiving most of what *he* perceives to be the rewards. He has the love of his wife and family. They meet his basic needs for relating, which are minimal. Thus, he is operating very close to the ceiling of the reward schedule. There is little anyone can promise him that is likely to motivate him to be more intimate. The rewards of improved self-awareness and increased personal power may be too abstract and alien for many men to identify with. The main motivational avenues available to women are the withholding of rewards, such as sex, and the threat of punishment. Some women have attested to the effectiveness of threats in bringing about changes in men:

- "I told him if he didn't start making me feel loved, I was leaving. It was as simple as that. He got the message and I got what I wanted."

- "When he understood just how unhappy I was, and when he understood that I was prepared to go elsewhere and get happy unless he came around, that's when he got serious about being as loving as I need him to be."

- "I blackmailed him with sex. I'm not exactly proud of what I did, but it seems to have worked. I told him I was only going to make love to him when I felt loved by him. There were some long dry spells in there. I think it was harder on me than it was on him, but I stuck to my guns and gradually he came around. Every now and then I have to remind him of what the deal is, but usually I get what I want, and when I do, then we both get what we want."

- "It's terrible to think that you have to threaten someone to love you 'or else,' but I honestly don't think that he would have heard me any other way. When I finally did say, 'Love me or I'm leaving,' he started listening and now he's started changing. I don't know if he'll keep it up, though, because I don't know how long I can threaten to leave before I either have to leave or it becomes just another empty threat."

The coercive reward/punishment strategy to motivate a man to be more intimate is a very high-risk strategy for two reasons. First, a man is not without his own rewards and punishments in a relationship, and threats against him may evoke threats from him. It's difficult to keep in touch with the love in a relationship when you are lobbing threats at each other. The second risk associated with threatened punishment is that you must be prepared to exact the punishment if change is not forthcoming. Otherwise the threat is empty and ineffectual.

One also has to ask if the ends justify the means. How loving is a relationship where one party lives under constant threat? Rewards and punishments *can* motivate change, but they exact a great cost to the relationship in the process. There may be more interpersonally inexpensive ways to make men want to be more intimate.

Guilt/Anxiety

Jack York wanted to change because he felt anxious about having to face another personal crisis without the support of close, loving relationships. Terry Minderman set out to be more loving because he felt guilty that he had received so much love and given so little in return. Guilt and anxiety are two very powerful motivators of change. Much of our behavior is dictated by what we think it means for us (anxiety) or what we think that others might think (guilt). Men can be made to feel anxious or guilty about their own loving behavior and thereby motivated to change.

Anxiety is perhaps the most common cause of a man's desire to be more intimate with those around him. Usually a man's anxious state is induced by some event or series of events that bring about a personal crisis in which he finds his own resources inadequate. In those times, women can turn to caring others, but men have no such relationships to draw upon. Uncertain about his ability to handle future crises, a man may turn to closer relationships with others as a kind of insurance policy. These personal crises cannot be manufactured, and judging by the reports of some, when they do occur, helping relationships often have to be almost forced upon a man.

- "He would not talk to me about his father's death, but I could see that it was eating him up. I just badgered away at him until he had to unload just to get me off his back. Once he started, it all came pouring out. He ended up saying, 'Why didn't I turn to you sooner?'"

- "A man will never ask for help—never, no matter how much he needs it. You just have to force him to take help. You make it harder for him to say no than to say yes. The way you do that is you just never pay attention when he does say no. You just keep on moving in closer and closer. Next thing he knows, he can't do without you and he doesn't know how it happened."

There is a less common but more compelling form of anxiety that leads men to seek out others. This is personal anxiety that comes from self-searching probes of one's own goals, abilities, and desires. The more deeply a man gets into trying to understand himself, the more likely he is to turn to others. Again, this sort of anxiety cannot be induced so much as encouraged:

- "When he started questioning his career, what he had

done and what he was going to do, I saw an opportunity for us to get close. I hadn't been much of a part of who he had been, but I saw a chance for me to be a part of who he was going to be. I really encouraged his self-examination. I told him it was important, and more than that, I *showed* him I thought it was important every way I could. I questioned him about how it was going. At times I even confronted him when I thought it was appropriate. The result was that he opened up to me, mostly, I think, as a way of finding himself."

■ "He's always been so self-directed and so proud of it that I think he was more surprised than I was when he started experiencing some self-doubts. He was really worried about what was happening to him and what was going to happen to him. I didn't let him off the hook too easily. I suppose I could have given him all sorts of reassurances and built him up, but I thought if he stayed with his fears for a while, he might learn something about himself. I think what he learned was that he really loved me and he wanted to be sure of our relationship above all else. From my standpoint, it couldn't have worked out better."

It is difficult and even potentially dangerous to induce anxiety, but there are enough anxious moments in the life of any man that an attentive other can seize the opportunity to encourage self-inquiry. Disclosing what you see happening to a man validates his experience of himself. Your perspective gives him information he can use in his self-inquiry and invites him to pursue more from you; it also offers a way of alleviating the anxiety he feels.

Guilt is not nearly so effective as anxiety as a motivator of increased intimacy for men. Guilt is a socially induced response, and most men claim to be little affected by what others think. Any appeal to a man's sensitivity to others is likely to be met with a counterdependent response: "Who cares what they think!" Even more futile is the argument that begins, "After all I've done for you . . ." This typically brings about his listing all that he thinks he has contributed to the relationship. Few men feel guilty about the way they relate to their spouses. One occasion in which some success has been achieved in motivating a man through guilt to be more loving was when the love of his parents or his children was invoked:

- "I've pretty much given up on him ever loving me the way I would like, but it's not too late for him to have a decent relationship with the children. Actually, I try to shame him into getting close to them. My best line is, 'They love you so much and they ask for so little in return.' Even if he does love them more out of guilt than anything else, at least he does love them. It's *how he is* that counts to them, not why he is that way."

- "The only way I've been able to get him closer to his parents is to harp at him that they don't have much longer to live. I tell him that if he doesn't show them now that he cares, he may always regret it. I'm not sure how much it really works, but he does go to see them more than he used to. Maybe he'll eventually get the idea that I want some love from him, too. I can only hope."

Anxiety and guilt are effective motivators of change, but it is difficult to sustain these states over long periods of time. Prolonged anxiety without reprisal gradually dissipates. Guilt without retribution similarly loses its motivational punch over time. One needs to be careful, too, that one does not become identified as the source of guilt or anxiety. A simple way for a man to escape guilt or anxiety is to remove the source by withdrawing from the relationship. Guilt and anxiety provide excellent ways to get a man to want to be more intimate, but other strategies may be needed to bring about a sustained desire to change.

Disconfirmation
One reason that we change the way we behave is that we come to the realization that our current behavior is not pro-

ducing the results we intend. Our belief about the link between our goals and our behavior is disconfirmed, typically by new information. Disconfirmation has powerful potential as a motivator of more intimate behavior in men. The reason for this is that disconfirmation requires no goal change. For example, men generally desire to be seen as manly by others. If men were suddenly to perceive that the way to be manly was to be open, self-disclosing, and loving, they would behave in those ways. They don't need to set aside the goal; it remains important to them. They have only to change their behavior. If, on the other hand, men were asked to give up the goal of being manly, we can predict that there would be very little in the way of change.

To use disconfirmation as a means to motivate men to be more loving requires starting with what men value, what their goals are. Men value control, and they avoid the disclosures required for intimacy because they are seen as a threat to control. If men can be made to see that intimacy increases their self-awareness and therefore their control, they will be motivated to behave in more intimate ways. Some women have come upon this strategy almost by accident.

■ "I pointed out to my husband that the reason he always gave in to me was that he couldn't deal with my emotions. When we fight, he's always so detached and rational, while I'm yelling, crying, laughing. He can't match my emotional level, so he gives in. When he realized that was what was happening, he started to try to be more expressive of what he was feeling. He's not as far as I am yet, but he's moved in a long way from where he was. Now he's more comfortable with my emotionality because he's showing his emotions, too. Now he even wins sometimes."

■ "If you don't know what you are feeling, you can't know what you want. How can you be in control if you don't even know where you're going? That kind of logic is the only thing that gets through to him, but it does get through. He's at least trying to open up."

■ "I think he finally realized that if I gave him more than he gave me, I was always going to have the upper hand. It's the same with the kids. If they get more of the love they need from me than they do from him, it's only natural that they are going to be more influenced by me. He finally saw that if he was going to be the man he wanted to be in this family, he was going to have to open up and let us in. He has, and we couldn't be happier."

The secret to making a man want to be more loving may lie in making him see that that is how he must behave if he's going to be the man he wants to be. A helping other can be a source of information that disconfirms how he is and re-affirms intimacy as a path to how he would like to be. Challenges to what he values will evoke only defensiveness and withdrawal. The key to the effective use of disconfirmation is to help him to see that by not being intimate he is not achieving *his* goals.

Psychological Safety

The final way in which men can be motivated to become more intimate is through psychological safety. Psychological safety describes that condition in which there are no risks associated with change, or in which whatever risks are associated with change are manageable. This strategy should be familiar to any parent who has encouraged a child to try out a new behavior, such as eating a new food, or jumping into a swimming pool. "Eat your vegetables. They won't hurt you!" Or, "Jump, it's okay. Mommy will catch you."

As with children, psychological safety as a means to motivate men to change requires great trust. In the case of adults, if men are to be intimate they must believe that they have nothing to risk or that the risks are fully within their control. Sensitive as men are to interpersonal vulnerabilities, it is not often that they believe intimacy is risk-free, but there are some instances where the risks appear to be removed by virtue of the situation they find themselves in:

- "After my divorce, I felt a lot freer to tell things to my ex than I did when we were married. Maybe it's because I wasn't afraid anymore of doing or saying something that would really screw up our marriage. I mean, we'd already split, so what more harm could be done? And now that I say just exactly what I feel, we seem to get along a whole lot better than we did before. Even she says how open I am now. She wonders what happened to make me change."

- "A lot of men are uncomfortable around children—I mean the really small kids, one, two, three. I love them at that age because they take you just as you are. They don't ask for explanations or bring a lot of expectations. You can be whoever you really are with them and get away with it. I date a lot of young divorcees, and I get along a lot better with their kids than I do with them. I'm always a little afraid to be really honest with women."

- "I like the freedom of totally anonymous situations. In my job I travel constantly. If I meet someone, I'm never with them for more than a day or two before I have to be off again. Chances are, we'll never see each other again. I suppose to some people that would be frustrating, but I find it freeing. I can be real because there's no risk at all. Of course, the relationships I form have no future, either, but that's why there is no risk. It's perfect for me."

Situations that give a man a sense of psychological safety, the idea that it's okay to change, are somewhat unusual. Intimacy carries such inherent costs for men that a situation must be extraordinarily risk-free for a man to feel safe. The assurances of others are seldom convincing enough. Women can tell men that it is okay to be open and loving, that their disclosures won't be used against them, but few will believe it. Men may accept that no risk is intended, but as long as they see the potential for harm in self-disclosure, they are not going to open up. It is fair to say that for most men in relationships, there is no such thing as a risk-free disclosure.

An alternative strategy for those who would help men is

to convince them that whatever the risks associated with being more loving, together they can handle them. For example, a wife may say to her husband, "I know it's going to be difficult for you to open up to the children, but I will help you." Men who have successfully become more loving frequently give credit to someone else who helped them shoulder the burden of changing:

- "I simply would not be the way I am today if my wife hadn't stood by me every step of the way. It was still hard to set aside years of socialization and actually become a new, loving man, but knowing that I had someone by my side to help me get over the rough spots made all the difference in the world. There were a lot of rough spots, too; anybody who thinks that there won't be is fooling himself. To my way of thinking, anybody who tries to go it alone is just as much of a fool. It simply can't be done. As much as any man likes to think he can do things on his own, when it comes to being more loving, a man has to have help. There are just too many things that can go wrong."

- "My whole family was in on this with me, and thank God they were. It is a scary thing when you try to change your whole way of being. Nobody can make the scary parts go away, but if you've got some supportive, loving people around you, you can at least lessen the scare. It's a lot like swimming in deep water. It's never completely safe, but it can be safer if you swim with a buddy. Being more open and honest with people is never completely safe, but if you have some help, it can be safer."

- "The best thing is if you can find a man who's already been through it to help you. I was lucky that way because my dad was a big help. My wife was supportive enough, but being a woman, she couldn't really understand what I was going through. My dad had experienced it all firsthand, so I could really rely on him. If you can't get help from another guy, I guess a woman would be okay. Any help is better than none at all."

Men are resistant to intimacy for so many reasons that it

is unrealistic to think they can be made to feel that being more loving is completely risk-free. It may even be irresponsible to suggest such a thing. There are, after all, some real risks associated with loving. Situations may arise that ameliorate these risks, but the utility of psychological safety as a motivator lies principally in the notion of "manageable risks." Even here, a tremendous degree of trust is required. A man must trust that the helping other has his best interests in mind, that the risks are truly manageable, and that the other is capable of helping. Most men do not have this degree of trust in their relationships, even with their spouses. Trust must be built as intimacy is pursued.

This has some implications as to when and what a man begins to disclose as he attempts to become more intimate. As he successfully confronts the manageable risks of minor disclosures, he gains confidence in his own ability to handle risk. At the same time, he learns that the rewards of intimacy outweigh the risks. As a man accumulates experience with small intimacies, he gains confidence, and future disclosures seem that much safer.

All of these methods of motivating a man to want to become more intimate *can* be effective. The appropriateness of any one approach will vary with the man, the situation, and the man's relationship with a helping other. At times, rewards or the threat of punishment can push a man toward intimacy. At other times, for other men, guilt and/or anxiety may be the motivators. In general, disconfirmation and psychological safety are the most sustaining motives for a man to change his loving behavior. Just as important, these strategies offer the most constructive roles for a "helping other."

Each approach can create the conditions under which a man will *want* to change, and thus bring him to the threshold of intimate behavior. Many men have come to this point only to back away. Some shy away from change because they lack conviction. Typically, these men have not wanted to change for themselves but rather for another. At the moment